KU-306-816

WITHDRAWN

N 0002226 8

*Educational objectives
and the teaching of
educational psychology*

The research reported in Part One of this volume
originated in the psychology steering committee
of the Colleges of Education Research Group of the School
of Education, Birmingham University, and was supported
by a grant from the Social Sciences Research Council.

Educational objectives and the teaching of educational psychology

E. STONES

IN COLLABORATION WITH D. ANDERSON

NEWMAN COLLEGE
BARTLEY GREEN
BIRMINGHAM, 32.

CLASS	370.15
ACCESSION	35246
AUTHOR	STO

METHUEN & CO LTD

11 NEW FETTER LANE LONDON EC4

First published 1972
by Methuen & Co Ltd
11 New Fetter Lane London EC4
© 1972 by E. Stones
Printed in Great Britain by
Richard Clay (The Chaucer Press) Ltd
Bungay, Suffolk

SBN 416 61130 3

Distributed in the USA by Barnes & Noble Inc

Contents

Contents

vi

Acknowledgements

We wish to acknowledge the invaluable help of colleagues in colleges of education who took great trouble in administering the survey to their students. We also wish to thank the many tutors, students and teachers who completed our schedules and the educational psychologists who gave their time to reply to our request for comments about objectives. In particular we wish to mention the assistance of the psychology committee of the Birmingham School of Education Colleges of Education Research Group who bore with our obsession about objectives with remarkable patience. Within the Birmingham School of Education we should like to acknowledge the help of Mrs Henrietta Batchelor, Mrs Pamela Cotton, Dr N. C. Graham, Mrs Beatrice Nagel and Mr M. J. Tobin.

E.S.   D.A.

The authors and publishers also wish to express their thanks to the following for permission to reprint the papers collected in Part Two of this volume:

Association for Supervision and Curriculum Development for 'The relevancy of educational psychology' by Arthur P. Coladarci. Clinical Psychology Publishing Co. for 'Instrumentation of Bloom's and Krathwohl's taxonomies for the writing of educational objectives' by Newton S. Metfessel, William B. Michael and Donald A. Kirsner, and for 'Is there a discipline of educational psychology?' by David P. Ausubel. *Journal of Teacher Education* for 'Stating objectives appropriately for program, for curriculum and for instructional materials development' by David R. Krathwohl. National Society of College Teachers of Education for 'The objectives of educational psychology in the education of teachers' by Harry N. Rivlin. Dr W. James Popham for his paper 'Probing the validity of arguments against behavioural goals'. The British Psychological Society for 'A suggested outline of topics for inclusion in a course of educational psychology' by The British Psycho-

Acknowledgements

logical Society and Association for Teachers in Colleges and Departments of Education. The Ontario Institute for Studies in Education for 'Psychology in the teacher-preparation program' by John Herbert and Donald Williams. University of Chicago Press and the author for 'Educational objectives: help or hindrance?' by Elliot W. Eisner. University of Chicago Press and the author for ' Comments on Eisner's paper' by J. Thomas Hastings. University of Pittsburgh Press for 'Some persistent questions on the defining of objectives' by Ralph W. Tyler.

Preface

This book comprises two main parts. Part One reports an investigation into the perceptions held by different interested populations of the appropriate aims of a course in educational psychology for teacher preparation. This part also includes analyses of the literature on the subjects of educational objectives and educational psychology in teacher preparation. A final section of Part One presents a proposal for an approach to the specifying of objectives in educational psychology for teacher preparation. References for Part One are collected and presented in a Bibliography at the end of the part. Part Two comprises eleven papers reprinted from various sources dealing with the questions of educational objectives and educational psychology in teacher preparation. These papers have been minimally edited and in general appear as they were originally published. They are, however, referred to in Chapters 1 and 2 and some of them in Chapter 5. References for these papers are presented at the end of each paper. A set of appendices referring to the investigations carried out in Chapters 3 and 4 follows Part Two, and comprises information about instruments used in the investigation and statistical material related to the analysis of results.

It is hoped that the mode of presentation adopted will enable the reader most conveniently to follow the drift of the discussion and provide him with ready access to some of the key literature in the field.

Introduction

On objectives

This book is concerned with the question of educational objectives as they apply to the teaching of educational psychology to student teachers. For our purposes we take a much more specific view than is usually implied when teachers talk about the aims and objectives of education or particular teaching programmes. There is no lack of pronouncements of aims such as the all-round development of the individual, or the development of the 'whole personality', or the development of a 'happy atmosphere' (Plowden, 1966). What is lacking in many spheres of education are the more specific, down-to-earth statements of teaching intentions which are possible of translation into teaching programmes. Not that we deprecate general statements of aims (indeed we make use of some fairly general statements later on), but that we are convinced that we shall be unable to proceed effectively in our teaching or research without some more objective and more specific statement of pedagogic intent. Our purpose, then, is to examine the problems of identifying the specific objectives in the teaching of educational psychology and to systematize them as much as possible. In our approach we shall inevitably proceed from some very broad views of our own (which many would probably consider all-important in their implications for the more specific ones), but we take these essentially as points of departure. We then proceed to the more specific, more objective statements, which, we believe, are essential in the guiding and planning of teaching procedures and in achieving genuine consensus about objectives rather than spurious consensus based on imprecise generalities.

On educational psychology

It is some time since Anderson (1948) wrote of courses on psychology: 'The curriculum is confused because psychology is confused'. However, there seems little doubt that in the field of teacher preparation there is still a good deal of truth in the remark. One problem is the use of the one term *educa-*

tional psychology to refer to clinical practice and to that element in a college course that might properly be termed *pedagogy.** Another important reason seems to be that imprecision is self-perpetuating. Since the boundaries are so vague, instructors are reluctant to exclude any subjects on the grounds that they may be important, or possibly, that someone scrutinizing the course might infer ignorance and so present a threat to professional status. Thus the subject has developed by a process of accretion which has resulted in courses of ill defined structure and imprecise boundaries.

In the pages that follow we review a variety of opinions as to the proper objectives of a course in educational psychology. We also present our own views in which we attempt to come to grips with the problem of the subject's encyclopedic eclecticism and to delineate those topics that we think truly germane to college courses. It is our hope that by formulating these views and presenting some exemplars in specific and objective form we shall provide a basis for discussion and possibly eventual consensus.

* *pedagogy*: the science of teaching *(Concise Oxford Dictionary)*.

Part One

Objectives in Education

A great deal has been written and said about instructional objectives in recent years. The impact of programmed learning and the ideas of curriculum development have been two major specific influences, and there is an extensive literature about the subject. The number of exemplifications of systems of objectives related to particular fields of study, on the other hand, is extremely small. There is, therefore, little of direct practical value in the literature; there are, however, some useful general arguments that bear on the subject and provide a context within which to approach the question. Some contributions are more help than others and suggest guidelines for the working out of a specific set of objectives related to a practical teaching task. In order to establish a context within which to work and also to make as much use of promising approaches as possible, we examined a wide spectrum of views about the question of objectives. We found that there were a number of issues that attracted attention and these we now consider.

The debate about objectives

There is by no means universal consensus that the specifying of objectives is 'a good thing'. Eisner (1967) believes that there are four main weaknesses in the argument for specifying objectives. First: educational outcomes cannot be predicted with the accuracy claimed. Second: the possibility of specifying with precision is a function of the subject being taught and some subjects are not amenable to this treatment whereas others may be to some extent. Third: in some circumstances objectives can only be used as a criterion of judgement, but attempts are made to use them as standards of measurement. Fourth: he believes there is confusion between the logical requirement of relating means to ends in the curriculum as a product and the psychological conditions useful for constructing curricula. He also argues that specific objectives can be as much 'window dressing' as broad syllabus aims. They may also, if stated in great detail, become so numerous that teachers would need to spend more time in writing objectives than teaching. Stenhouse (1969) takes up some of Eisner's points and considers also that objectives stress convergent rather than divergent thinking and may imprison students within a set pattern of objectives rather than allow them to work out their own purposes. They may also destroy the quality of opportunism in teaching.

Atkin (1968) urges a number of reservations about objectives, some of which are allied to the points already made but have a somewhat different slant. For Atkin an important difficulty is the fact that any learning situation will most likely have unforeseen and possibly unperceived elements; elements that could not have been included in a list of objectives specified *before* instruction. He feels that if precisely stated objectives become commonly accepted and expected the curriculum will emphasize those elements that are identifiable in this way, and other important outcomes less amenable to such treatment will disappear. He also feels that the curriculum will regress towards objectives reflected in test items, and that certain worthwhile learning activities may disappear. This would apply particularly to activities for which we have not succeeded in establishing a one-to-one correspondence between the curriculum elements and educational results which are rather difficult to measure. Atkin also believes that there is a danger that promising trends in curriculum development will be frustrated by an insistence on behavioural specification, since the essence of some types of developments is their tentativeness and fluidity. Finally, there is the danger that objectives will be chosen by the extent to which they can be readily measured rather than by the extent to which they are derived from our needs and philosophies. Stones (1969a) also draws attention to the fact that instruction may lead to unspecified outcomes. In an experiment using a programmed psychology text he found that seminar discussions allied to the study of the programme did not produce superior scores on the post test allied to the programme objectives, but nevertheless he suggests there might well have been unspecified and undetected learning as a result of the seminar discussions.

Popham (1968) in an examination of the arguments against behavioural goals is of the opinion 'that those who discourage educators from precisely explicating their instructional objectives are often permitting, if not promoting, the same kind of unclear thinking that has led in part to the generally abysmal quality of instruction in this country [U.S.A.]'. He accepts the fact that in some subjects it is particularly difficult to formulate aims precisely, and instances the fine arts and the claims made by many teachers in these fields that it can't be done. He points out that in fact teachers in these subjects are doing this all the time. On the one hand they say: 'How can you

6

stipulate precise behavioural objectives for artists?' On the other hand they do make critical judgements of their students' output. Instructional objectives merely make explicit the criteria of such judgements. If it is impossible to identify such objectives, how can it be possible for teachers in these fields to have evaluative criteria? Other views advanced by Popham are that behaviourally stated objectives need not lead to unanticipated outcomes of instruction being overlooked. Really important outcomes should never be overlooked anyway. He also points out that only when aims are behaviourally stated is it possible to determine whether they are trivial or not. All too often trivial behavioural outcomes lurk behind high-sounding façades of profundity. In reply to the argument that the demand for measurable outcomes reduces learning to the assimilation of quantifiable bits of data, he points out that consensus evaluation of highly complex skills such as high diving is extremely common and manages to avoid such reductionism. Developmental work is needed in areas where evaluative measures are primitive. Other points dealt with are that teachers do not operate like this anyway. This is really a non-argument: they should. That they cannot, because of shortage of time and the difficulty of the operation, is countered by arguing that the teacher's load should be so reduced that he is able to become a professional decision-maker rather than a custodian. Perhaps we should give him objectives rather than force him to generate his own. 'Many of the federal dollars currently being used to support education would be better spent on agencies which would produce alternative behavioural objectives for all fields at all grade levels.'

Another interesting point for those involved in teacher education relates to assessment of practical teaching. Precise statement of objectives may be seen as threatening by the teacher at whatever level, since, with objectives specified in terms of learner behaviour, the assessment of teacher competence shifts from the maze of folklore and mysticism that exists at the moment regarding teacher evaluation and is focused on pupils' actual attainments. This is a potent reason for some of the resistance to precisely stated objectives but it is important that educators promote this kind of accountability instead of the current indices of competence. Popham concedes that there are elements of truth in most of the criticisms made of precisely stated objectives but that these criticisms should be regarded as pointers to possible problems in specifying objectives, not as reasons for abandoning the practice. 'Any risks we run by moving to behavioural goals are miniscule in contrast with our current state of confusion regarding instructional intentions.'

De Cecco (1968) takes a similar point of view. He recognizes that over-explicit statements of objectives could lead to a multiplicity of meaningless aims. He also agrees that explicit statements may overemphasize conformity and inhibit such complex behaviours as critical judgement, creative innovation and adaptive individual behaviour. However, whereas some writers seem to consider the arguments against the specifying of objectives to be so compelling as to rule them out as instruments in course preparation, De Cecco sees the arguments as referring to real problems, which must be faced and guarded against but do not preclude the use of objectives. In fact De Cecco himself sets out a fairly elaborate set of objectives in his textbook *The Psychology of Learning and Instruction.* In a discussion of objectives in the teaching of mathematics, Wood (1968) accepts the fact that there are problems in this approach but argues that it is up to other methods of course planning to show that they have more to offer in making the teacher aware of what he is doing and why he is doing it.

In a seminar involving both Eisner and Popham (Popham *et al.*, 1969), Eisner develops a somewhat different approach to the question of objectives. He distinguishes between two kinds of objectives: instructional objectives and what he calls *expressive objectives.* Of the two, expressive objectives are, for him, the more important. An expressive objective is envisaged by Eisner as 'the outcome of an encounter or learning activity which is planned to provide the student with an opportunity to personalise learning. It is precisely because of the richness of these encounters or activities and the unique character of the outcome that the expressive objective becomes so difficult to describe in advance.' He argues that probably the overwhelming majority of teachers think of objectives in these terms and appraise their teaching by the extent to which the children are engaged and interested in the classroom activities. He declares: 'The reason for using this criterion rather than instructional objectives is because, as I view the situation, teachers believe that engagement, intellectual and emotional immersion, is a better indicator of educational value than achievement test scores.' However, since there is some difficulty in distinguishing between the *encounters* contributing to expressive objectives and learning activities, Eisner considers that either one takes the risk of such confusion or of describing what has occurred *after* the encounter.

Popham and Sullivan, commenting on Eisner's formulation, are unconvinced by his arguments on expressive objectives which they consider as being difficult to distinguish from learning activities geared to outcomes which at present cannot be assessed. Popham develops this theme and presents a schematic view of two continua related to the results of instruction. The first continuum relates to the degree to which the results of instruction were intended. The second relates to the degree of measurability possible. He explains: 'In cell A we find operationally stated instructional objectives. In cell B are those unanticipated outcomes which, if important, would obviously influence one's evaluation of an instructional sequence. In cell C, I believe, are the "expressive objectives" referred to by Eisner. He may even wish to use cell D to describe these kinds of results. To some degree, of

	Intended results	Unanticipated results
Measurable results	A	B
Unassessable results	C	D

course, results which are both unanticipated and unassessable are next to impossible to identify. Results associated with cell D are therefore of no utility.' While Popham does not discount the value of teaching and learning encounters where objectives are not prespecified, he believes the emphasis should most definitely be on the other type. He considers that the proportion of worthwhile results which should be classified in cells C and D is relatively small and he considers that 'hard inventive thinking can usually allow instructors to use cell A almost exclusively'.

Justification for specifying objectives

In his critique of 1967, Eisner listed the three main reasons advanced for the specifying of objectives. They are: to provide goals towards which the curriculum is aimed; once stated they facilitate the selection and organization of content; when specified in behavioural terms they make it possible to evaluate the outcomes of the curriculum. Much of the literature that we shall be considering in this section takes up aspects of these points and enlarges on them. It takes the point conceded by Eisner that the argument for specifying objectives is a disarming one because it implies logic and 'who can argue in favour of irrationality?' And in fact the attractions of logic and rationality are so great that the literature arguing in favour of the specifying of objectives is much more extensive than that arguing against it. However, there is little doubt that Eisner is correct when he says that the arguments have so far failed to convince teachers. It is our view that this is more likely a result of their being unacquainted with the detailed rationale of the process than because they have given very serious attention to the problem. And, of course, the point made by Popham about the possible threat to teachers of such activity is extremely relevant, and it is not surprising that Ammons (1964) found that teachers base their procedures on what they have done before rather than on the identification of objectives.

To a great extent traditional 'Aims' have helped perpetuate the practice of doing what was done before rather than working to clearly defined goals. Dearden (1969) points out that although aims should provide overall orientation and direction for a highly complex activity (teaching or learning), in fact the aims of child-centred theorists such as the cultivation of a 'happy atmosphere' or the developing of 'full and satisfying lives' or the 'full development of children's powers' cannot possibly give procedural guidance. In his view the currently clouded aims are the products of traditional education in eclipse. With aims such as this almost any instructional procedures can be advanced as appropriate, and in view of the impossibility of evaluating student final performance in such amorphous fields they could not be shown to be inappropriate.

It was in fact concern with the systematic approach to evaluation and testing that led to pioneer work on objectives in the 1920s and 1930s (Lindvall, 1964). R. W. Tyler is generally considered to be a seminal writer in the field at that time and up to the present. In 1934 he was already writing critically of vague high-sounding generalities, which were proposed as aims and which, although they may sound well, 'prove to be glittering generalities which are of little value as guides in teaching and useless in making examinations' (Tyler, 1934). In place of such grandiose but fruitless generalities Tyler considered it essential to state the objectives in such clear and definite terms that they can serve as guides in the making of examination questions. He goes on to make points which enunciate a principle still central to work in the field of objectives.

> Each objective must be defined in terms which clarify the kind of behaviour which the course should help to develop among the students; that is to say, a statement is needed which explains the meaning of the objective by describing the reactions we can expect of persons who have reached the objective. This helps to make clear how one can tell when the objective is being attained since those who are reaching the objective will be characterised by the behaviour specified in this analysis. (Tyler, 1934; Klausmeier and Swanson, 1950)

Lindvall (1964) considers that work in the fields of testing and evaluation since Tyler's early work has stressed features of the statement of objectives, which can be summed up in two main points.

1   *Statements of specific objectives should be worded in terms of the pupil.* The question cannot be what the teacher has lectured on but what the *pupil* is able *to do* at the end of the course.
2   *Statements of specific objectives must include the exact behaviour that the pupil is to be expected to exhibit.* Lindvall points out that such criteria have had their effect not only on testing practice but also on curriculum development.

We would add that they have also had an important, possibly a profound effect on thinking about modes and processes of instruction, especially through the influences of experimentation in the devising of self-instructional programmes.

In a more recent contribution to the discussion about objectives Tyler (1964) argues that unless objectives are clear the student will not know what he is supposed to learn and will therefore be likely to learn something else. For example, he may memorize the teacher's lecture notes, which is very likely a form of rote learning, whereas the teacher could well have had in mind that the student should learn principles that would be of general application. Later, Tyler (1969) urges that even if we concede that good teaching may be intuitive the planning of instruction is dependent upon goals.

One of the first fruits of the discussions about objectives, which made tangible some of the ideas that had been mooted, was the *Taxonomy of Educational Objectives: the Cognitive Domain*, by B. Bloom *et al.* We discuss this later at some length but at this stage we think it apposite to refer to Bloom's views on the purposes of objectives. In his view the Taxonomy will help to ensure accuracy of communication, will help in the clarification of goals, and will be of value in the building of curricula. Emphasis on the usefulness of objectives in facilitation of communication is referred to by Beard (1968) and by MacKenzie *et al.* (1970). Beard and MacKenzie also stress the point referred to by other writers that the stringent specification of objectives facilitates the efficient selection of teaching and learning activities. They also both refer to the need for objectives in the evaluation of instruction. An allied point with a slightly different emphasis is made by Wood (1968) when he argues that the specification of objectives is a powerful agent in making the teacher aware of what he is doing and encourages him to ask himself why he is doing it. Gagné (1967) accepts the general tenor of the arguments for objectives referred to above but goes on to suggest that 'the most fundamental reason of all for the central importance of defining educational objectives is that such definition makes possible the basic distinction between content and method'. Content must be derived from objectives, method cannot be.

There is in the above comments on the desirability of carefully specifying objectives a rough consensus of opinion about the valuable features of such an activity. Increasingly for curriculum reformers, for test constructors and for the constructors of learning and teaching materials and sequences, the need for carefully defined objectives is taken for granted. Thus, for example, we find that Maclure (1968), in discussing curriculum innovation, does not question that one of the characteristics of such innovation is that it focuses on ends, aims and objectives. Similarly, the report of the National Council for Educational Technology in 1968 takes it as axiomatic that the two first steps in the design of any learning system are the thorough analysis of the objectives of the learning in question and the clear specification of the initial requirements demanded of the learner before embarking on this design.

Characteristics of objectives

An examination of the literature suggests that there are a number of elements that may be considered criterial attributes of instructional objectives. Furst (1957) suggests that objectives should have the following characteristics. They should be clearly stated in terms of pupil behaviour; they must not overlap; they should include all the important aspects of behaviour related to the problem; they should specify the kinds of response that may be accepted as evidence of these aspects of behaviour; they should specify the limiting conditions under which the learning is likely to take place. These points would gain acceptance from most writers in the field. In particular there is a general consensus that objectives should state clearly what the *student* should be able to *do* at the end of instruction. Mager (1962) has made a very influential contribution in this field by pointing out the pitfalls in the use of expressions such as 'know', 'understand' and 'appreciate' when used in the specification of objectives. What, he asks, is meant when we say that we want a learner to 'know' something? Stones (1968) has given some examples of the use of this type of terminology in public examinations. Recent A-level syllabuses have expressed their aims in such terms as 'will have a sound knowledge of', 'will be able to show an awareness of', 'will show such knowledge of . . . as is necessary for the appreciation of'. In teacher education, examples from recent college prospectuses include such pearls as 'to provide each student with the opportunity to extend his creative potential to the full and to develop understanding and critical appreciation of the visual arts: to extend his constructive imagination and encourage curiosity and acute perception'. This from an art course. An example from mathematics is terser but of comparable precision: 'The aim of the course will be to help the student to appreciate mathematical thought.' And a glance at any collection of such documents will yield a rich harvest of similar formulations. The point is, of course, that any of these statements could be agreed by people who had very different ideas about what constituted the proper aims of the various courses. The terms used are so open to misinterpretation that they can mean just about anything to anybody. Even with more precisely stated objectives it is important to be quite explicit in specifying required student behaviour since the danger of spurious consensus is quite high. The one phrase may symbolize very different concepts for different tutors unless it is both precise and as explicit as is necessary for complete unambiguity. In view of the comments by Eisner, who seems to have confused precision with specificity, it is perhaps worth stressing that precisely stated objectives are not necessarily highly specific and do not necessarily imply that the student behaviours related to a given objective are molecular or trivial. In order to give the needed precision Mager suggests that we use terms such as *construct*, *state* or *solve* in relation to the desired student activity when we frame objectives and eschew expressions such as *understand* and *appreciate*.

Although objectives should be specific, they can be specific at different levels. Tyler (1964) believes that the problem is to avoid being too specific or too global. On the one hand it is important to avoid spelling out the minutiae of course content; on the other hand it is necessary to avoid the spurious consensus through vague generalities exemplified in traditional syllabuses. Tyler gives an example to illustrate this problem. He suggests that the aim, 'the ability to read French', is too general, but that spelling out in detail that a student should be able to give the meaning of the most common 2500 French words, or have knowledge of the meaning of each of a number of common French idioms is being too specific. Often it is possible to state an objective and to give it precision by providing examples of the behaviours involved in achieving the objective. Thus, for example, an aim such as that the children should be able to solve quadratic equations can be made more precise by adding 'of the type' and providing one or two examples (Stones, 1968).

Krathwohl (1965) presents the arguments for the need for objectives at different levels of specificity. He suggests that there is a first, most abstract level of objectives such as the broad general statements that correspond to generalized educational goals and may refer to the work of several years. At

cf.
Wheeler

a second level a *behavioural* objectives orientation helps to analyse broad goals into more specific ones, useful in specifying the goals of an instructional unit, a course or a sequence of courses. The third level is the level needed to create instructional materials. Almost invariably these materials are the operational embodiment of one particular route to the achievement of a curriculum planned at the second, more abstract, level. Objectives at the third level bring into focus the objectives of specific lesson plans. Krathwohl argues that the different levels of specificity in the preparation of objectives are essential and that it is not possible to move at once into the objectives at the most specific level. All levels of specification are essential to guide planning. Only as each level is reached can the next be begun. Furthermore, not all objectives lend themselves to *complete* specification at the third level. He instances the example that there are only forty-five sums of two numbers from o to 10 that need to be learned and these could be specified with perfect accuracy, but often we cannot specify all the instances of behaviour implied in the objectives. He uses Gagné's term, 'mastery' objective, to apply to learning of the former kind, and 'transfer' objective to apply to learning of the latter type. Transfer objectives seem to constitute the major ultimate goals for the bulk of the educational process. A third reason for having objectives at several levels of specificity is to enable us continually to examine their interrelation to one another. This introduces a measure of flexibility so that the agreed core of more general objectives continues to guide the preparation of the more specific objectives when, as is likely for various reasons, they change. This argument is based on the fact that consensus is more likely on broader objectives, which will tend to remain, even when the more specific ones are questioned. Similarly, while agreement may be reached on the broader objectives, it may well be that different course planners will have different ideas about the specific ways of achieving those objectives and there may, in fact, be several different sets of highly specific objectives all legitimately leading towards the achievement of the same broader ones.

We believe that the question of level of specificity and the arguments about the need for them are of key importance and we will return to them when we discuss our own approach. So also is the question of mastery or transfer objectives. Markle and Tiemann (1970) take up this point and argue that the distinction between mastery and transfer objectives is the key distinction when classifying educational objectives. To some extent we share these views and will return to them in more detail later.

To give even more precision to the stated objective, the level of student final performance is often specified. In the case of the example given on the specification on solving equations, we might add 'without making any errors', or 'correctly in nine out of ten problems'. The level of competence written into the objectives, like the objectives themselves, is a function of one's attitude to teaching and the evaluation of learning. Traditional syllabus-bound instruction will often be satisfied with student achievement of say 50 per cent, whereas a teacher working to objectives such as we have been discussing is more likely to go for achievement at least at the 70 per cent level. (It is true, of course, that the issue of norm-referenced tests and criterion-referenced tests is much wider than the debate about objectives, but there is little doubt that the increased attention to objectives, which flowed from the development of programmed learning, has been crucial in making this an important focus of attention in the development of evaluative techniques.)*

Some writers consider the question of entry behaviour as part of the problem of preparing objectives. This refers to the capabilities of the student in the field in question before instruction is started. Clearly it is possible to produce objectives without considering this problem, but it would not be possible to generate teaching sequences to accomplish these objectives without taking into account the prerequisite skills and concepts for the learning in question. In general the point at issue is that we aim to ensure that the learner has the necessary competence to start the course of instruction. However, Mager and Clark (1963) addressed themselves to another problem, the problem that many students come to a course of instruction already competent in some aspects of the proposed learning. They found in several investigations that merely by providing students with detailed specifications of course objectives and access to a tutor, the students learned more efficiently than they did on orthodox courses. An important reason for this result is that students in this kind of learning situation demand only the information they need to achieve the stated objectives, and therefore the activities that merely rehearse existing skills, which may be regarded as redundant, are omitted with the result that learning time is reduced.

---

* In norm-referenced tests an individual's performance is measured against the performance of the group. In criterion-referenced tests an individual's performance is assessed according to the extent to which he has mastered the learning related to the test. Thus a score of 50 per cent in a norm-referenced test might be considered satisfactory because it is the average score of the group. It would probably be unsatisfactory in a criterion-referenced test because it would indicate that the student had learned only half of his assignment.

There seems little doubt that the findings of Mager and Clark should be seriously considered, especially at the level where students can take a large amount of responsibility for their own learning. However, in so far as the actual preparation of objectives is concerned, it is undoubtedly of greater importance to determine a minimum level of entry competence. Without this competence the student would be unlikely to achieve the objectives at all.

Whether or not entry behaviour should be taken as part of the job of specifying objectives will probably remain a question of personal preference, and to some extent the same applies to other aspects in the preparation of objectives. In the last analysis objectives themselves are matters of personal preference, the considered value judgements of those responsible for the teaching, but this is not to say that intuitive teaching is sufficient. An instructional programme must be a functioning instrument; its cutting edge has the sharpness that results from careful analysis of its purpose (Tyler, 1969). And even if we have no truly objective criteria for determining objectives, at the least they should be consistent with our theories of learning (Tyler, 1964). They should also be precise, and they should be consistent, i.e. the achievement of one should not render the achievement of others difficult or impossible (Ammons, 1964).

There is one final and most important feature of objectives: they should constitute a dynamic system. Tyler expresses this important point succinctly:

> . . . as you work with objectives and your efforts to teach them you frequently have a basis for the re-definition of your objectives. As you see what is really possible, you may see more clearly the kinds of things the pupils need in addition to those that you thought of in your original planning. The process of clarifying goals, then working towards them, then appraising progress, then re-examining the goals, modifying them and clarifying them in the light of experience and the data is a never ending procedure. (Tyler, 1964, p. 83)

The systematizing of objectives

In the discussion of objectives so far there has been little reference to the way in which objectives might relate to one another. It is, of course, possible to conceive of a set of objectives that are not related to one another in any systematic way. Such a completely atomistic system might well be useful but it would have limitations, which could produce problems at the planning, teaching and evaluative stages of any instructional process. A problem common to all these stages would be the difficulty of deciding on the relative importance of the objectives. At the evaluative stage there would be the problem of determining the appropriate test instrument for each objective out of an undifferentiated collection. At the teaching stage there would be problems of sequencing and emphasis, which would virtually force the teacher into some attempt at systematizing his aims, even if only at a very rudimentary level. In the actual process of clarifying objectives it would be difficult to be sure that the field had been comprehensively covered, that there was no duplication and that the objectives were at the appropriate levels of generality. A logically consistent model for the generation of objectives would clearly be a boon to all concerned with teaching, whether in research, in the classroom or in the construction of evaluative instruments.

Few would deny that the taxonomies produced by Bloom *et al.* (1956) and Krathwohl *et al.* (1964) have gone some way to providing assistance in the clarification of objectives along the lines mentioned. The Bloom taxonomy has indeed been seminal in its influence in several spheres of education. Cox (1966) reported that at that time he had reports of fifty-six studies involving the use of the Bloom taxonomy and was in contact with sixty people working with the taxonomy, and the mailing list was increasing daily. In the U.K. the first publication of the taxonomy created little stir, but in recent years there has been considerably more interest and currently the taxonomy is influencing thinking and activity among groups such as the public examining bodies (Joint Matriculation Board, 1969) and the Society for Research in Higher Education (Beard *et al.*, 1968) not to mention the impact it is having in many unrecorded curriculum construction discussions. In the Birmingham School of Education Colleges of Education Research Group it has been used as a guide in the thinking of tutors concerned with the objectives of a variety of courses in colleges of education (Stones, 1970b).

Krathwohl (1965) has produced a useful exposition of the rationale of the taxonomy. He explains its structure and function.

> The taxonomy of educational objectives is basically a classification scheme just as the biological taxonomy is a classification scheme for animals into class, order, family, genus, and species. In the educational objectives taxonomy, the kinds of behaviours we seek to have students display as a result of the learning process are classified. Every behavioural objective is composed of two parts – the behaviour the student is to display and the subject matter or content that is then used in the display. The taxonomy deals only with the behavioural part of the

objective; the content or subject matter classification is left to the Library of Congress, the Dewey Decimal System, and such other similar classifications.

For purposes of convenience the taxonomy was divided into three domains, the cognitive, affective, and psychomotor. Handbook I, *The Cognitive Domain* . . . deals with objectives having to do with thinking, knowing and problem solving. Handbook II, *The Affective Domain* . . . includes objectives dealing with attitudes, values, interests, appreciation, and social-emotional adjustment. The psychomotor domain covers objectives having to do with manual and motor skills. [Not yet published]

Basically the taxonomy is an educational–logical–psychological classification system. The terms in this order reflect the emphasis given to the principles upon which it is built. It makes educational distinctions in the sense that the boundaries between categories reflect the decisions that teachers make among student behaviours in their development of curriculums and in choosing learning situations. It is a logical system in the sense that its terms are defined precisely and are used consistently. In addition, each category permits logical subdivisions which can be clearly defined and further subdivided as necessary and useful. Finally the taxonomy seems to be consistent with our present understanding of psychological phenomena, though it does not rest on any single theory.

The scheme is intended to be purely descriptive so that every type of educational goal can be represented. It does not indicate the value or quality of one class as compared to another. It is impartial with respect to views of education. One of the tests of the taxonomy has been that of inclusiveness – could one classify all kinds of educational objectives (if stated in student behaviours) in the framework? In general it seems to have met this test.

The authors of the taxonomy make the point that their scheme is more than a simple classification of objectives by common attributes. They preface their handbook with a dictionary definition: 'Taxonomy – "Classification, esp. of animals and plants according to their natural relationships . . ." ' The hypothesized 'natural relationships' that transform the collection of objectives into a taxonomy are those of a hierarchy. There are six main categories of objectives in the cognitive domain and five in the affective domain. Each category is assumed to involve behaviour more complex and abstract than the previous category. Thus the categories range from simple to complex behaviour and from concrete to abstract behaviour. Each category has a main heading, which is broken down into more specific subheadings, which can themselves be further subdivided into still more particular areas. An abbreviated version of the taxonomy follows, but the reader is referred to the full taxonomy to see the detailed working out of the hierarchical principle in actual examples of test items.

Summary of the taxonomy of educational objectives, Handbooks I and II

I   The Cognitive Domain

1.00 *Knowledge*

1.10 Knowledge of specifics
    1.11 Knowledge of terminology
    1.12 Knowledge of specific facts

1.20 Knowledge of ways and means of dealing with specifics
    1.21 Knowledge of conventions
    1.22 Knowledge of trends and sequences
    1.23 Knowledge of classifications and categories
    1.24 Knowledge of criteria
    1.25 Knowledge of methodology

1.30 Knowledge of universals and abstractions in a field
    1.31 Knowledge of principles and generalizations
    1.32 Knowledge of theories and structures

2.00 *Comprehension*
    2.10 Translation
    2.20 Interpretation
    2.30 Extrapolation

3.00 *Application*

4.00 *Analysis*
    4.10 Analysis of elements
    4.20 Analysis of relationships
    4.30 Analysis of organizational principles

5.00 *Synthesis*
    5.10 Production of a unique communication

5.20 Production of a plan or a proposed set of operations

5.30 Derivation of a set of abstract relations

6.00 *Evaluation*

6.10 Judgement in terms of internal evidence

6.20 Judgement in terms of external criteria

II   The Affective Domain

1.0 *Receiving (Attending)*

1.1 Awareness

1.2 Willingness to receive

1.3 Controlled or selected attention

2.0 *Responding*

2.1 Acquiescence in responding

2.2 Willingness to respond

2.3 Satisfaction in response

3.0 *Valuing*

3.1 Acceptance of a value

3.2 Preference for a value

3.3 Commitment

4.0 *Organization*

4.1 Conceptualization of a value

4.2 Organization of a value system

5.0 *Characterization by a value or value complex*

5.1 Generalized set

5.2 Characterization

Scrutiny of the full taxonomy will reveal a number of expressions that would not meet the criteria referred to in the discussion on specificity and precision. The number of concrete illustrations is limited and could well be challenged, according to Mager's criteria, for lack of specificity. In an attempt to provide a more clear cut description of how the taxonomy can be implemented in the school setting, Metfessel *et al.* (1969) have prepared a scheme for the instrumentation of the Bloom and Krathwohl taxonomy. The scheme comprises a set of behaviourally orientated infinitives, which, when combined with given objects, would form a basis for meaningful, cohesive and operational statements.

The instrument devised to achieve this aim comprises a table with three columns. The first column contains the taxonomic description following Bloom and Krathwohl. The second contains infinitives appropriate to the precise stating of the behaviour desired. The third contains general terms relative to subject matter properties. These are direct objects and may be expanded to furnish specificity at a desired level. They may also be permuted with one or more of the infinitives to yield the basic structure of an educational objective. Although the preparation of this scheme may not, at first blush, appear to be a particularly high level activity, the act of attempting to specify objectives in behavioural terms is likely to convince one otherwise and we suggest that the scheme is worthy of the attention of those involved in this type of activity. We provide below an illustrative sample of the tables described.

Extract from Table 1 of the Instrumentation of Educational Objectives Cognitive Domain (Metfessel *et al.*, 1969)

Taxonomy classification	*Examples of infinitives*	*Examples of direct objects*
1.11 Knowledge of terminology	to define, to distinguish, to acquire, to identify, to recall, to recognize	facts, factual information (sources) (names) (dates) (events) (persons) (places) (time periods), properties, examples, phenomena
5.30 Derivation of a set of abstract relations	to produce, to derive, to develop, to combine, to organize, to synthesize, to classify, to deduce, to develop, to formulate, to modify	phenomena, taxonomies, concepts, schemes, theories, relationships, abstractions, generalizations, hypotheses, perceptions, ways, discoveries

The cognitive domain of the taxonomy of educational objectives was developed before the affective domain, since the authors considered it likely that this domain would be more useful to educationists. There was also the fact that curricular trends were moving away from emphasis in the affective areas (Krathwohl, 1964). This trend was undoubtedly a reflection of the reappraisal of the warm and woolly aims that had constituted the staple of many American schools and not a few British schools. In the desire to inject rigour into the curriculum, affective aims were looked upon with suspicion. Undoubtedly this reappraisal had very beneficial effects, but at the same time it cannot be denied that some affective aims are extremely important and, in addition, even if the woolly aims of yesteryear were predominantly affective, it is by no means true that woolliness is an inevitable feature of all affective aims. R. Mager (1964) makes some cogent points on affective aims. After careful study of educational objectives prepared by nationally recognized educators, Mager and his associates found that these aims had one thing in common: they all intended for the student to be able to do something after the instruction has ended, at some point after the influence of the instructor is terminated. After considering the best way of achieving this particular objective, they concluded that 'no matter what the nature of the instruction, no matter what the subject matter, no matter what the age level of the student, there is a universal objective appropriate to all instruction; that *at the very least* it should be the intent of the instructor to send the student away from the instruction with an attitude towards the subject matter at least as favourable as that with which he arrived.' (Richmond, 1968, p. 32) He goes on to point out that, if education is for the future, teachers should endeavour to send the student away from instruction anxious not only to use what he has learned but anxious to learn more about it as time goes on. In fact, he points out, it is generally agreed that

> *every* teacher wants to send his students away more favourably disposed towards his subject than when the student arrived . . . if this is true, then for the most part it is a hollow wish, it is talk not followed by action, it is little more than another example of good intention. Because, you see, to act to achieve this goal requires that the objective be specified in a way that would allow one to recognise success. Some sort of measuring instrument would have to be prepared and administered to ascertain whether attitudes have been improved or degraded by the teacher, course procedures would have to be analysed for techniques that tend to adversely influence attitude (approach tendency), and the course would have to be constantly monitored for its affective effect on the student. How many are demonstrating that much interest in reaching this objective? 'There can't be many,' we were told by one ex-student. 'After all,' he said, 'not all of us millions dropped out of school because we were pregnant.'

It seems to us that this comment provides an important gloss on the relationship between the cognitive and affective domains of the Bloom and Krathwohl taxonomies.

The analysis of cognitive behaviours, ranging from the simple memorizing of facts (level 1 cognitive domain) to the ability to deploy complex bodies of concepts in processes of evaluation (level 6 cognitive domain), is effectively counterpointed by the range of behaviours from acceptance (level 1 affective domain) to the complete involvement of level 5 of the affective domain, where the individual is so committed to a given outlook that it is part of his total philosophy or world view. It is possible that the level of commitment alluded to by Mager does not necessarily reach this level, but it certainly seems to correspond to level 3. Thus, for example, an objective at this level suggested in the affective taxonomy is 'Devotion to reading as an avenue for self improvement'. A correlated objective in the cognitive domain, which might be considered to be functionally related to it, is at level 4.30, 'The ability to recognize form and pattern in literary or artistic works as a means of understanding their meaning'. An example of a correlation at a different level may be found in level 1.11 of the cognitive domain, 'Knowledge of the vocabulary of the fine arts sufficient to be able to read and converse intelligently', which is related to an example of an objective at level 1.1 in the affective domain: 'Develops some consciousness of colour, form, arrangement and design in the objects and structures around him and in descriptive or symbolic representations of people, things and situations'. Such matches can, of course, be found at the different levels of the taxonomy.

Scriven (1967) has suggested a classification scheme, which is closely related to the Bloom taxonomy but which, in the opinion of MacKenzie *et al.* (1970), adds an important dimension by identifying three levels of description for educational objectives. They are:

a   A relatively abstract or *conceptual* description of the parameters (of the field of knowledge).
b   A *manifestational* description, which is the next stage towards the specification of the particular tests to be used.
c   The *operational* description, i.e. the stage at which the actual tests are specified.

MacKenzie points out (and our experience in specifying objectives in various fields of the education course in colleges leads us to concur) that, if one tries to go straight to the manifestation level, 'one is liable to arrive at rather segmented and unrelated groups of objectives and to have no clear guidelines for deciding upon priorities'. On the other hand, if one begins at the conceptual level one gets an overall view of the structure of the subject, which enables one to determine the kind of global view of the subject that one wishes the student to attain. From this one can derive the manifestational level where one has to specify the precise nature of the skills, concepts and attitudes one hopes the student will have acquired, and, finally, at the operational level one has to prescribe the actual instruments that will evaluate the extent to which the student has achieved the objectives set. This formulation is, of course, very similar to Krathwohl's (1965) argument (p. 14).

Gerlach and Sullivan (Sullivan, 1969) devised a method of classification for objectives in the cognitive domain, which differs from the Bloom taxonomy particularly in that it is based on overt learner behaviour. In their scheme they argue that it is possible to classify nearly all learner behaviours of a cognitive nature under six headings as follows.

IDENTIFY: The learner indicates membership or non-membership of specified objects or events in a class when the name of the class is given.

NAME: The learner supplies the correct verbal label (in speech or writing) for a referent or set of referents when the name of the referent is not given.

DESCRIBE: The learner reports the necessary categories of object properties, events, event properties, and/or relationships relevant to a designated referent. The teacher should decide in advance the learner responses which will serve as acceptable descriptions, although he should also accept other given descriptions which he deems correct but did not anticipate.

CONSTRUCT: The learner produces a product (e.g. a drawing, article of clothing or furniture, map, essay, examples of a particular concept, etc.) which meets specifications given either in class or in the test item itself.

ORDER: The learner arranges two or more referents in a specified order. The learner may be required to name or describe the referents in order himself, or a group of referents may be provided for him to order.

DEMONSTRATE: The learner performs the behaviours essential to the accomplishment of a designated task according to pre-established or given specifications. The learner may be required to provide a verbal description to accompany the performance.

Sullivan points out that while the conceptual framework of this system of classification suggests optimum sequencing procedures for instructional tasks, validation of their efficacy awaits empirical evidence on their use in the teaching situation. And this applies to all such systems at present not excluding the one we propose in a later chapter.

Another extremely important contribution to our thinking about the objectives of instruction has been provided by Gagné (1965). Gagné's classification is more directly related to behaviour than the Bloom and Krathwohl taxonomies. Whereas the Bloom and Krathwohl taxonomies relate to the

24

outcomes of learning, the Gagné classification relates to the types of learning that might be conceived of as leading to the outcomes described in the other taxonomies.

Gagné's classification may be considered to be a taxonomy, since it has a logically consistent scheme of relationships among its constituent elements. As with the Bloom and Krathwohl taxonomies, the relationships among the elements are hierarchical. Proceeding from the simple to the complex we observe that the elements higher in the hierarchy subsume and depend upon the elements lower in the hierarchy. As with the other taxonomies, we cannot regard the Gagné scheme as a definitive statement, which will command universal acceptance as a theory of knowledge in this field; rather it is a working model, which seems to accord quite closely with reality as we presently conceive of it. Clearly this model will be modified or superseded as knowledge in the field expands.

The Gagné model suggests a hierarchy of learning types, proceeding from those types of learning that are common to man and the other animals and progressing to the types of learning that are characteristically human. His scheme in abbreviated form is as follows.

The types of learning that can currently be distinguished are as follows:

Type 1 SIGNAL LEARNING. The individual learns to make a general, diffuse response to a signal. This is the classical conditioned response of Pavlov (1927).

Type 2 STIMULUS RESPONSE LEARNING. The learner acquires a precise response to a discriminated stimulus. What is learned is a connection (Thorndike, 1898) or a discriminated operant (Skinner, 1938), sometimes called an instrumental response (Kimble, 1961).

Type 3 CHAINING. What is acquired is a chain of two or more stimulus-response connections. The conditions for such learning have been described by Skinner (1938) and others, notably Gilbert (1962).

Type 4 VERBAL ASSOCIATION. Verbal association is the learning of chains that are verbal. Basically, the conditions resemble those for other (motor) chains. However, the presence of language makes this a special type because internal links may be selected from the individual's previously learned repertoire of language.

Type 5 MULTIPLE DISCRIMINATION. The individual learns to make n different identifying responses to as many different stimuli, which may resemble each other in physical appearance to a greater or lesser

25

degree. Although the learning of each stimulus-response connection is a simple Type 2 occurrence, the connections tend to interfere with each other's retention.

Type 6 CONCEPT LEARNING. The learner acquires a capability of making a common response to a class of stimuli that may differ from each other widely in physical appearance. He is able to make a response that identifies an entire class of objects or events.

Type 7 PRINCIPLE LEARNING. In simplest terms, a principle is a chain of two or more concepts. It functions to control behaviour in the manner suggested by a verbalized rule of the form 'If A then B', where A and B are concepts. However, it must be carefully distinguished from the mere verbal sequence 'If A, then B', which of course may also be learned as Type 4.

Type 8 PROBLEM SOLVING. Problem solving is a kind of learning that requires the internal events usually called thinking. Two or more previously acquired principles are somehow combined to produce a new capability that can be shown to depend on a 'higher order' principle.

Gagné enters one *caveat* in respect of the supposed dependence of each different type of learning on the acquisition of learning at the level immediately before it in the hierarchy, in recognizing that there is lack of agreement among American psychologists that learning of type 2 is necessarily dependent upon learning of type 1. There is also a body of opinion that argues that the distinction made between these two types of learning is unreal anyway (Razran, 1965).

There are clear correspondences between the Bloom and Krathwohl proposals and the Gagné taxonomy. The lower level learning types in the Gagné model relate to the 'learning of facts' objectives in the lower levels of the Bloom taxonomy: i.e. they indicate the type of learning likely to be required to achieve the objectives at level 1 of the Bloom taxonomy. At the higher levels, principle learning and problem solving are clearly related to such objectives as the 'ability to plan a unit of instruction for a particular teaching situation' (Bloom level 5.30) or 'The ability to indicate logical fallacies in arguments' (Bloom level 6.10). To a great extent the two approaches are complementary. The Bloom taxonomy helps to clarify the goals and provides a tool for the effective analysis of objectives, while the Gagné scheme does the same for the learning behaviours.

In concluding this section we would stress that we consider the various models aimed at systematizing objectives as of considerable heuristic value

26

and our work owes a great deal to the stimulating concepts referred to. Nevertheless, we believe that the curriculum constructor, or the designer of learning sequences, is well advised to keep an open mind as to the optimum approach for his particular project. We have found, for example, that in certain circumstances the Bloom taxonomy has become the Bloom tramlines, which has had the effect of stultifying thinking about objectives rather than stimulating it. In our experience this seems to have been in part the result of the organization of the taxonomy, going as it does from the atomistic lowest level objectives and progressing to the higher order objectives later on in the taxonomy. The problem has been the difficulty of seeing the level 6 wood for the level 1 trees. In our own approach, which we discuss later, we have tried to avoid this difficulty.

2

Educational psychology in teacher preparation

As it has been

As long ago as 1835 concern was expressed about the practice of teaching, which adumbrated a very contemporary concern to equip student teachers with some general pedagogical principles upon which to base their classroom practice. The *Quarterly Journal of Education* commented at that time: 'We press moral principles upon the young mind relying upon the efficiency of precept at a time when children are only affected by sensible objects.' Shades of Piaget! Unfortunately, however, 'charity school teachers possess no talent beyond the nursery maid'. The twin themes are with us today.

Official pronouncements on the training of teachers have consistently taken up the theme that subjects, which would be classified by many as in the realm of educational psychology, should be accorded a major part in the preparation of teachers. Thus in its regulations for the training of elementary teachers, the Board of Education in 1909 suggested that students should be introduced to such topics as attention, memory, the growth of imagination and reasoning. The syllabus for 1918 developed these suggestions further and recommended that student teachers study the successive stages of child life from infancy to adolescence, the physical and mental characteristics of children at these stages, children's interests and activities, the means of obtaining attention, the handling of backward or precocious children, the causes of inattention, means of classifying and promoting scholars, discipline and order, the formation of good habits, the means of learning at the disposal of children at different ages and the framing of questions and dealing with children's answers. Unfortunately these topic headings are not enlarged upon.

Subsequent reports laid greater stress on physical development in their recommendations about child study. The Hadow Report (1931) gave roughly the same weight to the physical aspects of child development as it did to

28

what might be termed the psychological. The subjects it recommended were: sensory capacity, reasoning, aesthetic appreciation, emotion, children's interests as revealed in play, the 'working contents of the child's mind', the child's 'definition of his ideas' and the influence of the environment. The Spens Report (1938) devotes nine sections to physical development and one each to attention, memory, imagery, reasoning, the transfer of training and emotional development. The Newsom Report (1963) stressed the importance of sociological factors and social psychology. The Plowden Report (1966) makes little direct reference to the education of teachers beyond calling for a full inquiry into the system. Neither 'Psychology' nor 'Educational Psychology' appear in the index to this report. It does mention, however, that child development and the problems of handicapped children are areas of study of the greatest importance.

In professional circles it is reasonable to consider that the book by E. L. Thorndike, *Educational Psychology*, which appeared in 1903, was the first statement that claimed the existence of a body of knowledge under that name (Travers, 1969). At that time the field seemed to be virtually coterminous with psychology in general. Subsequent texts have been less universal in scope and have tended to focus on particular areas, but even so, many texts have tended to be wide ranging if not encyclopedic in their coverage. This is more characteristic of American books than of British. British books tend to be considerably shorter than American ones, which has probably had a restricting influence on their coverage. There has also, however, been a cultural difference. British texts have until recently devoted a major proportion of their contents to the consideration of individual differences with a pronounced emphasis upon intelligence and intelligence testing. The University of Hull *Library Bulletin* (1966) reviewing Stones's (1966) *Introduction to Educational Psychology*, draws attention to this fact and gives the proportions of the main British books in the field devoted to this subject. It finds that 27 per cent of Peel's (1956) *Psychological Bases of Education* was devoted to testing, with 31 per cent devoted to learning and thinking. Lovell's (1958) *Educational Psychology and Children* had 24 per cent devoted to testing and 18 per cent devoted to learning and thinking. Stones had 12 per cent on testing and 54 per cent on learning and thinking.

It would be very misleading, however, to suppose that there are clearly definable views as to what educational psychology is. Blair (1941) analysed eight contemporary psychology texts and found such a lack of overlap of the vocabulary from text to text that one could only conclude that there was little agreement on the areas of research in psychology that have maximum potential for educational application. In 1965 the situation was essentially the same. In the *Handbook for Instructors of Educational Psychology*, published in 1965 for the Division of Educational Psychology of the American Psychological Association, the authors take the view that there is still a substantial lack of agreement on what should constitute a course in educational psychology for prospective teachers (Della-Piana *et al.*, 1965). They quote from the *Annual Review of Psychology*: the field of educational psychology is in a 'general state of disorder' and 'in this field it is extremely difficult to organize the material around a central theme because of the wide range of subject matter and the diversity of methods employed'. Faced with this situation the committee concerned with the compilation of the *Handbook* decided not to attempt to specify the content of educational psychology courses.

The nearest British equivalent of the American *Handbook* is the joint report of the British Psychological Society and the Association of Teachers in Colleges and Departments of Education issued in 1962 (Birch, 1962). In an examination of what was taught under the rubric of educational psychology and of its place in the education course they produced the following picture.

Percentage of the education course devoted to psychology

%	Number of colleges
Impossible to answer	28
0–10	1
11–20	2
21–30	12
31–40	18
41–50	14
51–60	12
61–70	7
71 and over	4
Mean of 70 colleges = 39·9 per cent	

Topics in existing psychology courses

1 Development psychology (1660 units)
2 Psychology of learning (980 units)
3 Adjustment (780 units)
4 Educational attainment (760 units)

30

5 Intellectual abilities (610 units)
6 Personality (540 units)
7 Psychological functions: thinking, sensation, perception, imagination (430 units)
8 Statistics (170 units: negligible treatment apart from the normal curve)
9 Physiological psychology (120 units)
10 Others: aesthetics, temperament/physique (very few units each)

The high proportion of returns declaring it impossible to determine the proportion of time devoted to educational psychology underlines the hazardous nature of data collection in this field. It is more than likely that this problem is a consequence of the 'mother hen' principle of course organization, under which a group of students is allocated to a tutor who is responsible for the bulk of their tuition in education, be it philosophy, history, psychology or 'method'. Under such a system it is clearly impossible to get an accurate picture of the nature of the course, since there will be as many courses as there are tutors and the nature of the courses will reflect the tutors' interests and capabilities.

The list of topics taught presents us with an allied problem. Precisely what is involved in the headings given is virtually impossible to determine: each college will have its own idea of the actual nature of the instruction appropriate to the rubrics.

This report, like the American one, refers to the shortage of tutors adequately qualified in the subject to conduct rigorous courses. This problem is not one that we discuss at this time, but it is clearly one to be considered in planning teaching. It is also one that bears on our own inquiry into tutors' perceptions of appropriate objectives in educational psychology to which we will return later.

Hollins (1963) takes up some of the key points from the B.P.S./A.T.C.D.E. report and concludes that the general impression to be drawn from it is a very unfavourable one. The colleges had a high proportion of unqualified lecturers (39 per cent). The teaching was outdated: for example, examinations asked questions on McDougall's list of instincts, but there was little reference to Piaget. He thought there was a danger of students being indoctrinated by the excesses of the child-centred school without a dispassionate, scientific view. The report provided little evidence that students 'were expected to possess scientific knowledge in educational psychology as they might be expected to possess it in geography or physics or English'.

Other writers at different times have drawn similar conclusions as a result of scrutinizing college courses. Susan Isaacs (1924) drew attention to the paucity of knowledge about learning and instruction in colleges. She found a variety of views among college staffs concerning the value of educational psychology in college courses. Some thought that a teacher could not develop independently without it, others that it arouses the spirit of inquiry. It was considered by some to be too bookish but by others to help teachers to understand individuals. It was considered to be poorly taught, mainly by spoonfeeding in lectures. Some years later the focus in British colleges was on 'human relationships'. Fleming (1954) considered that attention had turned 'from externals such as class size, S.E.S. level, place or order of birth, to the more subtle relationships contributing to the satisfaction of the basic human need to receive appreciation and to make a contribution to an intimate circle of friendly human beings'. Brearley (1957) considered that the colleges taught observational techniques and aspects of development 'as a means of developing the primary qualities of sympathy and intuition which we assume in an intending teacher. . . . We aim at a professional training which will open up channels through which this sympathy and insight will flow more effectively and reliably, and to better purpose.' It was this kind of orientation that was presumably influential in bringing about the soft-centred approach referred to by Hollins.

The American experience in the same field has been somewhat different but still unsatisfactory. Glaser (1962) comments on the unsatisfactory nature of the relationship between developments in educational psychology and in teaching method. Instead of one informing the other, the two have developed along parallel tracks and feedback is quite missing. Schoben (1964) considered that much of what was presented in teacher education was a dull display of complicated but trivial research dealing with concepts remote from the would-be teacher. Many texts, he considered, are sound methodologically but substantially trivial. Skinner (1968) declares that the past history of educational psychology cannot be related to classroom teaching. Teachers rely on rules of thumb and experience, learning and teaching are not analysed and almost no effort is made to improve teaching as such. Indeed, he remarks, 'learning theorists insist that their work has no practical value'. Stiles (1969), reviewing teacher education programmes in America, declares that educational psychology, the most frequently required professional course, still suffers from lack of research and adequate standardization of subject matter.

Examination of the B.P.S./A.T.C.D.E. report suggests that the same lack of standardization was a feature of British college curricula at the time. The problem is that the correlation among courses in different colleges cannot be determined. Thus, although we can get an idea of the range of subjects taught, we cannot determine the ways in which they are combined and in fact the actual constituent elements in college courses could be quite varied. A scrutiny of a sample of college prospectuses suggests that variety is a feature of current courses. The course in one of these colleges consists of four major elements: child development, theories of maturation and learning, the recognition and treatment of difficulties in children and the psychology of groups. In this college educational psychology is one of four elements in the education course. In another college in the same area training organization, psychology of education is one of eleven elements in the education course. Some of the other elements would be considered by some colleges as belonging to educational psychology, viz. intelligence and intelligence testing, the developmental psychology of Jean Piaget and personality theory. A third college allocates educational and social psychology (bracketed) one fifth of the education course. In this college the psychological component comprises: the physical, intellectual, emotional and moral development of children; individual differences and their measurement; learning, including motivation, reasoning, reinforcement; elementary educational statistics. Within these different courses the individual tutors will interpret these headings in their own way and within their own spheres of interest and expertise. It is interesting to speculate whether we are likely to find the situation reported of a certain Canadian college where a husband and wife enrolled in the same educational psychology course found they could not discuss any substantive issues in the subject because they were enrolled in different sections with different instructors (Corman, 1969).

The justification for educational psychology

It seems to us plausible that the lack of agreement about the substantive content of educational psychology courses is very much a consequence of the lack of a body of clearly defined objectives. This, in turn, may reflect an uncertainty about the function of educational psychology as a course of study in the training of teachers. One gets the impression from official reports and similar publications that the main aim is to help the teacher to do his job better, but precisely what this entails is usually left unclear. In some cases the implications are that a theoretical study is not the best tool to help teachers in their work. Thus Dewey (1929) urged that student teachers would be well served if methods were developed which would 'enable us to make an analysis of what the gifted teacher does intuitively, so that something accruing from his work can be communicated to others'. Stolurow (1965)

33

puts a different point of view. He argues that the complexity of behaviour being observed is such that different observers may fix on different factors like analysts of the Rorschach projection test! Other considerations to be weighed are the ease with which superstitious behaviour (in the Skinnerian sense) can be acquired, that there are more ways of teaching ineffectively than there are of teaching effectively and even expert teachers engage in ineffective behaviour. If this is so, how can the observer pick out that which is effective? And, of course, many things now being done ineffectively might be done effectively. An analysis of the job and the use of a variety of techniques are more likely to improve teaching. In Stolurow's words, 'Master the teaching model', rather than 'Model the master teacher'.

Darroch (1911) was in a similar tradition. He considered that principles without psychological bases are mere empirical generalizations, which produce a formalistic approach with teachers following rules rather than deploying a body of pedagogical principles. In his view, educational psychology could provide the basis for such a body of principles. Darroch was of the opinion that there were four needs in this field, viz.: the need for a science of group psychology; the need to understand motives and incentives; the need to understand how experience is acquired and organized; the need to understand pupils' capacities. Lloyd-Evans (1935) argued that, whereas early in the century academic work was entirely separated from the professional, what was needed (1935) was a course in psychology that would help students to understand themselves, to understand their relationships with others and to understand their relationships towards children. This approach he opposed to earlier practice where masters of method taught methods of imparting information where the stress was on recall. Drever (1935) argued that since education is the process by which the behaviour of the child is controlled and modified by a variety of influences, and since psychology is the study of behaviour, then teachers must be informed about psychology. In his view, the great problem at the time was teachers' tendency to react in a global way to children's global behaviour: there was no attempt at the psychological analysis of behaviour: 'They tell you a child is inattentive in the same way as they tell you a piece of paper is white.' However, Drever considered that the psychological analysis, which could help teachers, should not be simplified psychology for teachers but a discipline in its own right. Trow (1948) takes a similar line to that of Drever. The teacher's function is to promote learning; learning is a psychological process; therefore teachers should understand psychology. He considers that the alleged gap between theory and practice is not a real one but one that can be removed by action

34

on the part of the colleges. Colleges should identify their objectives in terms of facts, generalizations and skills to be learned. Writing later, Trow (1949) suggests four areas that could prepare the prospective teacher to deal intelligently with the children he has to teach. We consider his suggestions later.

More recent writers have taken a similar point of view. Skinner (1968) declares that since teaching is the arrangement of the contingencies of reinforcement, a knowledge of reinforcement theory will be of help to teachers. Gage (1967) sees teaching as the exertion of psychological force. Learning is considered to be a change in capabilities or behaviour and as such must, by definition, come from psychological experience not physiological or mechanical – hence the need for teachers to have a knowledge of educational psychology. Ausubel (1968) discusses the pros and cons of educational psychology as an important study for prospective teachers. He suggests that the argument is based on two fundamental premises: (1) the nature of classroom learning and the factors influencing it can be reliably identified; (2) such knowledge can be systematized and transmitted. Against these two propositions he suggests there are two counter arguments: (1) knowledge of subject matter automatically gives competence to teach that subject; (2) teaching skill is innate. Ausubel believes that counter argument (1) is invalidated by common observation of teachers. To (2) he rejoins that native aptitude obviously varies but normal intelligent people must benefit from systematized instruction. He goes on to suggest that in the absence of valid psychological principles teachers can adopt two alternative procedures. Either they follow traditional prescriptions from educational folklore, or they discover effective techniques through trial and error. The first procedure, he points out, is likely to lead to following rules when what is needed is a body of principles. The second procedure is extremely wasteful of time. The study of educational psychology makes it possible to avoid these problems, since it can provide principles that enable the teacher to choose rationally in varying circumstances and test the validity and success of his choice. These principles, he believes, are derivable from relevant psychological theory and from relevant research conducted in an educational context. This view is interestingly reminiscent of the views of Darroch sixty years earlier.

Views on the nature of educational psychology

If we accept the point that educational psychology can be a teacher's guide to good pedagogical practice, and also the fact that there has been, and still is, considerable variation in the nature of the discipline as presented in

35

colleges, there is an undoubted need to attempt some sort of clarification as to what the educational psychology course should consist of. Writers in the field have taken up points of view which fall roughly into two categories. Some make rather global suggestions, which delineate a fairly general field, while others make more specific suggestions covering narrower fields.

GLOBAL VIEWS

Wolters (1935) is a representative of the global approach. He suggests that psychology for teachers must be a psychology of human beings, a branch of social psychology. It should not be narrowly professional in the psychological sense and, whereas the work of Thorndike might be considered the psychologist's territory, Buhler, Burt and Isaacs are the teacher's territory. The areas he proposes as meriting the chief emphases are problems of development and personality, how to deal with individual children, especially maladjusted or refractory children. There should also be a study of the psychology of teachers. He also stressed that the course should be demonstrably respectable intellectually. Anderson (1949) considered that a teacher who studies educational psychology should know and understand a body of information and principles, have an objective, experimental approach to educational problems, and possess skills in dealing with children and people in social settings. Freeman and Snygg (1953) propose that the content of educational psychology courses must be designed specifically to attain objectives. Concepts such as 'the whole child' must be given substance and concrete meaning and the content should always be in a state of development. That is, it is not enough for content to be narrow and limited to past solutions of past problems. Teachers must be more than technicians, they must be able to tackle new problems: no course can provide students with all the problems they will meet as teachers. Some selection of subject matter will have to be made in view of the limited time available. They suggest that the content of the course should provide answers to the basic questions: Why do people in general act as they do? What are the motives and goals of human behaviour? And how and why do people develop their individual personality and patterns of behaviour and how can these be changed? Some subsidiary questions suggested were nature/nurture, factors in mental development, the effect of social development and factors that influence learning. Writing at the same time, Murphy (1952) gives a selection of specific objectives, which he considered appropriate to a course in educational psychology. He suggests that students should know such things as: how babies learn to suckle, climb out of high chairs, command the attention of adults;

how children learn to speak single words and phrases; the learning processes involved in dressing, making a model, painting pictures; why 7 year olds play in groups when 5 year olds cannot; what the differences in perception, interests, motivation, are between a 6 year old who has learned to read and one who hasn't. In the same genre, Trow (1949) suggests four areas of study necessary to enable the prospective teacher to deal intelligently with children. (1) Biological growth: genetic factors, heredity, embryological growth, neurological processes, striated muscle systems, organization of drives and motives. (2) Environment: groups, family, community, school. (3) Development: growth, intelligence, individual differences. (4) Personality: temperament, mental hygiene, adjustment, conflict and frustration. These, and other examples, suggest a very broad view of educational psychology.

A somewhat different approach, but one that still takes a broad view, was presented by Rivlin (1953). He considers that educational psychology had failed in the past because it had been a 'college course' instead of a truly professional education. The content was factual and it was tested by recall, which did nothing to enable the students to relate theory and practice. Rivlin puts forward a number of global objectives:

1 Develop students' interest in people so that they understand children and adults.
2 Have favourable effects on attitudes, behaviour, and psychological understanding of the students in both personal and professional relationships.
3 Enable students to use the body of knowledge derived from research and explain the way in which learning occurs.
4 Improve the students' ability to learn.
5 Foster students' appreciation and understanding of research.

From these objectives flow the following implications:

1 Students should have respect for children as individuals.
2 Students should realize that education is a social process.
3 Students should realize that education is dynamic, not a static bag of tricks.
4 Educational psychology must be the yardstick of good teaching.

Browne *et al.* (1957) also put forward a number of global objectives:

A: To help students achieve a better understanding of:

1 themselves;

D

2   children as individuals and members of groups;
3   the process of learning;
4   the uses of psychological tests;
5   the principles of leadership and authority in social groups;
6   scientific method in human studies.

B: To help students to cultivate habits of clear and rigorous thinking and articulate expression.

C: To foster certain attitudes or values in students:

1   in the academic field, e.g. in relation to precise observation or logical thinking;
2   outside the academic field, e.g. by cultivating in students a sympathetic attitude to children or a desire for democratic group structures.

The major objective of the educational psychology course in training college according to Collier (1960) is 'to cultivate the students' insight into the thoughts and motives of ordinary children'. More specifically, he thought they should know how to use standard checks on surmises, tests inquiring into background, relationships, reactions to various types of control, response to various kinds of leadership. He believes that this cannot be acquired from lectures and urged the need for observation.

The B.P.S./A.T.C.D.E. report (1962) is on the borderline between the global statements and the more restricted views of educational psychology. It suggests ten requirements of a course in educational psychology for the training of teachers.

1   To enable the teacher to make use of psychological knowledge, not to be a second rate psychologist.
2   To provide knowledge of the major aspects of child development and the nature and conditions of classroom learning.
3   Provide skills in using tests and other evaluative devices, diagnostic procedures, case history techniques.
4   Provide skills in recognizing when specialist help is required.
5   Produce a desire for further and deeper study.
6   To stimulate an interest in inquiry and research.
7   Provide an insight into methods of psychological thinking.
8   Explain facts and procedures in teaching techniques that have proved their value.
9   Develop an understanding of individual behaviour and development.

38

10 To provide knowledge of up-to-date therapy of handicapped and maladjusted pupils.

The report also suggests an outline of topics for inclusion in a course on educational psychology.

1 Learning: motivation, goal directed activity, reinforcement.
2 Factors influencing learning and retention: nature of the material, method of presentation, the individual differences of learners.
3 Learning difficulties in school: characteristics of failing children, causes of failure, remedial education, readjustment of failing children to the school learning situation.
4 Developmental psychology: nature of development, nature/nurture, maturation/learning, development in emotional, social, cognitive, symbolic, aesthetic fields.
5 Factors influencing development of personality: biological, individual differences, social factors, frustration.
6 Educational measurement: the concepts of validity, reliability, sampling; limitations of traditional methods; characteristics of standardized tests; scales, units of measurement, norms; the scientific method in social sciences.
7 Psychology and the teacher's job: the teacher's role, personal problems; psychology of leadership and authority.

Commenting on the report, Thyne (1963) declares that the key problem is not finding relevant psychology to include in education courses but deciding what to leave out. An order of relevance should be decided upon according to the time available, the claims of other subjects, the students' abilities and the psychological maturity of the students. As an example he suggests that it would be more realistic to have students know about tests but not attempt to teach them how to apply them. This comment chimes with one in the *Suggestions for a Three Year Course* (Ministry of Education, 1957), that education is a comprehensive and difficult study capable of indefinite extension in which the need is not to extend but to prune.

Which brings us back to Tyler's remark apropos of the problem of selection of objectives: 'You can't learn everything.'

LESS GLOBAL VIEWS

A harbinger of more specific approaches to the teaching of educational psychology in teacher preparation courses was provided by Anderson in 1950.

Writing in the *Journal of Educational Psychology* on the 'Content of Learning Section' in educational psychology courses, he suggested a number of topics all under the general rubric of 'Learning'.

1   The general nature of learning
2   The motivation of learning
3   Transfer, retention, forgetting
4   Motor learning
5   Intellectual learning
6   Social and attitudinal learning

Anderson was writing of one important element in the psychology course. There has been an increasing tendency in recent years to take a similar focus and propose this as the exclusive area of study in such course. Carroll (1965) approaches this position when he declares that educational psychology is the study of the school learning process in all its aspects. He points out that most studies and researches in the field of educational psychology are snapshots. New curricula are being devised, which occupy up to 400 hours of pupils' learning time. What psychological experiments, he asks, can utilize time like that? He considers there is a need for panoramic studies to examine all interrelated aspects of educational growth over a major part of the time spent in school by a significant number of pupils. He spells out what he considers to be the variables in school learning and his list, we may presume, itemizes the subjects that a course in the subject should consider.

1   Time variables
    a: Aptitude: how long will the pupil take to learn it?
    b: Opportunity to learn: how much time is available?
    c: Motivation: how much time is he willing to give it?

2   Quality of instruction
    a: Adequacy of communication.
    b: Proper schedules of reinforcement.
    c: Feedback.

3   Ability to comprehend instruction.

Bruner (1966) summed up most effectively the problems and possibilities of educational psychology when he commented on how it had failed to be of much help to education in the past but looked forward to its making an important contribution in the future.

Something happened to educational psychology a few decades ago that brought it to the low status it now enjoys. . . . Part of the failure of educational psychology was its failure to grasp the full scope of its mission. It has too readily assumed that its central task was the application of personality theory or of group dynamics or whatnot. In fact, none of these efforts produced a major contribution to educational practice, largely because the task was not really one of application in the obvious sense but of formulation. Learning theory, for example, is distilled from descriptions of behaviour in situations where the environment has been arranged either for the convenience of observing learning behaviour or out of a theoretical interest in some special aspect of learning – reinforcement, cue distinctiveness, or whatever. But a theory of instruction, which must be at the heart of educational psychology, is principally concerned with how to arrange environments to optimise learning according to various criteria – to optimize transfer or retrievability of information, for example.

Gage (1967) believes that in the past courses in educational psychology have focused on issues that are essentially peripheral to the kind of training teachers need. In his view, what is needed is a course that deals with the psychology of the different methods of teaching and with the characteristics and behaviour of teachers. Educational psychology should develop concepts, principles and theories of methods of teaching and thus the course should be a course in the general methodology of teaching. That is, a general course from which specifics could be derived. He stresses, however, that teaching is based on an understanding of learning processes. But the study of learning should not stop short at the descriptive level, attempts should be made to derive implications for teaching. The most helpful way of looking at the subject is to regard learning-teaching as an interrelated procedure needing interdependence and interadaptation, and to avoid the twin dangers of considering learning as an autonomous process to which the teacher should adapt, or teaching as an autonomous process that decides what the learner should do.

Anderson *et al.* (1969) stress the centrality of learning and teaching in the study of educational psychology. In their view:

> Traditionally educational psychology courses have aimed to give the student some exposure to virtually all of the aspects of psychology which could have relevance for the educational process and for an understanding of youth. Courses of study run the gamut from infant physiology

to the sociology of institutions, from personality development to aptitude testing, and from classical conditioning to social psychology. While undeniably it would be good for the student to know something about each of these topics, the really essential issues are inevitably slighted with such broad coverage. We hold that learning and instruction are at the heart of educational psychology. It is our conviction that educational psychology and educational psychology courses should be directed mainly toward answering two questions: Under what conditions is student learning maximized? What features of instructional materials and teaching procedures facilitate student learning?

Ausubel (1969) takes a very similar view. He has a very low opinion of educational psychology as it has been in the past thirty years. He considers that it is 'a superficial, ill digested, and typically disjointed and watered down miscellany of general psychology, social psychology, psychological measurement, psychology of adjustment, mental hygiene, client-centred counselling and child-centred education'. His conception of the field of educational psychology is that it is that branch of psychology

> concerned with the nature, conditions, outcomes, and evaluation of school learning and retention. As such the subject matter of educational psychology consists primarily of the theory of meaningful learning and retention and the influence of all significant variables – cognitive, developmental, affective, motivational, personality, and social – on school learning outcomes: particularly the influence of those variables that are manipulable by the teacher, the curriculum developer, the programmed instruction specialist, the educational technologist, the school psychologist or guidance counsellor, the educational administrator, or society at large.

It follows therefore that educational psychology should discover appropriate and efficient ways of organizing and directing learning towards specific goals (Ausubel, 1968).

Since the study of school learning is the province of educational psychology its subject matter can be inferred from the problems facing the classroom teacher. The teacher

> must generate interest in subject matter, inspire commitment to learning, motivate pupils, and help to induce realistic aspirations for educational achievement. He must decide what is important for pupils to learn, ascertain what learnings they are ready for, pace instruction

properly, and decide on the appropriate size and difficulty level of learning tasks. He is expected to organise subject matter expeditiously, present materials clearly, simplify learning tasks at initial stages of mastery, and integrate current and past learnings. It is his responsibility to arrange practice schedules and reviews, to offer confirmation, clarification, and correction, to ask critical questions, to provide suitable rewards, to evaluate learning and development, and, where feasible, to promote discovery learning and problem solving ability. Finally, since he is concerned with teaching groups of students in a social environment, he must grapple with problems of group instruction, individualisation, communication, and discipline.

Ausubel is at pains to point out the irrelevance of most of the work on learning carried out in psychological laboratories, dealing as it does with types of learning far removed from human learning in the classroom. Hilgard (1964), Gage (1967), Stones (1966) and Lunzer (1968) also make this point. Stones (1970b) raises an issue that is particularly applicable to the British scene. The term *educational psychology* is used to refer both to work in clinical psychology in child guidance, and to work in the field of pedagogy. In fact, the recent report of the training of educational psychologists (Summerfield Report, 1968) deals entirely with the training of clinical psychologists. While there are undoubtedly areas of common interest in the two fields, their main concerns are very different and the use of the common term can lead to confusion.

One of the most useful sources of information about current thinking about the place of educational psychology in teacher preparation is to be found in Monograph No. 5 published by the Ontario Institute for Studies in Education (Herbert and Ausubel, 1969). In this, Herbert and Williams report the views of a number of educational psychologists on what the outcomes of a course in educational psychology should be. A list of seven general aims was compiled. It was a composite list and did not represent a consensus of opinion. The educational psychology course should:

a   Enable teachers to obtain orderly information about the classroom processes, using the disciplined resources of psychology.
b   Enable teachers to take a new look at classroom events, formulate hypotheses about students and learning, and test them to arrive at professional decisions.
c   Enable the instructors to screen out from teaching those students incapable of reaching professional decisions.

43

d   Help students to feel positively orientated towards psychological knowledge and skills, so that they will continue to apply them and to learn about them.

e   Enable teachers to assume the role of the teacher expected by administrators, parents and fellow teachers, and to possess the knowledge commonly commanded by professionals.

f   Provide the teacher with techniques for handling individual students and groups of students, with ways of shaping their behaviour, and with knowledge of how students go about shaping the teacher's behaviour.

g   Sensitize the teacher to his own students' feelings; for example, those of hostility, insecurity, altruism and helpfulness, and to the ways of considering them in the classroom.

Herbert and Williams report the comments of a number of psychologists on the subject of objectives in the teaching of educational psychology. Ripple considered only the first two objectives to be critical and the remainder secondary. Miles considers the problem not to be one of providing courses for teachers, but of providing experiences such as sensitivity training, the use of observation techniques, interaction recording systems, and audio and video tapes to obtain information about their own teaching. Teachers should be familiar with various ways of shaping behaviour and with techniques that produce changes in people's attitudes and conduct. Kounin feels that help in group management should precede or accompany any work in psychology.

Herbert and Williams point out, however, that in spite of the great divergencies of opinions about the proper concern of the educational psychology course, they all stressed the need for a 'more appropriate relationship between the academic study of educational psychology as a field of enquiry and the professional study of psychology in the preparation of classroom teachers'. Similarly everyone 'expressed strong doubts about the adequacy of the standard lecture course as a means to that end or else totally condemned the traditional course offerings'.

In view of the wide ranging nature of the debate about objectives in the teaching of educational psychology in teacher preparation courses, and in view of the widespread dissatisfaction with courses as traditionally conceived, it seems to us that any proposals for objectives in the field are more likely to be radical than conservative, even in the case of our present inquiry, which is aimed essentially at delineating objectives to be used in experiments in teaching and learning in colleges of education and could, therefore, have taken existing courses as a datum. However, in the process of grappling with the problem of deciding on what our objectives should be, even within a relatively small group of tutors, we were very conscious of the unsatisfactory nature of objectives as currently set out in college syllabuses and felt very much in sympathy with Travers (1969) who, talking of research in educational psychology, likened the subject to a country that has no identifiable boundaries, but whose sovereignty flows into other sovereignties. Eventually our own predilections and the views of the leading workers in the field, referred to above, disposed us to consider *de novo* what our objectives should be. We naturally considered carefully all the points made about objectives and about educational psychology in deciding on our own approach, but we were also convinced that it was essential to take the views of tutors, students and teachers on the subject before proceeding and in the next chapter we report on their reactions.

3

The survey of perceptions of preferred objectives

The last section ranged widely over what has been said about the proper concerns of educational psychology in teacher preparation. Nowhere is there any reference to the views of students on the subject, little reference to college tutors' views generally, and nothing on British college tutors' views particularly. It would have been perfectly feasible, of course, to have prepared a set of objectives based on proposals made in the literature and our own predilections without taking other counsel. We did not favour this approach for two reasons. First: we wanted as much evidence as we could possibly get covering all aspects of educational psychology as it is currently conceived, and clearly it would have been inexcusable to have overlooked the populations for whom we were presuming to legislate. Second: had we not taken the views of tutors, we could in theory have produced a set of objectives that left us in the same position *vis-à-vis* college tutors as the two Canadian students referred to in the last section. We could have finished up with a specification of objectives in educational psychology which had a zero correlation with the views of the practitioners.

We were, of course, aware of the dangers of taking the opinions of populations so closely involved in existing procedures. The *einstellung* effect was almost bound to bias responses towards practices that are familiar and currently considered to be 'educational psychology'. We hoped to cater for this problem by providing a reasonably wide range of alternatives. A related problem, which seemed difficult of solution by comparable means, was that of dealing with objectives that were likely to be novel, about which tutors and students would be in no position to judge. Some such cases emerged in the survey and are referred to below.

The schedule of objectives

In order to get the information we needed it was necessary to conduct a data collection exercise and after preliminary discussions with college tutors we

46

decided to construct a schedule of proposed objectives. The schedule was intended to cover the widest possible spectrum of possibilities consistent with the objective treatment of the data so obtained. We therefore carried out pilot studies, which laid virtually no constraints on respondents.

The first step was to conduct open-ended discussions with college tutors involved in teaching the subject. The suggestions made in these discussions were used in devising a schedule of proposed objectives. The main sources for the objectives included in the schedule were the B.P.S./A.T.C.D.E. report of 1962 and the N.S.C.T.E. monograph of 1953, together with currently used textbooks in the subject. The pilot schedule comprised ninety-four items and asked respondents to add any objectives they considered to have been overlooked.

An attempt was made to couch the objectives in behavioural terms and each objective was prefaced by the statement 'At the end of the course it is essential that the student should be able to. . . .' Respondents were asked to express the extent of their agreement with the stated objectives by checking on a five-point scale ranging from strong agreement to strong disagreement. Respondents were also asked to indicate whether each stated objective was a current objective of their teaching.

The pilot schedule was completed by fifteen tutors concerned with teaching educational psychology. College tutors in the psychology committee of C.E.R.G.* then met to discuss the returns. As a result of this discussion and scrutiny of the specific items in the pilot schedule by the principal investigators, a revised schedule of fifty items was constructed. The presentation and format of the schedule were revised and slightly different covering instructions were prepared appropriate to different groups of respondents. These are referred to below and the full schedules are given in Appendix 1. The fifty items chosen seemed to us to cover the main areas of concern in the teaching of educational psychology as proposed by authorities in the field. The areas included physical development, learning, statistics and measurement, pedagogy, cognitive development, deviance (including maladjustment and delinquency), psychological development (including emotions and personality). In addition there was a group of affective objectives concerned with such things as commitment to the discipline of educational psychology.

An attempt was made to couch the objectives in behavioural terms but this was difficult with some objectives, particularly the affective ones. A few of a 'woolly' nature were almost by definition impossible to classify in this way.

* University of Birmingham Colleges of Education Research Group.

However, although some of the affective objectives may lack the rigorously behavioural format achieved in some other objectives, we believe that it should be possible to devise instruments to ascertain whether or not the objectives have been achieved.

One other general problem encountered in drawing up the schedule was the question of the specificity/generality of the items. It is probably impossible to decide definitively how the various items range on the specific-general continuum, but it is highly unlikely that they are all at the same level of generality. However, they are all less general than the broad statements of aims which are often used to characterize the general areas of study of a discipline. On the other hand, they are by no means highly specific and may probably be regarded most accurately as first order objectives, related to the general area of the discipline, which may be further analysed to yield more specific second and third order objectives.

Although it is possible to classify most of the objectives according to broad content areas, there is no taxonomic logic to the classification: the objectives are interrelated only on the basis of their being perceived traditionally as the proper concern of educational psychology. How they came to be so perceived is difficult to determine, but it seems unlikely that the process of historical accretion, which has produced the 'typical' course in educational psychology, has been guided by any coherent body of principles.

The administration of the schedule

1: TO TUTORS

The schedule was sent to 147 colleges of education in England and Wales and tutors involved in teaching educational psychology were invited to complete it. They were also asked to suggest any objectives that they considered had been omitted from the schedule. Replies were received from 92 colleges and a total of 280 individual tutors.

2: TO STUDENTS

The schedule for students had the same items as that for tutors. However, they were not asked whether the stated objectives were currently their own, as were tutors. Instead they were given a response category 'O' signifying 'I do not feel sufficiently familiar with the proposed subject matter to respond to this item'.

The schedule was administered to a random sample of students drawn from colleges in England and Wales. First a random sample of Area Training Organizations was drawn, then a random sample of colleges within the

A.T.O.s was taken. In addition a random sample was taken from colleges in the Birmingham A.T.O. All third year students in the colleges selected were asked to complete the schedule. It is difficult to say what percentage returns were obtained since college tutors acted as intermediaries and it is most unlikely that all inventories sent out were handed to students. However, since returns or non-returns were effectively a function of tutor rather than student interest, the percentage of returns actually made should be regarded somewhat differently from returns made to questionnaires where the respondent's own interest is the factor that decides whether a return is or is not made. In the event 60 per cent of the schedules sent out were returned. In all, 1332 students returned completed papers. These students were at the very end of their three year college course and were, in our view, the most suitably placed students to give opinions on our list of proposed objectives.

In addition to the main sample of students at the end of a three year course, 358 students at the beginning of their third year from two colleges were asked to complete the schedule. Our intention here was to check on any differences that might be attributable to 'year' differences.

3: TO TEACHERS

A random sample of 135 teachers in the Birmingham area were also asked to complete the schedule. They were given the same form as the students.

4: 'EXPERT' OPINION

The schedule was sent to a number of British academics involved in the teaching of the subject for their views. They were also invited to make open-ended comments on the proper objectives of a course in educational psychology. Comments were received from five people.

Analysis of the schedule

Returns were analysed to permit of comparisons among the various groups of respondents and within groups according to such criteria as sex, courses taught (for tutors) and year of course, sex, age (for students). Several modes of analysis were employed to examine different aspects of respondents' perceptions of the suggested objectives. We now present an outline of the different methods of analysis; subsequent sections extend and amplify the outline.

1: RANKING OF OBJECTIVES

Each respondent had accorded a score from 1 to 5 to each objective, according to its perceived importance. If the respondent considered the proposed

49

objective to be very important he scored it 5, if it was considered unimportant it was scored 1. These scores were used to compute the mean score awarded to each objective by the different groups of respondents: i.e. students, tutors or teachers. By arranging the mean scores in rank order, it was possible to arrive at an order of importance of the fifty objectives as the various groups saw them. By then comparing the rank orders of the three groups, it was possible to discover the extent to which the views of the different groups to each objective coincided. We were able to express the degree of coincidence by calculating the rank order correlation coefficients among the groups.

2: CLUSTERS OF OBJECTIVES

Factor analysis was used to determine whether there were coherent patterns among the choices made by the respondents. Using data from all students and all tutors, two analyses were made, one for students and one for tutors. Two matrices of intercorrelations between the objectives were derived and subjected to principal component analysis. Twelve factors with roots greater than unity were rotated to the varimax criterion. By inspection of the factor loadings it was possible to identify several clusters of objectives.

3: TUTORS' PERCEPTIONS OF OBJECTIVES COMPARED WITH CURRENT TEACHING

This analysis enabled us to ascertain the extent to which tutors actually taught to the objectives they considered desirable. We considered it possible that some tutors might, possibly for reasons of college policy or lack of time, be unable to teach for objectives they considered important. Low correlation between what was taught and what was considered important would reveal a problem which the present scrutiny of perceived desirable objectives might help to solve.

4: DIFFERENCES AMONG COLLEGE CHOICES AND OBJECTIVES

An analysis was made to investigate possible pronounced divergencies of choices among students in different colleges of the objectives and from students in all the colleges of each objective. This was done by computing chi squares for differences between the choices of objectives made by students from each college in turn and the rest of the colleges. Chi squares were derived from a set of 750 3×2 tables, which compared in turn the summed choices for, against or neutral to each objective, made by students in each college with student choices in the rest of the colleges in the sample. The chi squares so derived made it possible to pick out colleges with atypical choice patterns and also revealed the objectives about which there was leats consensus.

Results

1: MEANS, STANDARD DEVIATIONS AND RANKING

Inspection of the data for within group differences (e.g. for sex, age) revealed no important variation. The main groups are therefore taken as homogeneous throughout. Table A in Appendix 2 sets out the means and standard deviations of the choices of the main groups together with the rank order of objectives for each group, the mean of means for the three main groups and the rank orders derived from these means. Inspection of the table reveals the items most highly regarded by the different groups and those least highly regarded. The ten overall most highly regarded objectives are set out in Table 1. The ten least favoured objectives are set out in Table 2.

The views of particular groups of respondents diverged markedly from the others on a few of the objectives. These divergencies may be seen in Table A (Appendix 2) but the more pronounced ones are set out in Table 3 (p. 54).

2: CORRELATIONS AMONG GROUPS

We have just drawn attention to a small number of objectives where the views of different groups tend to be divergent. However, in the main the correlation among the views of the groups was quite high. Between the views of the July 1969 end-of-year sample and the October beginning-of-third-year sample the correlations are 0·97 between the national sample and the October sample from one college and 0·91 between the national sample and the sample from the other college. Because of the clear indication that we are dealing with the same population here, the choices of these groups are not shown in the various tabulations. Correlations among the opinions of the other groups are given in Table 4.

3: UNFAMILIAR TOPICS

Teachers and students checked each objective 'O' if they were unfamiliar with the topic. Inspection of the returns revealed several topics about which there was some doubt. Items 25 and 38 (interaction analysis and attitude scales) were unfamiliar to 30 per cent of teachers and 20 per cent of students (on their own admissions). In addition items 2 and 44 (conditioning and gestalt psychology) were also unfamiliar to 30 per cent of teachers. Twenty per cent of teachers also reported lack of familiarity with items 9, 26 and 30 (learning sets, Piaget, and hierarchical model of learning types).

TABLE I **Rank order of the ten objectives most highly regarded by the groups overall**

Rank	Objective	Means			
		Of means	Teachers	Students	Tutors
1	(14) . . . be willing to modify his teaching methods to allow for the varying needs of individual children.	4·76	4·79	4·63	4·86
2	(46) . . . be able to adapt himself to a variety of teaching situations.	4·56	4·68	4·39	4·62
3	(16) . . . be able to distinguish between rote and meaningful learning.	4·43	4·49	4·14	4·67
4	(18) . . . be able to identify children who are failing at school and propose effective remedial treatment.	4·39	4·54	4·25	4·39
5	(35) . . . responding to children's interest, acting as leader in learning situations rather than as source of information.	4·39	4·41	4·37	4·41
6	(11) . . . be able to prepare effective instructional procedures in the teaching of reading.	4·34	4·47	3·96	4·59
7	(28) . . . have the psychological insight to make professional judgements which are objective, realistic and tolerant and not fixed by dogmatic precept or emotional thinking.	4·31	4·22	4·17	4·55
8	(34) . . . be able to outline the major factors which influence the emotional development of children.	4·31	4·37	4·23	4·44
9	(48) . . . be able to outline the most important social influences on children's learning.	4·26	4·19	4·07	4·54
10	(13) . . . be able to assess the influence of play upon children's development.	4·23	4·22	4·11	4·37

* With S.D. = 1·0 the S.E. of the means of the different groups is as follows. Teachers 0·08, tutors 0·06, students 0·04. Smaller S.D.s yield smaller S.E.s, so that we can be reasonably confident that the ranking proposed is meaningful.

TABLE 2 **Rank order of the ten objectives least highly regarded by the groups overall**

Rank		Objective	Means			
			Of means	Teachers	Students	Tutors
41	(44)	. . . be able to evaluate the importance of gestalt psychology in the development of learning theory.	3·46	3·36	3·40	3·64
42	(12)	. . . be able to replicate some of Piaget's experiments with children.	3·39	3·19	3·05	3·95
43	(30)	. . . be able to define a hierarchical model of types of learning and give examples of classroom behaviour which might be related to each type.	3·39	3·29	3·24	3·64
44	(10)	. . . be able to state the characteristics of the normal curve of distribution and compute the standard deviation of a group of scores.	3·36	3·37	3·09	3·62
45	(17)	. . . be able to translate a group of raw scores into standard scores.	3·32	3·45	3·06	3·45
46	(37)	. . . be able to describe learning experiments with simple animals and relate the essential features of reinforcement to the classroom.	3·31	3·31	3·04	3·59
47	(21)	. . . be convinced that the solution to many professional problems may be found in the principles of psychology.	3·30	3·24	3·07	3·61
48	(1)	. . . be able to state the essential aspects of the physiology of the nervous system and relate them to human personality.	3·30	3·12	3·14	2·92
49	(38)	. . . be able to describe the construction and use of attitude scales.	2·98	3·00	2·87	3·08
50	(50)	. . . be able to state the most important features of Freudian and neo-Freudian psychology.	2·95	2·81	2·72	3·34

E

A *Objectives about which tutors hold views divergent from other groups*

Objective 5   . . . be able to explain the currently held most important psychological views on the nature of intelligence.
Tutors rank this objective 7, whereas college students rank it 25 and teachers 33.

Objective 26   . . . be able to list the characteristics of Piaget's model of cognitive development and relate them to classroom situations.
Tutors ranked this 19, whereas students ranked it 36 and teachers 47.

Objective 6   . . . be able to identify a maladjusted child and decide on the psychologically most desirable way of treating him.
Tutors ranked this 45, whereas college students ranked it 9 and teachers 9.

B *Objectives on which teachers hold views divergent from other groups*

Objective 32   . . . be able to list the characteristics of programmed instruction and prepare instruction in this form.
Teachers rank this 26 whereas tutors rank it 38 and college students 42.

TABLE 4 Rank order correlations of the ranking
of the fifty objectives by different groups

	Students	*Tutors*	*Teachers*
Students		0·78	0·89
Tutors	0·78		0·71
Teachers	0·89	0·71	

4: CLUSTER ANALYSIS

a : Tutors' views

Using the procedures referred to earlier, the clusters of objectives set out in Table 5 were identified. These clusters represent meaningful patterns in the data from tutors, indicating the relationships that exist between 43 of the 50 variables. Three variables fall into two clusters. These variables are asterisked on the table. The rank order, mean score and factor loading of each variable are also given.

b : Students' views

Using the same technique, the clusters of variables from the data from the national sample of students were obtained. These are set out in Table 6.

TABLE 5   Cluster analysis: Tutors' summary table

Asterisks indicate items appearing in more than one cluster

Cluster			Objectives	Loading	Rank order	Mean score (5 point scale 1–5)
1	1	(27)	Ability to interpret professional research reports.	0·5941	34	3·86
	2	(19)	Outline nature of language and its relationship to learning.	0·5370	8	4·45
	3	(16)	Distinguish between rote and meaningful learning.	0·5240	2	4·67
	4	(23)	Distinguish between reception and discovery learning.	0·5017	19	4·29
	5	(28)	Psychological insight for making professional, objective, realistic judgements.	0·4891	5	4·55
	6	(14)	Adapt teaching to varying needs of individual children.	0·4759	1	4·86
2	1	(39)	Ability to maintain classroom order and obtain satisfactory work from class.	0·7508	8	4·5
	2	(46)	Adaptability to various teaching situations.	0·6829	3	4·62
	3	(35)	Responding to children's interest, acting as leader in learning situations rather than as source of information.	0·5837	11	4·41
	4	(49)	Able to judge educational policies on psychological grounds.	0·3144	32	3·90
3	1	(26)	Knowledge of Piaget's model of cognitive development and ability to relate this to classroom situations.	0·7195	19	4·29
	2	(12)	Replicate Piaget's experiments.	0·6489	28	3·95
	3	(40)	Outline experimental studies on intellectual development of children.	0·5899	22	4·18
	*4	(33)	Describe main elements in concept formation and strategies involved in concept attainment.	0·5230	15	4·33
	*5	(47)	Outline views on nature of thinking.	0·4959	27	4·04

55

TABLE 5 *continued*

Cluster			Objectives	Loading	Rank order	Mean score (5 point scale 1–5)
	*6	(36)	Describe how child learns to perceive world.	0·4080	18	4·32
	7	(48)	Outline social influences on learning.	0·4052	6	4·57
4	1	(8)	Describe sequence of physical development of pre-school children.	0·7853	31	3·92
	2	(15)	Describe sequence of physical development of middle childhood.	0·7811	26	4·08
	3	(13)	Assess influence of play on children's development.	0·4460	14	4·37
	4	(34)	Outline factors influencing emotional development of children.	0·4329	10	4·44
5	1	(6)	Identify and decide upon the most psychologically desirable way of treating a maladjusted child.	0·7706	45	3·59
	2	(20)	Identify possible causes of delinquency and relate these to individual children.	0·7139	28	3·95
	3	(18)	Diagnosis/treatment of failing children.	0·6823	12	4·39
	4	(43)	Identify deviant behaviour at various ages between birth and adolescence.	0·4438	24	4·11
	5	(11)	Prepare instructional procedures in teaching of reading.	0·4318	4	4·59
6	1	(4)	Analyse teaching task, construct teaching sequence and devise suitable test for it.	0·5963	21	4·23
	2	(25)	Outline current work on classroom interaction analysis.	0·6591	42	3·62
	3	(9)	Describe necessary conditions for learning sets.	0·5260	30	3·94
	*4	(33)	Describe main elements in concept formation and strategies involved in concept attainment.	0·4520	15	4·33

TABLE 5 *continued*

Cluster			Objectives	Loading	Rank order	Mean score (5 point scale 1–5)
7	1	(3)	Compute and apply mean, median and mode of groups of scores.	0·7695	39	3·69
	2	(17)	Translate raw scores into standard scores.	0·7456	47	3·45
	3	(10)	Understand normal curve of distribution; compute standard deviation.	0·7424	42	3·62
	4	(24)	Principles underlying test construction, validity, reliability, and compare standardized tests with traditional methods of evaluation.	0·7061	36	3·82
	5	(31)	Administer and mark intelligence tests, compute IQs, interpret results, knowing their characteristics, advantages and disadvantages.	0·5888	33	3·88
8	1	(50)	State features of Freudian and neo-Freudian psychology.	0·6309	48	3·34
	2	(29)	Concept of critical periods of development in relation to its usefulness for teachers.	0·5765	25	4·10
	3	(44)	Evaluate Gestalt psychology in development of learning theory.	0·5461	40	3·64
	*4	(36)	Describe how child learns to perceive world.	0·4646	18	4·32
9	1	(37)	Relate essential features of reinforcement in animal learning experiments to the classroom.	0·7076	45	3·59
	2	(2)	Describe necessary learning conditions for classical and operant conditioning and distinguish between them.	0·5734	37	3·78
	3	(32)	Characteristics of programmed instruction and prepare instruction in this form.	0·5405	38	3·72
	*4	(47)	Outline views on nature of thinking.	0·4740	27	4·04

57

TABLE 5 *continued*

Cluster			Objectives	Loading	Rank order	Mean score (5 point scale 1–5)
10	1	(45)	Construct sociograms with practical aims in mind.	0·7454	35	3·85
	2	(38)	Construct and use attitude scales.	0·4980	49	3·08

TABLE 6 **Cluster analysis: students' summary table**
Asterisks indicate items appearing in more than one cluster

Cluster			Objectives	Loading	Rank order	Mean score (5 point scale 1–5)
1	1	(46)	Adaptability to various teaching situations.	0·7622	2	4·39
	2	(35)	Responding to children's interests, acting as leader in learning situations rather than as source of information.	0·6222	3	4·37
	3	(39)	Ability to maintain classroom order and obtain satisfactory work from class.	0·5253	23	3·66
	4	(48)	Outline social influences on learning.	0·5096	10	4·07
	*5	(14)	Adapt teaching to varying needs of individual children.	0·4553	1	4·63
2	1	(6)	Identify and decide upon the most psychologically desirable way of treating a maladjusted child.	0·7419	9	4·09
	2	(18)	Diagnosis/treatment of failing children.	0·6544	4	4·25
	3	(20)	Identify possible causes of delinquency and relate these to individual children.	0·6474	11	4·05
3	1	(16)	Distinguish between rote and meaningful learning.	0·5522	7	4·14
	2	(11)	Prepare instructional procedures in teaching of reading.	0·4857	15	3·96

58

TABLE 6 *continued*

Cluster			Objectives	Loading	Rank order	Mean score (5 point scale 1–5)
	3	(19)	Outline nature of language and its relationship to learning.	0·4460	20	3·77
	*4	(13)	Assess influence of play on children's development.	0·4371	19	3·78
	*5	(14)	Adapt teaching to varying needs of individual children.	0·4166	1	4·63
	6	(23)	Distinguish between reception and discovery learning.	0·4036	18	3·79
4	1	(8)	Describe sequence of physical development of pre-school children.	0·7145	28	3·56
	2	(15)	Describe sequence of physical development of middle childhood.	0·6587	22	3·67
	3	(22)	Describe development in adolescence.	0·4828	17	3·85
	*4	(13)	Assess influence of play on children's development.	0·4048	8	4·11
5	1	(41)	Describe development and ways of assessing personality.	0·6330	21	3·75
	2	(34)	Outline factors influencing emotional development in children.	0·5442	5	4·23
	3	(40)	Outline experimental studies in intellectual development of children.	0·5015	33	3·45
	*4	(47)	Outline views on nature of thinking.	0·4898	32	3·47
	5	(36)	Describe how child learns to perceive world.	0·4362	13	3·98
	*6	(33)	Describe main elements in concept formation and strategies involved in concept attainment.	0·4147	19	3·78
6	1	(31)	Administer and mark intelligence tests, compute IQs, interpret results knowing their characteristics, advantages and disadvantages.	0·5605	29	3·52

TABLE 6 *continued*

Cluster			Objectives	Loading	Rank order	Mean score (5 point scale 1–5)
	*2	(11)	Prepare instructional procedures in teaching of reading.	0·5484	15	3·96
	3	(32)	Characteristics of programmed instruction and prepare instruction in this form.	0·5133	42	3·33
7	1	(42)	Consider educational problems and practices in light of psychological knowledge.	0·6956	26	3·62
	2	(49)	Able to judge educational policies on psychological grounds.	0·5540	40	3·38
	3	(21)	Conviction that solution to many professional problems to be found in principles of psychology.	0·4524	45	3·07
	4	(28)	Psychological insight for making professional, objective, realistic judgements.	0·4485	6	4·17
	5	(27)	Ability to interpret professional research reports.	0·4341	36	3·37
8	1	(5)	Be able to explain the currently held most important psychological views on the nature of intelligence.	0·7008	25	3·63
	2	(7)	Enjoys discussing educational psychology.	0·6136	34	3·44
	*3	(47)	Outline views on nature of thinking.	0·4248	32	3·47
9	1	(1)	Able to state aspects of physiology of nervous system and relate them to human personality.	0·5431	44	3·15
	2	(2)	Describe necessary learning conditions for classical and operant conditioning and distinguish between them.	0·6477	27	3·61
10	1	(25)	Outline current work on classroom interaction analysis.	0·7133	36	3·39

TABLE 6 *continued*

Cluster			Objectives	Loading	Rank order	Mean score (5 point scale 1–5
	2	(38)	Construct and use attitude scales.	0·6128	49	2·87
	3	(9)	Describe necessary conditions for learning sets.	0·5023	24	3·65
11	1	(44)	Evaluate Gestalt psychology in development of learning theory.	0·6237	35	3·40
	2	(26)	Knowledge of Piaget's model of cognitive development and ability to relate this to classroom.	0·5800	36	3·39
	3	(37)	Relate essential features of reinforcement in animal learning experiments to the classroom.	0·5671	48	3·04
	4	(12)	Replicate Piaget's experiments.	0·5336	47	3·05
12	1	(10)	Understand normal curve of distribution; compute standard deviations.	0·7346	41	3·09
	2	(17)	Translate raw scores into standard scores.	0·6971	46	3·06
	3	(3)	Compute and apply mean, median and mode of groups of scores.	0·6685	36	3·39

5: THE ACTUAL AND THE IDEAL: WHAT TUTORS TEACH AND THE OBJECTIVES THEY CONSIDER DESIRABLE

In order to examine the degree of correlation between what tutors teach and what they consider desirable objectives, product moment correlation co-efficients were calculated between the scores of tutors on each item of the objectives schedule and their statement as to whether or not they taught to the objective. A tutor who claimed to be teaching to an objective by checking YES on the schedule was scored 1 and a tutor who checked NO was scored 2. Since highly regarded objectives scored highly on the schedule of views about objectives, tutors who taught what they considered desirable would score high on the schedule of views and low on the YES/NO scale and vice versa. Table 7 sets out the correlation coefficients between tutors' views

Educational objectives and educational psychology

about each objective and their statements as to whether or not they teach to
the objectives. The mean scores of each objective on the two scales are also
given. Objectives that are taught to by a large number of tutors will approach
a score of 1, objectives that are taught to by few tutors will approach a score
of 2. A high negative correlation between these two scores will indicate that
tutors are teaching what they consider to be desirable, a low negative correlation may suggest a high 'index of frustration'. No attempt has been made to
compute an average 'index of frustration' since it would be of doubtful
statistical or conceptual validity.

TABLE 7 Correlation between choice scores made by tutors to objectives
and whether or not they teach to the objectives

Objective	A Choice scores	B Whether taught or not	Correlation AB
1	2·919	1·693	−0·4656
2	3·785	1·189	−0·5042
3	3·696	1·437	−0·4236
4	4·237	1·456	−0·3749
5	4·478	1·063	−0·2984
6	3·596	1·470	−0·5826
7	4·381	1·178	−0·3624
8	3·930	1·181	−0·3694
9	3·948	1·407	−0·4515
10	3·630	1·452	−0·3580
11	4·596	1·267	−0·4321
12	3·952	1·278	−0·5579
13	4·378	1·152	−0·3979
14	4·863	1·063	−0·1627*
15	4·089	1·193	−0·4128
16	4·670	1·044	−0·3200
17	3·448	1·667	−0·3946
18	4·393	1·244	−0·3208
19	4·452	1·115	−0·3328
20	3·956	1·344	−0·3675
21	3·615	1·404	−0·5796
22	4·341	1·126	−0·2232
23	4·285	1·148	−0·4812
24	3·822	1·407	−0·4446
25	3·622	1·667	−0·4385
26	4·296	1·104	−0·2415
27	3·863	1·552	−0·4012
28	4·552	1·148	−0·4389
29	4·104	1·226	−0·4362

TABLE 7 *continued*

Objective	A Choice scores	B Whether taught or not	Correlation AB
30	3·641	1·452	−0·4861
31	3·889	1·470	−0·4604
32	3·726	1·463	−0·3196
33	4·333	1·141	−0·3690
34	4·444	1·093	−0·2535
35	4·415	1·122	−0·4099
36	4·322	1·089	−0·3289
37	3·596	1·219	−0·4944
38	3·081	1·759	−0·3511
39	4·456	1·163	−0·5644
40	4·181	1·170	−0·4150
41	4·130	1·200	−0·3209
42	4·381	1·167	−0·4504
43	4·119	1·259	−0·3999
44	3·641	1·270	−0·4157
45	3·859	1·244	−0·3042
46	4·630	1·104	−0·4064
47	4·044	1·252	−0·4663
48	4·541	1·048	−0·1482*
49	3·900	1·430	−0·5454
50	3·337	1·519	−0·4943

Items indicated by asterisk (*) are significant at the 0·05 level; all others are significant at the 0·01 level. A *high* score on column A indicates approval for the objective, a *low* score on column B indicates that the majority of tutors teach to that objective. A high (negative) correlation between A and B indicates that tutors are teaching what they think desirable.

6: PATTERNS OF STUDENT CHOICES OF OBJECTIVES BY COLLEGES

The chi square analysis referred to earlier was preferred to a comparison of means to investigate the difference in choices among colleges since it yielded information about the pattern of choices of objectives, which might otherwise have been obscured. Table B in Appendix 2 sets out the choices made by students in the different colleges and also give the value of chi square derived from a comparison of the choice of each college to each objective with the choices of the rest of the colleges combined. Levels of significance are given in the table but the point should be borne in mind that, with such a large array, a number of values of chi square will be significant by chance. Perhaps the most useful way of examining the data is to look at those chi squares that are particularly high. Reading down the matrix one is able to pick out the objectives about which patterns of choice are divergent or homogeneous. For our present purpose divergencies are more interesting. Such items, it may be inferred, are items about which there is least agreement among the choices made by colleges. That is, colleges value these items differentially to a significant degree. Reading across the matrix it is possible to pick out divergencies among patterns of choices among colleges. Thus colleges with many large chi squares may be considered to be divergent from the colleges as a body. However, we should not attempt to draw too much from this approach and we should bear in mind that all these data are interdependent. The objectives about which there seems to be most divergence of views are (11) teaching reading, (12) replicate Piaget's experiments and (26) knowledge of Piaget's model of cognitive development. One college diverges markedly from the group in its choice of eight objectives (College 7). Others show varying degrees of divergence, but it is probably true to say that there are no really startling differences overall.

7: FURTHER OBJECTIVES SUGGESTED BY TUTORS
(These objectives are given as they were suggested in returns and accompanying letters)

(1) The evaluation of research; distinguishing what is truly relevant and based on relevant sources.
(2) Understanding of the learning process in relation to group structures.
(3) Moral development; the ways in which children learn values and standards.
(4) Recognition of emotional responses to learning tasks: the cues that children give (boredom, etc.).
(5) The motivational process and its relation to classroom learning.
(6) Management and guidance in learning to achieve.
(7) Successful acquisition and retention of knowledge.
(8) Psychomotor skills.
(9) Teaching for transfer and application.
(10) Mental health in classroom learning.
(11) Brief historical introduction.
(12) Relation of 'educational technology' to psychology.

8: COMMENTS MADE BY TUTORS ON THE SCHEDULE OF OBJECTIVES

A number of tutors commented on various aspects of the schedule. Some of the comments were of a general affective nature, e.g. 'interesting'. Others expressed points of view about the shortcomings of the schedule. The latter statements were classified and are here presented in summary form. The number in brackets denotes the number of tutors making the comment. (Total number of tutors replying to questionnaire = 270)

Criticisms of a general nature

(1) Respondents objected to the use of the expression '. . . it is *essential* that the student . . .' in the rubric and would have preferred an expression such as *desirable* (4).
(2) The schedule ignores the relations with other disciplines (2).
(3) Phraseology is 'difficult' (1).
(4) The schedule does not define the level of understanding desired in the students (1).
(5) Schedule is incomplete (1).
(6) Schedule is dogmatic (1).
(7) Cannot accept terms such as 'list', 'state', 'describe', 'outline', which suggest mere verbalizing (1).
(8) Schedule is subjective; students should be aware of the whole child and whole self (as teacher and person) (1).

Criticisms of specific items

(1) Objective is double (12).
(2) Objective is covered in other courses (14).
(3) Objective is confusing or ambiguous (17).
(4) Objective cannot be taught (1) (relates to item 23).
(5) Objective is impossible to attain (1).
(6) Objective demands experience in schools which students lack (1).
(7) Objective not appropriate for students (1).
(8) Objective inadequate for the content involved (1) (item 36).

An interesting comment on item 28, which proposes that a student should be able to make professional judgements based on psychological insight, was the question: 'Why the special pleading for psychology?' And from the same college, referring to Questions 25 and 30 (interaction analysis and hierarchical views of learning): 'So American style worded as to lack clarity'.

9: SOME SPECIALIST VIEWS

The returns from this population were, as has been indicated, few in number, but the population itself is very small. A comment common to most of them concerned the great difficulty of the task; and in fact one respondent admitted defeat when asked to give an indication of his views on what should constitute the objectives of a course in educational psychology 'in brief compass' and was of the opinion that this would need a book. Three contributors gave their views on what the general aims of a course should be with supplementary comments about the more specific objectives that might be derived from these aims. The suggested general aims stress the need for students to acquire psychological insight in relation to their jobs. Respondent A stressed the need to distinguish between the aims in a course in education and a course in educational psychology, and also that 'objectives must be specific to particular kinds of performance, content, etc. If not they are so general as to provide little direction to either staff or students (e.g. "To give students insight into themselves" is so woolly as to be virtually useless. Precisely *what* information are they to have, *what* are they actually to do, and by what criteria do we distinguish "insight" from lack of it?).' He continues:

> I think the vast number of possible objectives can be seen as falling into two broad classes:
>
> (1) For the work of the teacher within the classroom itself – and for his preparation of such work [some specific items are mentioned].
> (2) For the teacher as a professional person in discussion with other people, parents, fellow teachers, administrators, examiners etc.
>
> How these objectives can be *achieved* is, however, more than a matter of the content of the psychology course. It is largely a matter of the student's thinking *with* certain appropriate concepts, a contingency often inhibited by certain attitudes (or prejudices) about education in general and themselves in particular.

Respondent B saw the overall objective as being:

> to make the students aware of the scope of psychological inquiry and its particular features – especially its intent to analyse problems in such a way as to reveal:
>
> (1) The various factors involved – social, personal, environmental etc.
> (2) The sorts of inquiry that could then be conducted so as to yield clear answers from empirical data.

Respondent C considered that the main aim of educational psychology courses should be

> *to develop* in the student-teacher *an understanding of the processes of learning and teaching, and to develop this understanding in the form of a*

66

coherent theory. Perhaps I should say theor*ies*, since we haven't got any satisfactory all-embracing theory in psychology and it is more effective to explain some of the processes involved in different ways.

This is the main aim, since the main contribution of psychology to a teacher's effectiveness is in giving him a means of understanding what he is doing, a means of thinking about his work and his problems, and of discussing it, and of adjusting to new ideas. You must have some theory, or you work merely by rule of thumb (which is to work ineffi- ciently in a job like teaching, where each situation, each class, each child is different).

And further:

Whatever else is included among the objectives of educational psycho- logy, this aim comes first. In your questionnaire, number 28 comes nearest to this. But spelling it out in behavioural terms results in losing a key point: that what is aimed at is a general understanding, a capacity to think about and discuss educational issues in terms of a science which has an integrated structure (or nearly so).

Respondent D checked the schedule and to a great extent seemed to be of a similar opinion, in so far as the important emphases are concerned, as respondent C. The items scored 5 (14, 41, 42, 46) all relate to the quality of open mindedness and the ability and willingness to consider educational problems in the light of psychological knowledge, except for item 41, which relates to personality and personality assessment.

Some specific proposals for course content from this group were: condi- tions for learning and implications for teaching; individual differences in intelligence, motivation, emotionality, rate of development; the rationale of testing; the means and validity of selection; the effects of punishment; the aims, intentions and motives of teachers; some general social problems (e.g. prejudice, violence); some actual researches on educational issues (e.g. streaming); certain areas of factual knowledge especially biological basis of development, cognition and language, human learning, social interaction, measurement, some consideration of the psychological contribution to special education, counselling and guidance, the school psychological service. These suggestions are not intended to parallel the items on our schedule and are at a higher level of generality resembling to some extent what we refer to later as first order objectives or, in some cases, suggested areas of interest from which to derive first order objectives.

Discussion

The schedule had been drawn up to include examples of objectives taken from all areas currently conceived of as being legitimately the province of the study of educational psychology. We had, of course, pared down the number of objectives as much as possible, in order to be as comprehensive as possible without being completely outfacing. In the event, it appears, we had been less comprehensive than we had thought, since tutors were still able to suggest further objectives. Not that there was any general disagreement with the selection we made; but objections to our choices did not hinge on our choice of wrong objectives, but on tutors' beliefs that we had omitted some that should have been included.

The general acceptance of our schedule of suggested objectives by tutors is evidenced by the fact that the mean tutor score for all objectives except number 1 exceeded 3, which is the mid point on the scale. From this we infer that tutors as a group accept the schedule without demur and embrace the whole gamut of proposed objectives as legitimate to the teaching of educational psychology.

The responses from teachers and students similarly show very wide general acceptance of all the objectives. However, two teachers returned papers with lines drawn across all the objectives and comments about the general worthlessness of psychology. These papers are referred to in the section of this report dealing with attitudes. One student checked most of the items but scored two out because 'they were not worth answering'. Apart from these few exceptions, the responses from teachers, students and tutors add up to the traditional educational psychology courses referred to in *Current Research on Instruction* (Anderson *et al.*, 1969), which aim 'to give the student some exposure to virtually all of the aspects of psychology which could have relevance for the education process and for an understanding of youth'.

This blanket approval of anything that smacks of psychology and children is, of course, the major problem. In the time available it is not possible to deal adequately with such a diverse range of subjects except in a most superficial way. Even were the time available we should still want to question such an indiscriminate acceptance.

We were able to cope with this problem by ranking the objectives on the basis of the scale values accorded to them by the different groups. This approach provided us with an index of discrimination even if it did not provide a criterion for deciding whether an objective should be included or not. In the final analysis the decision what to include must be judgemental, but

68

the rank order of scale values makes it possible to take into account the expressed perceptions of the three groups concerned of the objectives in the schedule.

Although tutors, teachers and students are in favour of almost all of the objectives, they are much more in favour of those concerned with problems of learning and teaching. Within this area they show an interesting preference for the attitudinal objectives. It would be easy to dismiss some of these objectives as woolly and pious and not amenable to quantitative evaluation. On the other hand we could consider them as to some extent congruent with the climate of the times where opinion is moving away from the idea of assimilating discrete bodies of factual knowledge towards a concern with the acquisition of broader concepts and general principles in a field and the developing of positive attitudes. The choice of objectives such as these within the context of overall approval suggests an outlook which offers promise for the development of new approaches related to these current concerns.

THE TOP TEN OBJECTIVES (GROUPS COMBINED)

A striking feature of the ten most highly regarded objectives is that with one exception they are accorded mean scale values in excess of 4 by all groups, and that the means of the mean scale values are well above 4 for all the objectives (Table 1). Such scale values indicate a very positive preference for these items. The fact that seven out of these ten objectives are concerned with learning and teaching is a very useful indication of the general orientation of perceptions of 'proper' objectives in educational psychology. It is interesting that two of the objectives relating to learning and teaching are attitudinal rather than cognitive (14, 46). The interest lies in the fact that they express a belief in the need for a commitment to a pervasive psychological approach to teaching rather than just a mastery of a body of conceptual knowledge. Of the three objectives not related directly to teaching and learning, two are part of the staple of traditional courses in educational psychology: play (13) and emotional development (34). In our view these items exemplify the 'old' course content of doubtful rigour referred to earlier, but they are without doubt highly regarded by the different groups. One other item, (35), 're-sponding naturally to children's spontaneous interests', is a touchstone of a pronounced interest in a child-centred approach and as such is a not unexpected choice. The choice of item 11 (teaching reading) may reflect current publicly voiced concern about the subject but it also answers some

F

of the criticism that suggests that the colleges are not sufficiently concerned (but see below, p. 75).

THE BOTTOM TEN OBJECTIVES (GROUPS COMBINED)

The low status of items of a statistical nature in this section is fairly predictable given the low level of mathematical ability of the majority of college students and the paucity of suitably qualified tutors. The lack of interest in gestalt psychology, Freud and animal learning probably reflects a change in the colleges over the past ten years, but this, in view of the lack of a base line, can only be speculative. It may well be that such a recherché item as 30, 'define a hierarchical model of learning', was not understood and therefore rejected with healthy scepticism because it appeared to be jargon (see the comment on p. 65).

GROUP DIFFERENCES IN CHOICES

Mean group differences are of considerable interest but they might well mask important differences between groups. However, the divergencies among groups outlined in Table 3 are relatively few and do not seem to indicate any important trends. In fact the main source of interest under this heading is not the differences but the similarities. The correlation between the three groups is surprisingly high: teachers, students and tutors produce a remarkable consensus. It might be argued that they are reacting to a stereotype, that the students and teachers are very much the prisoners of the course content they have experienced and that consensus is to be expected. We think that this is unlikely, since the schedule of objectives allowed plenty of freedom to manoeuvre and we believe that this correlation reflects a real like-mindedness among members of the three groups.

UNFAMILIAR TOPICS

It is not surprising that teachers are less familiar with the various objectives than tutors and students. Some of the items are of fairly recent vintage, e.g. interaction analysis, and one suspects that the percentage of teachers confessing ignorance of the subject is much lower than the true percentage of those who are not informed in the matter. It is of some interest to note the percentage of teachers unfamiliar with Piaget in view of the ubiquity of certain of his theses in English education. This may be due to the fairly recent percolation of his work into the education courses of colleges and textbooks.

THE ACTUAL AND THE IDEAL OBJECTIVES

We considered that a comparison between the objectives tutors considered to be important and those they actually taught would give an indication of possible growing points in the teaching of educational psychology. In addition, the correlation between what was considered desirable and what was actually taught would provide an 'index of frustration'; the lower the correlation the more likely it would be that tutors were teaching to objectives of which they did not approve, or were not teaching to objectives of which they did approve. In the event we obtained the data set out in Table 7 (p. 62). All the coefficients are significant at the 0·01 level except two, which are significant at the 0·05 level. In some cases correlation is very high indeed, which suggests a picture of tutors teaching what they think desirable, and not having to teach what they think undesirable. We consider it justified to conclude from this that the index of frustration in so far as the teaching of the subject is concerned is relatively low for tutors.

Looking at these data from a slightly different point of view, more in line with our remarks on page 68, we expose the same problem of indiscriminate acceptance of *all* objectives. We might, indeed, refer to the correlation coefficient as a high index of smugness rather than of low index of frustration!

CLUSTER ANALYSIS

Tutors

Although the table of rank orders and mean scores for the fifty objectives is valuable in providing an insight into the way in which individual objectives are appraised, the cluster analysis is more useful in indicating the kind of course tutors would favour, since it reveals their perceptions of the most appropriate mode of articulation of the various constituent objectives. Thus the inclination observed for tutors to favour objectives connected with teaching and learning referred to in the discussion (Table A, Appendix 2, and p. 69) becomes much clearer (Table 5, pp. 55–8). Recall that the clusters are arranged in order of the mean scale value of the constituent objectives. The first of these clusters has the phenomenally high mean scale value of 4·45 and the mean percentage of tutors teaching to the objectives is 82 per cent.

The elements in this cluster have a degree of homogeneity based on what might be termed 'pedagogical acumen'. This characteristic may be conceived of as expertise in the science of teaching in a general sense; the expertise being based on a knowledge of general psycho-pedagogical principles.

Cluster 2 is related to cluster 1. It is biased towards the affective and most of the items are attitudinal. Item 35, with its rather extreme child-centred orientation, may be considered woolly but the general preoccupation of the items in this cluster is clearly with practical classroom problems. The overt psychological content of most of the items is minimal but presumably it is implicitly understood in view of the fact that the items are being considered as elements of a course in educational psychology.

Cluster 3 is more theoretical and mainly concerned with cognitive matters. It is not concerned with teaching directly and suggests a fairly typical text-book approach to what might be called 'cognition and cognitive develop-ment', and in fact item 26, which refers to Piaget's model of cognitive development, has the highest loading of the group of objectives.

Cluster 4 is similar to 3 inasmuch as it is a 'knowledge' grouping rather than one that can be directly applied to a learning/teaching situation. It is, perhaps, further removed from teaching than 3 since it lays greater emphasis on development, with a bias towards 'unfolding' rather than of development involving the intervention of the teacher.

Cluster 5 is clearly identified with problems of coping with individual children with the emphasis on the deviant child.

Cluster 6 is not readily identifiable unless we take the view that the items are mostly of recent vintage in college contexts and therefore not well known to respondents. Alternatively, one could argue that this factor relates to work in the classroom. Possibly it would be most accurate to consider it as related to both fields and therefore concerned with recent ideas about class-room practices.

Cluster 7 is readily identified as being concerned with statistics and allied matters. The high loadings on the elements stress the homogeneity of this factor.

Cluster 8 may possibly be considered in a broad sense as a 'Schools of Psychology' factor, and this would accord with traditional ways of approach-ing the subject.

Cluster 9 is predominantly concerned with subjects usually associated with 'behaviourism'. 'Thinking' appears to be ill sorted here but it is shared with the 'cognitive' cluster and has the lowest loading of the constituent elements in cluster 9.

Cluster 10 brings together two psychological techniques and it may well be that these items are sorted together so low in the rank order because they refer to the students being able to apply the techniques.

Without ignoring the fact that one gets out of such an analysis largely what one puts in, it seems quite legitimate to comment that the general impression produced by an examination of the clusters is of a progression from factors concerned with principles of learning and teaching related to classroom intervention by the teacher to those more concerned with general psychological knowledge.

The grouping of items in the statistics/testing cluster and the comparatively low regard in which it is held confirms our subjective impression based on experience in colleges and a survey carried out in 1967 (Stones, 1967). Should a set of objectives for colleges include such a class, cognizance should be taken of this low status.

The location of programmed learning in cluster 9 is predictable in view of its early association with reinforcement theory. In our view this is unfortunate since it may account for its low status. Should this objective be included in a final set of objectives, the problem will be to shake it loose from its associations with the other objectives in the cluster that may be considered of less (or no) importance. Clearly the problem will not be solved in the mere act of stating or not stating the objectives—it will be solved, if at all, through a process of education.

Students

Much of what has been said about the clustering of tutors' objectives may be said about those of students. It may be argued that the coincidence between tutor and student grouping and ranking is only to be expected, in view of the fact that they share the same basic texts and that students depend largely for their image of what educational psychology is about on the picture presented by tutors. Nevertheless, it seems reasonable to suppose that, given the opportunity of expressing their views in an anonymous questionnaire, they would make idiosyncratic choices rather than conform to a pattern, even though they are constrained by a given frame of reference. It is important to remember, in addition, that we are dealing with a random sample of colleges drawn from all over the country and from a variety of localities and it is most unlikely that there is a monolithic consensus with regard to courses in this field.

When we examine the clustering of objectives by students, we find that their perceptions are very similar to those of tutors, both in the clusters they perceive and the ranking they accord to the clusters. There is, in fact, very little difference in the ranking of the clusters seen as being of most importance by tutors and students (Table 6, pp. 58–61).

Cluster 1 resembles the tutors' cluster 1 in that it is not concerned so much with specific skills as with general, almost attitudinal objectives. As was suggested above, the problem with objectives such as these is that they

73

so often verge on the woolly as to be suspect. At the same time they may well express valuable objectives of an affective character which are less obviously subject to rigorous treatment. Of the items in this cluster, probably 35 is the least rigorous and least informed with the ideas of systematic intervention in the teaching process. The others are more amenable to objective scrutiny. The cluster as a whole has essentially the 'pedagogical acumen' orientation of the tutors' number 1, but it also includes the 'survival' item of being able to keep order in the classroom.

Cluster 2 is very similar to the tutors' cluster 5: both identify these items as a homogeneous area of study. The interesting thing is that the students accord the area much more importance than do the tutors. Clearly students feel the need for guidance in dealing with the problems of exceptional children somewhat more than the tutors consider they do.

Cluster 3 is also related to 'pedagogical acumen,' resembling as it does the tutors' cluster 1. Item 13 (play and development) seems aberrant, but this is shared with cluster 4, which is concerned with development.

Cluster 4 is physical development and cluster 5, with an almost identical mean scale value, is psychological development. Between them they embrace most of the topics covered in the traditional development component of educational psychology courses. The relatively high scale value suggests that students see this area as of some importance.

Cluster 6 has little conceptual unity; the accordance of the elements springs rather from the fact that they refer to specific processes or psycho-pedagogical techniques.

Cluster 7 is commitment to a psychological outlook. It is attitudinal and, although fairly low in the rank order, it is valuable to know that students in fact see the items as an identifiable group if it is decided to include such items in any system of agreed objectives.

Cluster 8 links an interest in psychology with intelligence testing and thinking. Possibly this is a reflection of the emphasis laid on these subjects, particularly intelligence testing, in many British books on educational psychology in recent years.

Cluster 9 has only two items and has a physiological/behaviourist slant. Cluster 10 brings together items that are probably not well known to the students. Cluster 11 is concerned with different approaches to the study of psychology ('schools of?'). Cluster 12 is statistics and is quite the lowest ranking with a mean scale value only just above the mid point of 3·0. This low esteem indicates a considerable problem if it is decided to include these items in a course on educational psychology for college students.

74

PATTERNS OF CHOICES BY COLLEGES

As with many of the other analyses, the striking thing about the matrix of student choices of objectives in the various colleges (Table B in Appendix 2) is its relative homogeneity. However, by taking a succession of arbitrary values for chi square and examining the table for patterns, it is possible to bring out any meaningful differences among colleges and among objectives. Taking an arbitary value of chi square of 20 and scrutinizing all values above, we found only one college with any marked differences from the body of the colleges and even this one diverged only on one sixth of the objectives. The students in this college show less enthusiasm for systematic approaches to teaching and are in opposition to the trend of the colleges as a whole in that they rejected programmed learning, test construction and the use of tests (these items are not thought highly of by other colleges but the overall attitude to them is positive). On the other hand, this college is much more enthusiastic towards the pronouncedly child-centred item 35 (responding naturally to children's interests). We thus seem to have here an example of a college particularly strongly inclined towards child-centred methods and away from highly structured approaches. The picture changes somewhat if lower levels of chi square are used, but still reveals no overall trend.

The objectives about which there was most divergence in patterns of choices are probably of more interest than the variation among colleges. There is an interesting lack of consensus among colleges as to the importance accorded to the objective concerned with teaching reading (11). All the colleges except one, however, are in favour of the objective but in different proportions from each other. The college that differs is college 13, with a majority of students choosing against the objective. The Piagetian objectives are more diverse, as can be seen from the table. This pattern may well reflect an ambivalence among students who realize that Piaget is 'important' and yet find him difficult to understand and relate to the practical class-room task.

There seems little to be gained from pursuing this analysis further. The main finding is, as has been stated, the relative homogeneity overall.

COMMENTS, AND SUGGESTIONS FOR ADDITIONAL OBJECTIVES

In the main we feel that most of the suggested further objectives are implicit in the ones presented on the schedule and would emerge from a detailed analysis of those objectives. On the other hand, it might have been better, for example, to have had a separate item related to aspects of motivation, which was one of the suggestions. It is, of course, an impossible task to produce a definitive list that will cater for all tastes. We should, in fact, bear in mind that the suggestions and comments were made by very few colleges.

We accept some of the criticisms made by tutors. The point that the terms used to obtain behavioural statements of objectives may suggest mere verbalizing is just. Our rubric could have made clear how we hoped to avoid this problem, and in fact we do take up this point in a later section when we discuss our own approach to a statement of objectives.

The comments made about some of the items, that they were double-barrelled, are valid. Although most of them deal with topics usually linked, it would have made the schedule easier to complete had they been single, even though in the final analysis the clusters would probably have been very similar. With regard to comments about ambiguity it is not for us to judge. We did our best. Many of the other critical comments are, or course, statements of opinion and provide information about tutors' views on objectives even though they may be difficult to analyse. We take the point made by some tutors who would have preferred a rubric like 'At the end of the course it is *desirable* (rather than *essential*) that the student should be able to. . . .' However, we prefer our formulation. We think we should set our sights on *essential* and do our best. If we make it *desirable* there is not only less incentive but it becomes impossible *not* to achieve our objectives. The comment that we feel unable to answer is the one that considered the schedule to be subjective and thought that students should be aware of the 'whole child'.

THE VIEWS OF THE SPECIALISTS

The interesting thing about the contributions made by the specialists is the extent to which the priorities they suggest resemble those of the other groups with their emphasis on the importance of 'commitment' objectives, and the stress on the need for a clear relationship between the study of the discipline and the job of the teacher. Respondent B had a wider ranging view, which more resembles the overall acceptance of the schedule, while A and C suggest approaches more akin to the picture one gets when one considers the higher scoring objectives from the other populations. As is discussed in the section that deals with attitudes, there is a high probability that these two broad aims are closely bound up with each other and that commitment to the subject is likely to increase to the extent to which its objectives are related to the actual practice of the teacher in the classroom.

Conclusions

It is possible that had we spread our net wider and included an even wider range of objectives we would have obtained a much more miscellaneous collection of approved objectives than we did. However, our schedule as it stands educed an overall response, which tends to confirm the points made by many of the critics of courses in the subject. The somewhat indiscriminate approval suggests a course of considerable heterogeneity, which is perhaps nothing more than a polite way of referring to the 'disjointed miscellany' referred to by Ausubel (1969).

However, the relative degrees of importance accorded to the various objectives may be an encouraging augury. From this finding we get a picture of tutors, students and teachers with a general sympathy for and acceptance of educational psychology, which course planners and responsible tutors might well capitalize on. The importance attached to the attitudinal objectives and those concerned with the general principles of learning and teaching may indicate a readiness to accept more specific items if they can be seen to contribute to the favoured clusters of objectives. Finally, the comments made by the academics in the field are sufficiently akin to the items and clusters seen as particularly important by the other groups to encourage the belief that a fair degree of consensus is attainable, even though, in the last analysis, any proposed set of objectives is likely to be idiosyncratic.

4

The survey of attitudes

We intended the inventory of possible objectives to provide the bulk of the data concerning the perceptions held by the various groups of respondents on what constitutes a set of desirable objectives for a course in educational psychology for college students. However, we also considered it desirable to examine the context within which these choices were being made. Clearly if a hierarchy of choices were made within a general climate of overall rejection of the subject, the implications of any findings flowing from our investigation would be of a different sort of significance from those flowing from a climate of approval. The key group for the purposes of our objectives survey were the college tutors, but we did not include this group in our survey of attitudes for fairly obvious reasons: the most compelling one being that we considered that tutors would have a pronounced and abiding commitment for the subject and that to ask them to complete an attitude scale on the subject would not only have been supererogatory but would have been more than obliquely derogatory.

Student opinions were, of course, of key importance so far as attitudes were concerned. Since the whole aim of the course in educational psychology is to change students' conceptual structures along appropriate dimensions and to inculcate positive attitudes towards the subject, it is important to have some knowledge of the attitudinal base line from which any course would start. The teachers were also of interest in view of the frequent suggestion that the study of educational psychology is purely theoretical and divorced from the real job of teaching. Problems inherent in taking the views of this population are that many of them who left college some time ago will have very vague memories of their study of the subject and, of course, the subject itself has changed considerably in many colleges since they were students and any answers they might give to the questionnaire would refer to a subject that is likely to be considerably different from the one that students today are familiar with. A comparison between the views of teachers and

78

students might well provide some interesting insights into some of these problems.

We are aware of no published quantified data related to views about educational psychology in Great Britain. A recent publication (Kay, 1970) expresses an opinion that probably attracts some support and is not untypical of a certain genre in the field.

> Educational Psychology is included [in courses in education] because 'the students ought to know how children's minds work', though it is not unknown for the course to be chiefly concerned with the learning behaviour of rats. . . . The work of Freud and the psychoanalytic school, which has probably been more responsible than any other coherent psychological theory for our present view of child behaviour, may well be ignored altogether or simply referred to in an aside. (Kay, 1970, p. 47)

Another way of looking at the subject is exemplified by the teacher who returned the schedule of objectives with the questions scored through and the comment: 'After 30 years teaching I find this jargon mostly unintelligible, and in any case I have far better things to do with my time.'

In America attempts have been made to obtain quantifiable information about the views of students and teachers about educational psychology in relation to teacher training. A very useful source for this information is Monograph No. 5 of the Ontario Institute for Studies in Education (Herbert and Ausubel, 1969). They report three studies. One was by the National Education Association in 1967, which found that teachers with various kinds of training were, in general, favourably disposed to educational psychology in teacher preparation courses. Another survey in 1969 at Cornell University found that graduates in the Master of Education programme rated educational psychology as the most important course. A third survey at Reed College in 1967 found that, in general, students were favourably disposed to the educational psychology course. In this survey students' satisfaction with course coverage increased to the extent to which it became more relevant to teaching. We hoped that our investigations into teacher and student attitudes would provide similar insights into the way the subject is viewed by the consumers.

The design of the investigation

Whereas the investigation into perceptions of desirable course objectives had been concerned with the views of respondents on the value of specific items as constituent parts of a course in educational psychology, the investigation into attitudes was concerned with the views of students and teachers to

79

the subject as a whole. The most appropriate instrument to collect these data was judged to be a Likert type attitude scale, which makes use of the summed ratings of respondents to a number of statements about the subject being investigated.

The scale was devised to incorporate statements for and against courses in educational psychology in teacher education. The statements were drawn from the literature, from tutors working in the field and from teachers taking courses in educational psychology. The pilot version of the scale comprised fifty items. This version was administered to a sample of forty-eight college students and the individual items were analysed to establish their levels of discrimination. Twenty-five items were retained, each of which discriminated at a high level of significance between holders of favourable and holders of unfavourable attitudes towards educational psychology (see Appendix 3).

The essential function of the scale was to measure global attitudes towards educational psychology. A respondent's choice of a given statement about the subject is marked 5 if strongly in favour and 1 if strongly against. The items for and against the subject are carefully seeded in the scale to counteract response set. The key statistic obtained from an administration of the scale is the total score of the respondent. Maximum support for educational psychology would produce a total of 125, complete rejection would produce a total of 25. The individual items are of less importance than the summed scores. The revised scale was given to all the students and teachers who completed the schedule of objectives. Split half reliability was 0·88.

Results

The returns were analysed to establish the overall attitudes of students and teachers and also the attitudes of subgroups, as in the analysis of the replies

TABLE 8 **Mean scores of teachers on attitude scale**

Subgroups	N	M	S.D.
Male teachers	61	82·4	12·1
Female teachers	71	81·1	12·4
Secondary teachers	66	79·7	11·9
Primary teachers	66	83·8	12·3
Less than 5 years experience	58	81·2	13·6
More than 5 years experience	74	82·2	11·1
Total sample	132	81·7	12·3

to the schedule of objectives. Table 8 gives the means and standard deviations of the teachers' attitudes. Table 9 gives the means and standard deviations of the students' attitudes. These tables also give the data relating to the

TABLE 9   **Mean scores of students on attitude scale**

Subgroups	N	M	S.D.
Male students	323	81·3	13·0
Female students	1007	83·7	11·7
Below 25 years	1004	81·4	12·0
Over 25 years	286	86·7	11·5
Infant courses	124	86·2	11·0
Junior courses	240	83·8	12·0
Secondary courses	383	82·3	11·7
Infant courses	124	86·2	11·0
Total sample	1330	83·1	12·0

N.B. The total number of students in different courses does not total 1330 since combined courses and F.E. courses are not included.

subgroups within the student and teacher populations. A comparison was also made among the attitudes of students from the different colleges in the sample; this is given in Table 10.

TABLE 10   **Students' mean scores on attitude scale analysed by colleges**

College	N	M	S.D.
1	159	83	10·8
2	176	81	13·2
3	46	79	16·4
4	75	89	9·1
5	61	84	11·6
6	31	90	9·1
7	95	79	10·8
8	47	83	12·5
9	46	88	11·3
10	150	85	11·8
11	42	91	9·9
12	95	78	12·9
13	45	82	8·9
14	201	81	12·3
15	60	87	11·1

Discussion

The interesting thing about the overall means is the way both student and teacher scores come down positively in favour of educational psychology. The mean score for students is somewhat higher than that for teachers, but the difference is of no real moment. However, both are appreciably higher than the score of 75, which would be obtained if all respondents chose a neutral response for each item. The overall deviation from this point of 75 for both groups is significant, but, in view of the difficulties involved in considering it to be a 'true neutral point', we say no more than that there is a definite indication of favourable attitudes to educational psychology on the part of both teachers and students. Examination of the individual items tends to support this statement. Although, as we have suggested, the important and most significant statistic to be derived from the attitude scale is the summed score of responses to the separate items, some information can be gleaned from the average score accorded to each item. Table 11 sets out the mean scores for the twenty-five items of the attitude scale, each item having been taken separately and the mean response score to each item calculated. It is interesting that the items that obtained the highest mean scores from students are the items that stress the contribution the study of psychology can make to the work of the teacher in the classroom. This finding resembles that reported by Herbert and Williams and seems a clear indication that students are very much aware of the need for some theoretical underpinning of the practical work in the classroom. Among the specific items we may pick out for scrutiny is item 5, where the mean score of 3·87 (minimum 1, maximum 5) reflects a conviction that the statement 'Educational Psychology adds nothing to the experienced teacher's skill' is false. A score of 3·86 on item 9 indicates that a fair body of student opinion considers that the study of educational psychology is an essential study for all teachers. The score of 3·83 on item 23 denies that educational psychology cannot be related to class room learning and a score of 3·83 on item 25 denies that educational psychology cannot be related to teaching. Item 20 is an example of an item that is useful as a discriminator in the full attitude scale but provides little information on its own, since it makes a statement about educational psychologists which is open to question. Item 4 is interesting in that it picks up the most commonly reported attitude expressed by students and indicates that, despite the general acceptance of educational psychology, much remains to be done to point up its use in practical situations. It thus seems clear that, whatever the shortcomings of current courses may be, there is a reasonably

TABLE 11 **Mean scores of teachers and students to individual items on the attitude scale**

Item number	Mean score (students) N = 1330	Mean score (teachers) N = 132
1	3·36	3·25
2	3·46	3·32
3	2·64	2·34
4	2·13	1·99
5	3·87	4·01
6	3·42	3·19
7	2·90	2·90
8	3·51	3·42
9	3·86	3·75
10	3·50	3·51
11	3·23	3·19
12	3·38	3·25
13	3·50	3·01
14	3·01	3·04
15	3·42	3·54
16	3·65	3·56
17	3·72	3·51
18	2·89	3·27
19	2·75	2·45
20	2·81	2·43
21	3·54	3·63
22	3·78	3·90
23	3·83	3·85
24	3·15	3·16
25	3·83	3·99

clear conviction among students and teachers that educational psychology has something valuable to contribute to the professional training of teachers. This body of opinion indicates that the critical views referred to earlier do not reflect the views of the mass of students certainly, or probably the views of teachers. (We make this distinction in view of the different sizes of the two populations in our analyses.)

Scrutiny of the differences among the subgroups indicates that there are no very great differences of opinions between men and women teachers or students. The interesting differences among students seem to be age and type of course. The more positive attitudes evidenced by the over 25-year-old students is picked up in the analysis by colleges, where two colleges catering for mature students (Colleges 6 and 15) both have relatively high mean attitude scores. The high means for infant students are reflected in a similar difference in the mean scores of primary as compared with secondary teachers. The picture that emerges, then, is one of older students having more pronouncedly favourable attitudes to educational psychology and both teachers and students concerned with younger children being more positively inclined to the subject than those concerned with older children; all differences should, of course, be seen in a context of a generally favourable attitude by students and teachers as a whole.

Divergence of attitudes between students in colleges in the various institutes indicates that differences do not exist between the different Area Training Organizations as such, so much as between colleges. All the A.T.O.s have ranges of means of attitudes, which most probably reflect the diversity in approaches of the individual colleges. The two colleges catering for mature students referred to earlier (6 and 15) both return high means (90 and 87) and may indicate an age influence, but the highest mean (91) is returned by a specialist P.E. college. College number 3 is aberrant in having a much larger spread of scores than the others. This discrepancy seems more likely to be the result of a combination of a few extreme scores and a low N rather than of any peculiarity of the college. The mean is, of course, very similar to the rest of the colleges.

The results of the survey of attitudes, then, indicate fairly clearly that students and teachers in general consider that educational psychology has a useful contribution to make to the training of teachers. Teachers and students dealing with younger children tend to consider the subject of particular importance. In view of statements often made about the subject such as the ones quoted earlier, and anecdotal 'evidence', this is perhaps a somewhat unexpected finding, but it is one that squares with the results of the returns from the schedule of objectives and seems to us to be an encouraging augury for any serious scrutiny of the subject, aimed at enhancing its relevance to student teachers and improving the way it is taught.

5

Objectives in educational psychology: a modest proposal

The general approach

In this chapter we present our own conception of objectives in educational psychology. In the process we take up the points made by the many writers in the fields of objectives and educational psychology. We also consider the views of students and of colleagues in colleges and schools as we found them in our surveys. In doing so we find that we have taken up a position similar to that of De Cecco, in that we recognize that there are problems involved in the process of specifying objectives, but this does not preclude our using them. We are not ignoring the criticisms made of the practice, but we are convinced that many arguments made in their favour are valid and that a number of the arguments against them are open to serious questioning.

As we considered the arguments made against the specifying of objectives, we were struck by the similarity between the general import of most of the criticism and the criticisms often made of programmed learning. Not that the substantive issues are the same, but the underlying logic often is. Programmed learning, it was (and is) said, implies such things as rote learning, convergent thinking and conditioning. Behavioural objectives, it is alleged, bring in their train convergent thinking, oversimplification of the learning process and triviality. In our view the criticism of programmed learning is essentially a criticism of the *programmer*: rote programmes are produced by rote programmers (teachers). A teacher who constructs a convergent programme will most likely teach a convergent lesson. By the same token, whether or not objectives are concerned with trivialities, whether or not they stress convergent behaviour, whether or not they totally exclude the spontaneous, is not a function of the mere fact that the objectives have been specified, but of the nature of the person who has specified them.

Tyler's (1964) notes on the specification of objectives is an elegant testimony to the irrelevance of most of the criticism. In particular, his

G

remarks on the way objectives should be related to the philosophy of the school illustrate the point we are trying to make. As the *éminence grise*, in so far as the specifying of objectives is concerned, he should surely be the archetypical trivial-minded converger. Instead we find him arguing for objectives which leave the learner with the conviction that he *doesn't* know all there is to know. He urges the notion that:

> the learner is active, that he is looking at the world, and is trying to make something out of it. We are trying to guide him in his continued activity rather than trying to close the world for him by giving him all the answers. We don't want to tell him, 'You have learned what there is in this course. Everything was here in the textbook and now you have learned it all.' The student must see his learning as a constantly continuing process. To achieve this you will have to think of objectives of the sort that lead from the third grade to the fourth grade to the fifth grade and so on.

In similar vein:

> The hope is . . . that students will really become involved in a lifelong process of learning in which the school's role is to get them fairly well started. With such a view the problem of defining objectives becomes that of determining the behaviours, appropriate to the given grade level, that the pupil can carry out so that when he has done this he will have a feeling for the open-endedness of the situation, the new questions to be asked, the new knowledge to be gained and not feel that learning is finished.

We believe that the approach exemplified by Tyler's position can provide an adequate safeguard against the problems indicated by those who are not persuaded about the desirability of determining objectives. We are also convinced by Popham's (1968) argument that only by specifying objectives as precisely as possible does one become aware of the trivial, of the lacunae in the course, or of redundancies. On the other hand, we are also conscious that, so long as course descriptions follow traditional lines, we shall have very little indication of the real nature of the course or of whether we are achieving what we hope to achieve. In such a course almost all outcomes are unspecified and it is difficult to separate the unforeseen from the intended outcomes.

The problems of the vaguely specified courses are compounded by the problems dogging educational psychology. The combination of the ill-defined content of the discipline and the vestigial statement of aims to be found in most prospectuses provide a situation where the most hetero-

86

geneous activities could be subsumed under one general rubric. To the dedicated diverger this may be the most convincing argument for letting well alone. However, we take the view that the future development of courses in this field will be better served by attempting to define the boundaries of the discipline as clearly as possible and to arrive at some rationale for specifying objectives in the field. For our own purposes, in our examination of problems of teaching and learning in educational psychology it is an essential step in our research. If we are to evaluate the effects of our instructional procedures we must prespecify what we intend those outcomes to be. In the pages that follow we explain our approach to these problems.

Objectives in general

Our general approach to determining the objectives of a course in educational psychology has followed the lines suggested by a number of writers, including Krathwohl (1965), Tyler (1964), Scriven (1967) and MacKenzie *et al.* (1970), and also the concepts of behavioural analysis developed in the field of programmed learning (Mechner, 1961). Using this approach, we developed ideas as to what the broad, more general aims of the course should be. These we analysed into the elements that we considered as contributing to the achievement of these broad aims. At this stage we had moved into the field of behaviourally stated objectives but we were still talking in fairly general terms. This was the equivalent of Krathwohl's second level (see p. 14) or Scriven's *manifestation* level (see p. 23). This level is further analysed into more specific areas and the process is continued until we reach that level of a hierarchy that corresponds to individual units of instruction. On some occasions it will be necessary to pass through a number of levels of specificity before reaching the final stage; on others this might be reached immediately after the second level has been specified.

This approach does not necessarily demand that every course analysis has to be pursued down to the most particular detail. In a document such as this it is probably most undesirable to do so. An exhaustive, precise prescription could certainly be restrictive (but note the point made in Chapter 1 (p. 12); method cannot be derived from objectives, content can; the teacher has thus a good deal of freedom to manoeuvre even when objectives are spelled out in detail). We have in mind particularly the fact that, while consensus on the higher level objectives might be attainable, it would be less easy to get agreement at the lower levels even if it were desirable. We take the view that the lower level objectives should be determined by the individual teacher in relation to a specific teaching situation, a given group of students and his own pedagogic predilections. Since there are probably several different parallel sets of lower level objectives contributing to one higher level objective, any selection must in any case by idiosyncratic.

In our early work in the Colleges of Education Research Group on specifying objectives in different fields, we used the Bloom model as a framework. As suggested earlier in this report (p. 27), we found that there were problems attached to this approach which are related to the question of specificity that we have been considering. To some extent our problems were artefacts of the arrangement of the taxonomy. Going as it does from the lowest level of behaviour at the remembering of facts level to the most complex conceptual operations at level 6, it is very prone to induce a set to work at level 1 first and to progress towards the higher levels. The snag here is that the course planner can very easily get bogged down in the specification of innumerable low-level objectives not necessarily closely related. As MacKenzie *et al.* (1970) remark, this is because the taxonomy was designed as an instrument for analysing objective test items. There was in our case, therefore, a very clear indication that we should adopt a different approach from Bloom if we were to arrive at a set of objectives that would constitute some sort of ordered system and avoid producing a plethora of highly specific and atomistic items. Hence our decision to work from the more general objectives to the more particular ones that they subsumed.

A difficulty arose at this stage in the work of some of the committees of the Research Group, which is likely to be a feature of cooperative working of this kind. Few members of the groups had had experience of working with objectives, and to many the Bloom taxonomy was quite new. There was consequently a tendency to adhere closely to the taxonomy, using it almost like an algorithm rather than a heuristic model. Presumably greater familiarity with the concepts of specification of objectives and practical experience will help to overcome this difficulty, but unless it is overcome the possibility of rigidity of approach in this activity is a real one.

One other consideration inclined us away from the Bloom model. There are difficulties, when using this approach, in classifying some behaviours at the appropriate level, since the classification will depend upon what the student has been taught (Bloom, 1956; Stones, 1968; Ausubel and Robinson, 1969; Markle and Tiemann, 1970). Thus, if a student is given the same problem during instruction as he is later tested on, his learning could well be rote and classifiable at level 1 of the Bloom taxonomy. On the other hand, if he has been taught with different material, his correct solution of the problem would be evidence of meaningful learning and classifiable at level 6.

88

We took the view that, in general, we would wish to focus upon learning at the higher levels, regarding the lower levels as contributory. The evaluation of early learning in a given unit of instruction would then make use of test items at the lower levels of the Bloom taxonomy only, whereas the test items at the later stages in the instruction would make use of test items at the higher levels only. The learned behaviours necessary for the correct solution of problems at the conclusion of the unit of instruction would subsume the earlier, contributory learning. Using this sort of approach we hoped to achieve a more satisfactory meshing of teaching and evaluation than often occurs, and at the same time emphasize the nature of the student's learning rather than the nature of test items in any scheme of objectives that we produced.

We have made clear in earlier sections our acceptance of the desirability of stating objectives in behavioural terms and we do not pursue this further here, except to say that in our approach we attempt to implement our views on the subject. We should like, however, to comment in passing on the point referred to in our discussion of the views of tutors on the schedule of objectives. We refer to the point that the use of behavioural phraseology can, in some circumstances, give the impression that the contingent behaviour is 'mere verbalizing'. This comment is closely related to the question of rote and meaningful learning discussed above. If the process of achieving competence in the behaviours specified is related to the kinds of learning in the way suggested, the problem disappears. If the material used in the criterion test is the same as that used in instruction, then the behaviour being sampled is, indeed, mere verbalizing. If, on the other hand, the material is different, then the opposite is the case.

Finally, in our approach to objectives, we attempt to systematize. In grappling with this problem we were much taken by Blake's line in *Jerusalem*: 'I must create a system, or be enslaved by another man's.' We felt the truth of this in the early work with the Bloom taxonomy and soon saw the desirability of a flexible approach; not that we felt competent to take Blake's position fully as when he goes on to say: 'I will not reason and compare; my business is to create.' And, as is clear, we did reason and compare and owe a lot to other men's systems. Particularly, of course, our use of a hierarchical model reflects much of current thinking about problems of the design of instruction and evaluation, curriculum design and current views on the processes of learning.

Objectives in educational psychology: the general problem

Reference has already been made to the difficulty of defining the territory appropriate to the discipline of educational psychology.* Scrutiny of current college syllabuses points up the problem. Most curricula run the gamut of topics from physical development to creativity. 'Detailed studies' of motivation, of learning, of the causes of backwardness and delinquency, of different 'schools' of psychology, are but a few of the topics covered by one syllabus. And what are we to make of a syllabus that, having chosen to include 'Personality Theory', spells out the content by a list of substantives such as 'Freud' and 'Eysenck'. In our view, syllabuses such as the former are pious in their impossible ambition given the time available for the subject. The mode of specifying the content exemplified by the latter is further cause for concern. Its vagueness and open-endedness are, in general, more appropriate to projection tests than to guides for instruction. If we were to produce objectives that would be a real guide to the planning of our instructional sequences, we were convinced that it was imperative to make a realistic selection of what we considered to be the key areas in the field of educational psychology, in so far as the needs of student teachers are concerned, and to prepare objectives that avoided the vagueness and piety of current syllabuses.

In making our selection of objectives appropriate to the needs of student teachers, we are conscious of the fact that our job is not merely one of selecting from an existing body of procedures, although this may well be the main task. There is also the need to examine any new suggestions for their relevance and feasibility. For our part we think it important that pronouncements such as that of Kay (1970) should not be allowed to go unchallenged. To suggest that current weaknesses of educational psychology courses can be ameliorated by a return to Freud is a point of view, but one that we consider should be resisted in favour of more rigorous, research-based and validated procedures. We are, therefore, encouraged by the findings of our survey that this particular subject ('Freud') receives a very low level of priority in most tutors' and students' eyes. However, the subject is still included in many syllabuses as are many other subjects that we would consider peripheral or inappropriate. Indeed, the remarks made in earlier sections on the

* We refer from time to time to current college prospectuses when discussing objectives specification and the content of educational psychology courses. We are aware, of course, that such prospectuses are often of little use as guides to what actually goes on under the various rubrics. However, we think it not unreasonable to expect *some* correlation between professed aims and actual course content and, *faux de mieux*, to use them as exemplifications of the points at issue.

heterogeneous nature of the typical course in educational psychology are substantiated by scrutiny of current syllabuses.

The indications of the analysis of college choices of objectives set out in Table B (Appendix 2) suggest that the actual combinations of subjects constituting courses are idiosyncratic. We found no apparent A.T.O. effect: the differences were all at the college level. While bearing in mind the criticism of objectives that they can lead to undesirable uniformity, we take the view that on such subjects as the teaching of reading, to which colleges gave differential emphasis, there should be more agreement than there seems to be.

The B.P.S./A.T.C.D.E. report is some help in narrowing the field and focusing upon the most relevant topics. However, we consider that the suggestions made in the report are still too wide, although there is a welcome move towards topics specifically related to the job of the teacher in the classroom. A feature of the report, which bears on our present attempt to suggest objectives in the field of educational psychology, is the fact that the suggested topics for a psychology course in the report were set out in much the same way as a typical college syllabus. Thus the subjects are essentially very broad areas, from which behavioural objectives might be derived, but on their own they are capable of varying interpretations. Our aim is to be more precise and explicit than this so that we shall not only attempt to be more selective than the report, but also more specific, using behavioural terms where possible. We are, however, mindful of the fact that the mode of presentation of suggestions for courses made in the report may well be an indication of the difficulty of setting out objectives in this field, in a mode such as we propose.

We found that many of the suggestions made in the literature discussed in Chapter 2 were of little help, except in a negative sense, in that they make reference to subjects we considered were best excluded from courses. We are doubtful, for example, of the relevance of the suggestion by Trow that embryological growth (among other things) should be part of the course. The suggestions made by the American psychologists (see pp. 43–4) are of limited help for a different reason. They are very broad and, although they may provide a general orientation, some of them present problems of interpretation and all need considerable further analysis before they can be of practical help in course planning. We found the suggestions advanced by Rivlin of interest (see p. 37), particularly his point about educational psychology being regarded as more than just another college course. We also accept most of his broad aims, but there is still the problem that they are stated in very general terms and need much more precise analysis. Similarly, the views of the specialists in the field are of help mainly in suggesting the broad fields of concern rather than specific course objectives. In terms of the approach, we suggest these would be taken as general areas from which we would derive first order objectives. The general tenor of these contributions, however, encouraged us in the view that the important issues in courses such as we are considering are concerned with problems of learning and teaching. Perhaps Respondent C (p. 67) put it most succinctly when he suggested an understanding of the processes of learning and teaching based on coherent theories as being the main general aim. The problem of how best to achieve this aim, or, indeed, how to get agreement on the criteria of success in achieving the aim, is another question. However, we accept this general position and therefore try to set out the means by which we can best achieve the aim.

Objectives in educational psychology: the central concern

The area of central concern in the teaching of educational psychology to which we turned our attention was, therefore, the problems of learning and teaching. One of us has already set out our position on the subject (Stones, 1970a): 'the main concern of the study of educational psychology [should be] the nature and conditions of classroom learning'. Clearly this position owes much to earlier writers and the arguments that have been rehearsed by some of the authors cited in earlier chapters have been particularly influential. Thus we were impressed by Anderson's suggestions (p. 40) for topics under the rubric of 'Learning' in the psychology course; Carroll's proposition (p. 40) that educational psychology is the study of the school learning process in all its aspects; or Ausubel's: 'the study of school learning is the province of educational psychology' (p. 42); or Bruner's: 'a theory of instruction . . . must be at the heart of educational psychology' (p. 41); and, closely related to Bruner's position is Gage's proposition that educational psychology should constitute a general methodology of teaching (Gage, 1967). We are strongly attracted to this last proposal, since it provides a concept of the discipline which holds the potential for the development of a coherent theory capable of underpinning the practice of the teacher.

If we adopt an approach such as this, we provide ourselves with a touchstone that will help us to determine whether or not a given objective is appropriate to our course. It enables us to reduce the randomness and incoherence so much a feature of current courses. In examining the claims of any particular topic for inclusion in the course, we consider the extent to which it contributes to the greater understanding by the student of the processes of classroom learning and general principles of teaching.

Applying this principle of selection to some of the objectives in our survey, we are unperturbed by the low regard in which subjects such as the ability to construct attitude scales is held, in view of its peripheral relevance to the teacher's task in the classroom (that there may well be a good case for developing some types of attitude scales for assessing affective objectives is not being disputed here, but whether or not their construction should be part of a teacher's expertise). On the other hand, we are concerned at the low regard in which programmed learning seems to be held, since the concepts of programming are in our view central to the study of learning and teaching. In similar vein, we would assess the desirability of having objectives concerned with tests and test theory, only to the extent to which they contributed to the more effective evaluation of pupil's learning by the teacher. Esoteric and sophisticated theory would not be judged apposite. Any objectives concerned with statistics should similarly deal with the general ideas in relation to the problems of learning and teaching (generally the evaluatory monitoring of learning) and not with complicated arithmetical processes divorced from the classroom.

Important as is the use of an approach such as Gage proposes in selecting objectives, it is not the key aspect. Should it be possible to develop a coherent body of knowledge related to the theory of learning and teaching, we would be in a position to equip students with principles of general application in a variety of classroom situations. Teachers would then be less dependent upon rule of thumb, would be more adaptable and more capable of coping with problems they had not previously encountered. Such a body of knowledge would constitute a general theory of teaching relatable to specific disciplines and to specific classroom situations but transcending them: a possible body of pedagogic principles, rather than tips for teachers.

THE IMPLICATIONS FOR THE PROPOSED APPROACH
OF THE SURVEY FINDINGS

The findings of the survey of the perceptions of the most suitable objectives in the teaching of educational psychology are encouraging. It is true that the global approval of virtually everything suggested is not consonant with our proposals for a more restricted approach. However, the weighting attached to the objectives by the various groups suggests that there is already an inclination in the direction we propose. As has been pointed out, many of the objectives high in the choices of all groups are those concerned with learning and teaching and the ranking of the clusters confirms this theme. It is true that there are several objectives low in the choices of the groups, which could conceivably be taken as concerned with our general line, but the predominant trend is undoubtedly in the direction we propose.

The results of the attitude survey confirm in an interesting way, the need for relating the study of educational psychology to learning in the classroom. We agree with Mager (see p. 22) about the importance of the affective objectives. We consider that the results of the Canadian and American surveys, reported in Chapter 2, and the findings of our own survey, are encouraging auguries for an approach to educational psychology such as we suggest. There is, it appears, a general acceptance of the discipline as an important element in the preparation of teachers. There is also, from all sources, a strong indication that commitment to the subject will increase to the extent to which it is related to classroom learning, a finding that is interestingly buttressed by the indication from the survey at Reed College (Herbert and Williams, 1969) that, as the work in psychology becomes more relevant to teaching, the students feel less need for additional areas to be added to the psychology courses. It may well be, then, that by focusing upon the areas we propose, we shall not only increase students' commitment, but also solve the problem of the heterogeneous encyclopedic course. It was with factors like this in mind, together with the other points rehearsed above, that we turned our attention to suggesting appropriate objectives for a college course in educational psychology.

Objectives in educational psychology: specific suggestions

As a result of considering the arguments and evidence discussed above, it seems to us that a statement of objectives in a course in educational psychology for student teachers should have at its central focus the need for students to acquire a sound grasp of the psychological principles relating to human learning and teaching and the ability to apply them to classroom situations. This overall aim may be broken down into subsidiary aims, which, while not themselves constituting behaviourally stated objectives, lay down general guidelines from which such objectives can be derived. The areas we have chosen are set out in detail later in this section, but briefly they cover questions of human learning, teaching variables in cognitive and motor learning, the effects of organismic variables on learning and teaching, the structuring of instructional situations and the evaluation of learning. We also have an objective in the affective domain, which is of a global nature, aiming at the inculcating of positive attitudes towards educational psychology.

The areas we have chosen are not in themselves of great use as guides to teaching action: their main use is in pointing up general approaches to the

94

more precise statement of objectives. The main problem is, of course, in deriving sets of objectives from these areas according to some consistent criterion. As we have explained above, other systems of classification were of limited relevance for various reasons and eventually we developed our own approach, which seems most appropriate to our purposes.*

The first step in developing the classification was to convert the 'areas' into objectives stated more precisely and as far as possible in behavioural terms. At this stage of the operation we had in mind that learning situations typically comprise activity of different levels of complexity, instanced, for example, by the different levels of the Bloom taxonomy or the Gagné hierarchy of learning types. The first stage in our analysis derived three *types* of *first level* objectives from each main area. By *first level* we mean objectives of the greatest degree of generality. Type A objectives involve the most complex type of learning, generally at the very highest level of problem solving or 'creative' activity (Bloom level 5 or 6). Type B objectives are still at the problem solving level but less complex (Bloom level 3 or 4). Type C objectives are least complex and are at the level of principle learning or Bloom level 1. All level 1 objectives, whatever their type, are very general objectives. However, any type A objective at level 1 depends on the prior achievement of the appropriate type B objective at the same level and type B depends in turn on the achievement of type C at the same level (Figure 2).

We may illustrate the distinctions between the different types of objectives as follows. Type A objectives demand that the student be able to apply a body of learned knowledge in a given field to specific problem situations. Thus the type A, level 1 objective from area 2 states:

> Given a teaching objective involving cognitive learning, decide on the type(s) of pupil learning most appropriate to the objective and specify the teaching and learning activities most likely to optimize the pupils' learning.

Type B objectives demand the ability to assess teaching/learning situations and classify the elements according to some scheme. Type B, area 2, level 1 demands:

> Classify novel examples of teaching behaviour according to their appropriateness for different types of cognitive learning.

* The reader is strongly urged to consult Figures 1, 2 and 3 on pages 101, 102 and 103 as he reads the pages in this section.

Type C objectives are concerned with the learning of 'facts' and the type C objective that corresponds with the types A and B given states:

Recall the key principles in teaching for efficient cognitive learning.

Each type A objective at level 1 is dependent upon the skills acquired in achieving objective type B, which in turn depends on type C. Higher level objectives are dependent in a somewhat different way upon prior learning at the lower, more specific levels. Dependency here is conceptual: level 1 objectives being more general conceptually than lower level objectives and subsuming them. Thus objectives of different types at level 1 subsume objectives of the same types at levels 2 and 3 and below down to the most specific objectives derivable in this field. It is thus possible to take each area in turn and derive from each type of level 1 objective the lower level objectives it subsumes. This operation is done *by analysing the concepts* at different levels. Type C objectives are derived from type B objectives and type B from type A *by analysing the skills* at different levels to determine what subordinate skills they are based on. On the one hand we ask: 'What prerequisite concepts do the concepts relating to this objective imply?' On the other hand we ask: 'What are the important constituent skills of this higher level capability?' (Figure 2).

The general areas from which the objectives are derived are not related in the same way as the objectives and their numbering is nominal and implies no order of importance. They are not, however, independent and, as reference to the first order objectives in the different areas will show, there is considerable overlap and interdependence. It seems to us that the fact that the rationale of our taxonomy does not apply to the general areas is merely a specific instance of the general principle that the choice of course content cannot at present be derived from logical or psychological premises but at best will be based on consensus.

We have just referred to the rationale of our taxonomy, and, lest we should be thought to be begging the question, we should like to submit that our model is indeed a taxonomy by virtue of the derivation of the different types and levels of objectives. The derived elements may be orthogonal but the process of derivation is in broad principle the same. If we are deriving levels, the question we ask is: 'What concepts does the student need to know to be able to do this?' (the question is, of course, taken from Gagné's original formulation). If we are deriving types we ask: 'What skills does the student need to be able to do this?'

A consequence of this method of derivation of objectives is that the taxonomy is hierarchical in nature, and indeed, apart from the general areas, this is so. We believe that this is a perfectly reasonable way of ordering objectives and one that chimes well with current thinking about the structure of human knowledge and types of learning. We also believe that there are advantages in this type of approach to the specifying of objectives for the development of curricula and for research into learning processes. One important advantage, it seems to us, is that, by going from the general to the particular in the way we suggest, one is helped to shake oneself free from old concepts and content. When this approach is coupled with the behavioural specification of objectives, irrelevancies are more readily exposed than in most ways of proceeding.

The approach we suggest need not be inflexible. We suggest that it is possible not only to vary the number of areas within a given course of study, but that it is possible to vary the number of subordinate objectives at any level according to the depth of study required.

In our own analysis, which is set out below, we have exemplified our approach. We have not, however, attempted to produce a definitive taxonomy of the whole field of educational psychology, since no taxonomy could be definitive. We considered it more useful to develop a model that could be used by individuals and groups of tutors as a guide to their own activity than to develop a scheme complete to the last Nth order objectives. Thus our proposal presents the main outlines of the approach concretely in terms of the first order objectives in all the areas. This outline is supplemented by a complete analysis of two areas and the detailed specification of objectives of all types and at several levels for these areas. We hope that by adopting this approach there will be enough guidance to a tutor wishing to attempt an analysis to help him in his enterprise without prescribing his every step. Our aim was to stimulate and not to hand down tablets for all to follow.

However, apart from this, we think there is another safeguard against dull uniformity in the system itself. While the broad areas and the higher order objectives may be accepted and agreed by a number of tutors, there is considerable latitude at the lower levels of objectives. And since tutors will derive their teaching approaches from the lowest levels of objectives one can see that there are many routes to the achieving of the higher level objectives.

Although we are not concerned here with methods of achieving objectives (this, of course, is a matter of teaching principle and methods), there are several points where questions of objectives and teaching approach are particularly intertwined. One important example involves the interrelation of the general areas of study. As has been mentioned earlier and as is mentioned in specific sections of our taxonomy, at some levels the objectives in different areas are much dependent upon each other. The question for the tutor is, then, in which order to deal with these objectives. A case in point might be the relationship between lower level objectives in the area dealing with the evaluation of learning and that dealing with the psychology of teaching cognitive skills. The expertise of evaluation is needed in assessing the pupils' competence and a knowledge of the psychology of teaching is needed to provide the substance for evaluative exercises. The solution to this problem may well be, for example, to adumbrate the general principles of evaluation when teaching the principles of the psychology of teaching cognitive skills and explain the techniques at length later. In addition, analysis of different areas tends to produce convergencies as one becomes more specific and it becomes possible to deal with objectives from different areas but of the same type and level at much the same time.

It is possible to adopt several different approaches to teaching to the objectives. One could take an area at a time and within each area teach to all the C-type objectives first, then the B-type objectives and then the A-type. Or one could teach to all the C-types in several fields, followed by the B-types and then the A-types. Or, indeed, one could adopt varied approaches within these general ones. Note, however, that the teaching approach follows the opposite sequence from the sequence in specifying the objectives.

In the presentation of our scheme we have tried to bring out the structure of the taxonomy and at the same time make it possible to examine the possibilities of different approaches to analysing the teaching task.

We have mentioned the question of task analysis. We think that this is the next teaching step, which follows naturally from the taxonomy. The taxonomy should provide useful guidelines but the task analysis really gets down to the nuts and bolts of producing teaching sequences. At this stage decisions have to be made about specific teaching approaches and appropriate teaching materials: in fact the same kind of behaviour that we are specifying for students in several areas of the taxonomy!

Closely bound up with task analysis is the question of evaluation. We should like to make special reference to this in view of our earlier remarks on rote and meaningful learning and recall and transfer objectives. It will be clear to the reader that objectives of type C (recall) could quite well involve rote learning. However, the learning will not be rote if the tutor ensures that the subordinate concepts to the principles (facts) that are being learned are in fact really within the students' repertoires and not just remembered parrot fashion. Objective test items that use different examples from those used in teaching also ensure that rote learning would be detected. Much the same applies to the other types of objectives, although rote learning is perhaps less likely. The essential point all the way through is that any evaluative measures used to assess learning of whatever type should present the student with test material that is novel but also embodies the principles the student has been learning. This approach is assumed throughout our taxonomy.

We now present our suggestions for a taxonomy. Our proposals follow the rationale discussed above and to a great extent our model. However, we should stress that 'model' could well be understood literally in two of its meanings. One in the sense of its being a theory and the other in the sense of its being an ideal or 'perfect exemplar of some excellence' (*Shorter Oxford Dictionary*, 1968). Our proposals for a taxonomy are attempts to apply the theoretical approach to a practical problem and also strive to approximate to an ideal. On both counts, of course, our efforts are less than perfect and the exemplification we put forward is perhaps somewhat ragged round the edges in places and in other places may presume ideal rather than actual states of knowledge and instructional capabilities. Thus many of our objectives demand that the student specify the *optimum* conditions for this or that teaching or learning activity. We are aware of the fact that we may not know what the 'true' optimum conditions are, but we presume that the tutor or group of tutors who agree to teach to the objective will have their ideas of optimum conditions, which will be derived from the state of knowledge in the field at that particular time. Whether or not their own analysis of the teaching task is accurate will, one hopes, eventually be revealed at the evaluation stage of the teaching so that their views as to what constitutes *optimum* conditions will be monitored and amenable to correction. In other words, the objectives as stated must always be considered in the context of specific teaching situations with specific tutors and students. In another respect the exemplar we present does not match an ideal. While the theoretical basis of the derivation of the subordinate objectives from the first order ones is not transgressed in our exemplar, the reader who looks for symmetry among the different dimensions of the model will be disappointed. Thus some of the level 1 objectives will generate subordinate objectives down to, say, level 3, others may generate more or fewer. And, indeed, there are examples in our proposals where level 2 is the lowest level of objectives. In addition, the number of objectives at the same level derived from different first order objectives may differ. The reader should not, therefore, look for a one-to-one correspondence between objectives at all levels. We consider that these imperfections are inherent in the nature of the exercise of translating the ideal into actuality, but we should welcome proposals that would help with the translation or in the production of a more useful, perhaps more parsimonious model. With regard to the present enterprise, however, the reader should bear in mind that the model presented in Figures 1, 2 and 3 will not match perfectly the exemplification we provide.

SEQUENCE OF OBJECTIVES

One additional point should, perhaps, be made here. Although the model aims to be inclusive and general, it is perfectly possible for a tutor to decide that his needs would be served by his students achieving objectives below the levels of greatest generality or of type A skill. In other words, a tutor might well be satisfied if his students were to achieve quite specific low level objectives, such as remembering facts. It is conceivable that such an aim might well be desirable at early stages in the course, but a tutor is also at liberty to decide that in some circumstances he would require his students to acquire only the relatively low level skills and concepts even by the end of the course.

The objectives are presented under the headings of the various general areas of study and this sequence does not imply any order of priorities. Other sequences imply hierarchical relationships. Recall that there will be second and third order objectives for the first two areas only, since these are the two areas we chose to analyse. Other areas will have first order objectives, which may be used as sources for the derivation of subordinate objectives. The elements of the taxonomy are presented in the following sequence.

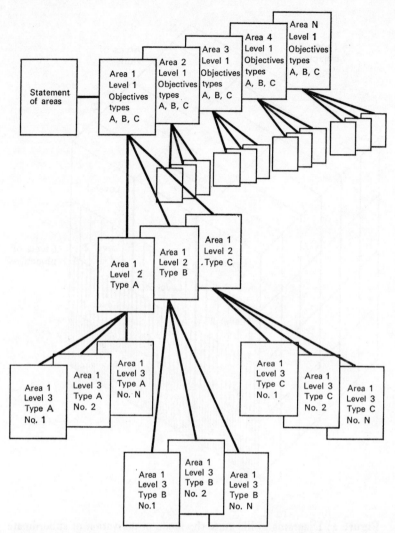

Figure 1: Diagram to show the relationship of areas of study, levels of objectives and types of objectives. According to our scheme the number of types of objectives is constant at 3, but the number of areas and levels may vary. Note that in this idealized diagram the implication is that each objective will generate the same number of subordinate objectives. This, of course, is unlikely.

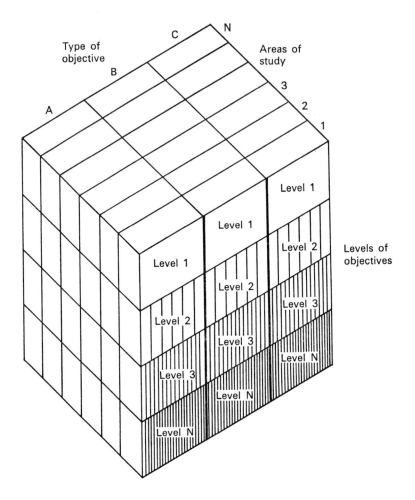

Figure 2: Diagrams to illustrate the mode of derivation of subordinate objectives within each main area of study. The nodes represent the objectives, the arrows indicate the direction of proceeding to derive objectives according to criteria in the text. Horizontal arrows move towards greater specificity of objectives, vertical arrows move towards less complex modes of learning. The number of types of learning remains constant at 3 (A, B and C) but the number of levels derived from each Level 1 objective can vary. In addition, the numbers of objectives at the same level but of different types may vary. *Note particularly that this is not intended as an analogue of the taxonomy, but as a heuristic device to illustrate the mode of deriving subordinate objectives.*

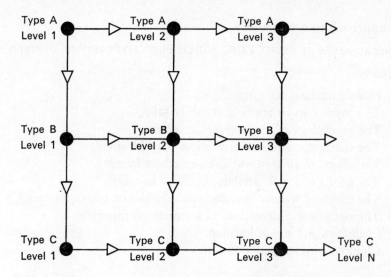

Figure 3: Diagram to illustrate the relationship of the various levels and types of objectives to each other and to the general areas of study.

An approach to a taxonomy

GENERAL AREAS OF STUDY FROM WHICH OBJECTIVES MAY BE DERIVED

Cognitive

1 Human learning.
2 The psychology of teaching cognitive skills.
3 The psychology of teaching motor skills.
4 The effects of cognitive variables on school learning.
5 The effects of affective variables on school learning.
6 The effects of social variables on school learning.
7 The effects of teacher characteristic variables on school learning.
8 The analysis and structuring of instructional materials.
9 Evaluation and school learning.
10 Children with learning difficulties.

Affective

11 Commitment to the use of psychological insights in teaching.

Note

In proposing these areas of study, we should like to repeat what we have mentioned before, that we think it important to avoid a dogmatic or rigid approach to their implementation. We would hope that students would be encouraged to weigh the evidence and exercise critical judgement in arriving at their own decisions. We do not include the development of this independence of mind as a specific objective since we believe it should be a general objective of all education and its spirit should inform whatever teaching methods are employed to accomplish the objectives we propose.

Area 1 : Human learning

LEVEL I   OBJECTIVES*

Type A   Propose the optimum conditions for different types of human learning.

Type B   Identify novel examples of human learning and classify the examples according to a coherent scheme of classification.

Type C   Recall the key principles relating to human learning as currently understood.

Notes

These objectives are closely related to those in areas 2 and 3, which deal with teaching. They are dealt with separately as an aid to clarifying the concepts involved. A general point of some importance is the fact that the objectives in this area are concerned with the acquisition of a body of knowledge about learning as an object of study, whereas the objectives of areas 2 and 3 are concerned with the manipulation of learning. All three areas draw on Gagné's suggestions for a hierarchy of learning types.

Many of the objectives which follow refer to specific learning situations. It should be taken on all occasions that the situations will not have been encountered by the students previously.

---

* In all objectives the reader should supply a prefatory clause of the nature of: 'At the end of instruction the student will be able to . . .'

Area 1 : The psychology of human learning

TYPE A   OBJECTIVES

Level 1:   Propose the optimum conditions for different types of human learning.

Which yields the following level 2 objectives

1 Propose the optimum conditions for adaptive behaviour in specific learning situations. [See the comments on p. 99 for the implications of formulations such as *the optimum conditions.*]

2 Formulate hypotheses which relate the principles of cybernetics to specific examples of human learning.

3 Propose the optimum conditions for classical conditioning in specific learning situations.

4 Propose the optimum conditions for instrumental conditioning in specific learning situations.

5 Propose the optimum conditions for learning response chains in specific learning situations.

6 Propose the optimum conditions for learning set formation in specific learning situations.

7 Propose the optimum conditions for concept learning in specific learning situations.

8 Propose the optimum conditions for principle learning in specific learning situations.

9 Propose the optimum conditions for problem solving in specific learning situations.

10 Propose the modes of language usage which could enhance learning in specific learning situations of different types.

11 Propose the optimum conditions for ensuring meaningful learning in specific learning situations of various types.

12 Propose the optimum conditions of reinforcement for enhancing learning in specific learning situations of various types.

Area 1 : The psychology of human learning

TYPE A   OBJECTIVES

Level 3   (derived from the level 2 objectives given in **bold**)

1 **Propose the optimum conditions for adaptive behaviour in specific learning situations.**
    1.1 Propose the learner behaviour most likely to be adaptive in specific learning situations.
    1.2 Propose the learning conditions most likely to enhance adaptive behaviour in specific learning situations.

2 **Formulate hypotheses which relate the principles of cybernetics to specific examples of human learning.**
    2.1 Explain how the principles of feedback are likely to operate in given learning situations.
    2.2 Explain how the 'movement towards equilibrium' may be involved in the motivation of specific pieces of learning.

3 **Propose the optimum conditions for classical conditioning in specific learning situations.**
    3.1 Propose the optimum forms and conditions of stimuli, responses and reinforcement for the establishment of classically conditioned responses in specific learning situations.
    3.2 Propose the optimum conditions for stimulus generalization, response generalization, stimulus discrimination and extinction of classically conditioned responses in specific learning situations.

4 **Propose the optimum conditions for instrumental conditioning in specific learning situations.**
    4.1 Propose the optimum forms and conditions of stimuli, responses and reinforcement for the establishment of instrumentally conditioned responses in specific learning situations.
    4.2 Propose the optimum conditions for stimulus generalization,

stimulus discrimination, response generalization, response discrimination and extinction in specific learning situations.

4.3 Propose the optimum conditions of the parameters of instrumental conditioning in specific learning situations involving shaping of behaviour.

5 Propose the optimum conditions for learning response chains in specific learning situations.

5.1 Propose the optimum prerequisite learning appropriate to specific learning situations involving response chaining.

5.2 Propose the optimum conditions of cueing, sequencing, repetition and reinforcement in specific learning situations involving chaining.

5.3 Decide whether forward or backward chaining is likely to be more effective in specific learning situations.

6 Propose the optimum conditions for learning set formation in specific learning situations.

6.1 Propose the optimum conditions of stimulus presentation, reinforcement and selection of subordinate discrimination tasks in specific learning situations involving learning set formation.

6.2 Deduce the prerequisite learner capabilities for learning set formation in specific learning situations.

7 Propose the optimum conditions for concept learning in specific learning situations.

7.1 Propose the prerequisite learner capabilities for the formation of specific concepts.

7.2 Propose the prerequisite learner capabilities for the attainment of specific concepts.

7.3 Propose the optimum modes of presentation of exemplars for concept formation and attainment in specific learning situations.

7.4 Propose the optimum conditions of reinforcement for specific examples of concept learning.

7.5 Predict the areas of generalizability of conceptual learning in specific learning situations.

108

Area   1
Type   A
Level   3

8 **Propose the optimum conditions for principle learning in specific learning situations.**

    8.1 Propose the prerequisite learner capabilities for the learning of specific principles.

    8.2 Propose the optimum learning conditions for the learning of specific principles.

    8.3 Enunciate the optimum conditions of reinforcement for specific examples of principle learning.

    8.4 Enunciate procedures of language usage which would optimize the learning of principles in specific learning situations.

9 **Propose the optimum conditions for problem solving in specific learning situations.**

    9.1 Propose the prerequisite learner capabilities for the solving of specific problems.

    9.2 Propose the optimum learning conditions for the solving of specific problems.

    9.3 Enunciate procedures of language usage which would optimize the solving of problems in specific learning situations.

    9.4 Enunciate the types of learning conditions most congruent with discovery learning in specific learning situations.

10 **Propose the modes of language usage which could enhance learning in specific learning situations of different types.**

    10.1 Explain how language could be used to cue various types of learning in specific learning situations.

    10.2 Explain how language might be used to provide feedback for various types of learning in specific learning situations.

    10.3 Explain how language might be used to direct activity in various specific learning situations.

    10.4 Formulate hypotheses which relate the syntactical aspects of language to different forms of learning in specific learning situations.

    10.5 Formulate hypotheses which relate the semantic aspects of language to different forms of learning in specific learning situations.

11 Propose the optimum conditions for meaningful learning in specific learning situations.

    11.1 Propose the prerequisite learner capabilities for meaningful learning in specific learning situations.

    11.2 Propose the optimum state of the situational variables to ensure meaningful learning in specific learning situations.

12 Propose the optimum conditions of reinforcement for enhancing learning in specific learning situations.

    12.1 Propose the types and conditions of reinforcement appropriate to specific learning tasks involving different types of learning.

    12.2 Propose the schedules of reinforcement (if any) appropriate to specific learning tasks involving different types of learning.

Area 1 : The psychology of human learning

TYPE B   OBJECTIVES

Level 1:   Identify novel examples of human learning and classify the examples according to a coherent scheme of classification.

Which yields the following level 2 objectives

1 Distinguish between instances of changes in human behaviour which exemplify learning and those which do not.
2 Distinguish between instances of adaptive and maladaptive behaviour.
3 Distinguish between instances of human behaviour which exemplify principles of cybernetics and those which do not.
4 Distinguish between instances of human behaviour which exemplify the principles of classical conditioning and those which do not.
5 Distinguish between instances of human behaviour which exemplify the principles of instrumental conditioning and those which do not.
6 Distinguish between instances of human behaviour which exemplify classical conditioning and those which exemplify instrumental conditioning.
7 Distinguish between instances of human behaviour which exemplify response chaining and those which do not.
8 Distinguish between instances of human behaviour which exemplify learning set formation and those which do not.
9 Distinguish between instances of human behaviour which exemplify concept learning and those which do not.
10 Distinguish between instances of human behaviour which exemplify principle learning and those which do not.
11 Distinguish between instances of human behaviour which exemplify problem solving and those which do not.
12 Distinguish between instances of human behaviour mediated by language and those which are not.
13 Distinguish between instances of rote and meaningful learning.
14 Distinguish between the effects of reinforcement on instances of human behaviour and the effects of other phenomena.

Area 1 : The psychology of human learning

TYPE B   OBJECTIVES

Level 3   (derived from the level 2 objectives given in **bold**)

1 Distinguish between instances of changes in human behaviour which exemplify learning and those which do not.
  1.1 Distinguish between examples of behavioural changes brought about by learning and changes brought about by maturation.
  1.2 Distinguish between examples of behavioural changes brought about by learning and brought about by lesion.
  1.3 Distinguish between examples of behavioural changes due to learning and changes due to temporary states of learner activity.

2 Distinguish between instances of adaptive and maladaptive behaviour.
  2.1 Classify examples of adaptation as morphological, behavioural at the species level, and behavioural at the individual level.
  2.2 Distinguish between adaptive and maladaptive behaviour in specific learning situations.
  2.3 Distinguish between specific situations which are likely to lead to adaptive learning and those which are prone to lead to maladaptive learning.

3 Distinguish between instances of human behaviour which exemplify the principles of cybernetics and those which do not.
  3.1 Distinguish between examples of bodily changes brought about by homeostatic mechanisms and changes brought about by other phenomena.
  3.2 Distinguish between examples of dynamic and static equilibrium.
  3.3 Distinguish between examples of behavioural change mediated by feedback and changes not mediated by feedback.

3.4 Identify samples of human learning which exemplify the concept of the 'movement towards equilibrium'.

4 **Distinguish between instances of human behaviour which exemplify the principles of classical conditioning and those which do not.**

4.1 Classify aspects of specific classical conditioning situations as: unconditional stimuli, unconditional responses, conditional stimuli, conditional responses, reinforcement.

4.2 In specific classical conditioning situations distinguish between examples of stimulus generalization, stimulus discrimination, response generalization and response discrimination.

4.3 In specific classical conditioning situations distinguish between examples of behavioural change brought about by extinction and those brought about by other phenomena.

5 **Distinguish between instances of human behaviour which exemplify the principles of instrumental conditioning and those which do not.**

5.1 Classify aspects of specific instrumental learning situations as unconditional stimuli, unconditional responses, conditional stimuli, conditional responses, reinforcement.

5.2 In specific instrumental conditioning situations distinguish between examples of stimulus generalization, stimulus discrimination, response generalization and response discrimination.

5.3 In specific instrumental conditioning situations distinguish between examples of behavioural change brought about by extinction and those brought about by other phenomena.

6 **Distinguish between instances of human behaviour which exemplify classical conditioning and those which exemplify instrumental conditioning.**

6.1 In specific learning situations distinguish between reinforcement used according to a classical conditioning paradigm from reinforcement used according to an instrumental conditioning paradigm.

6.2 In specific learning situations distinguish between unconditional responses which agree with a classical conditioning paradigm and those which agree with an instrumental conditioning paradigm.

6.3 In specific learning situations distinguish between conditional responses which agree with a classical conditioning paradigm and those which agree with an instrumental conditioning paradigm.

7 **Distinguish between instances of human behaviour which exemplify response chaining and those which do not.**

7.1 Classify specific examples of response chaining in terms of their constituent elements of simpler types of learning.

7.2 Classify the elements of specific examples of response chaining in terms of stimulus, response, reinforcement, cueing.

7.3 Distinguish between examples of verbal chains and other types of verbal learning.

7.4 Distinguish between examples of forward and backward chaining.

8 **Distinguish between instances of human behaviour which exemplify learning set formation and those which do not.**

8.1 Classify the elements of specific examples of learning set formation in terms of stimulus presentation, reinforcement, subordinate discrimination task.

8.2 Distinguish between the subordinate discrimination tasks and the main learning in specific cases of learning set formation.

9 **Distinguish between instances of human behaviour which exemplify concept learning and those which do not.**

9.1 Classify specific examples of concepts as conjunctive, disjunctive, or relational.

9.2 Distinguish between examples of the main strategies of concept attainment.

9.3 Distinguish between specific examples of transfer of learning mediated by concept formation and that mediated by primary stimulus generalization.

9.4 Distinguish between examples of concept formation and concept attainment.

9.5 In specific learning situations distinguish between the conditions relating to the learner and the situations which are appropriate for concept learning and those which are not.

10 **Distinguish between instances of human behaviour which exemplify principle learning and those which do not.**

10.1 Distinguish between responses based on learned principles and 'mere verbalizing'.

10.2 Distinguish between prerequisite learner capabilities which are appropriate to principle learning and those which are not, in specific learning situations.

10.3 Distinguish between situational variables which are appropriate to principle learning and those which are not, in specific learning situations.

10.4 Distinguish between language used in cueing principle learning and in providing feedback or reinforcement in specific learning situations.

10.5 Distinguish between principles at different levels of generality.

10.6 Analyse a principle in terms of its constituent concepts.

10.7 Distinguish between the transfer of learning based on principle learning and that based on other types of learning in specific learning situations.

11 **Distinguish between instances of human behaviour which exemplify problem solving and those which do not.**

11.1 Distinguish between prerequisite learner capabilities which are appropriate for problem solving and those which are not, in specific problem solving situations.

11.2 Distinguish between situational variables which are appropriate for problem solving and those which are not, in specific learning situations.

11.3 Distinguish between learning situations which are appropriate to problem solving and those which are not.

11.4 Distinguish between examples of problem solving by superstitious learning and by meaningful learning.

11.5 Analyse examples of problem solving situations in terms of their constituent concepts and principles.

11.6 Rank examples of problem solving behaviour according to their congruence with the concepts of discovery learning.

12 Distinguish between instances of human behaviour mediated by language and those which are not.

12.1 Distinguish between the labelling and process functions of language.

12.2 Distinguish between examples of the signal and semantic uses of language.

12.3 Distinguish between the symbolic and non-symbolic use of language.

12.4 Distinguish between examples of learning mediated principally by the combinatorial effects of language and those mediated principally by semantic effects.

12.5 Distinguish between exemplars and non-exemplars of learning mediated by the directive function of language.

13 Distinguish between instances of rote and meaningful learning.

13.1 Distinguish between situations where meaningful learning is essential and those where rote learning would be adequate.

13.2 Classify examples of learner and situational characteristics as being appropriate or inappropriate to ensure that a given piece of learning is meaningful.

13.3 Distinguish between material-to-be-learnt which is relatable to the learners' cognitive structure in a given learning situation and material which is not.

13.4 Distinguish between examples of learning material for specific teaching situations which is logically meaningful and that which is not.

14 Distinguish between the effects of reinforcement on instances of human learning and the effects of other phenomena.

14.1 Distinguish between examples of positive reinforcement, negative reinforcement and punishment.

14.2 Distinguish between examples of reinforcement, feedback and knowledge of results.

14.3 Distinguish between examples of reinforcement used in stimulus discrimination, response discrimination, stimulus generalization, and response generalization.

14.4 Distinguish between examples of different schedules of reinforcement.

Area 1 : The psychology of human learning

TYPE C   OBJECTIVES

Level 1 :   Recall the key principles relating to human learning as currently understood.

Which yields the following level 2 objectives

1 Give a generalized definition of learning.
2 Recall the differences between learning, maturation and native response tendencies.
3 Recall the essential characteristics of adaptive behaviour.
4 Recall the essential characteristics of cybernetic mechanisms as they apply to human behaviour.
5 Recall the essential features of classical conditioning.
6 Recall the essential features of instrumental conditioning.
7 Recall the differences between classical and instrumental conditioning.
8 Recall the essential features of response chaining.
9 Recall the essential features of learning set formation.
10 Recall the essential features of concept learning.
11 Recall the essential features of principle learning.
12 Recall the essential features of problem solving.
13 Recall the main influences of language on human learning.
14 Recall the main propositions on the nature of meaningful learning.
15 Recall the main propositions on the role of reinforcement in human learning.

Area 1 : The psychology of human learning

TYPE C   OBJECTIVES

Level 3   (derived from the level 2 objectives given in **bold**)

1 Give a generalized definition of learning.
> (There are no level 3 objectives from this item)

2 Recall the differences between learning, maturation and native response tendencies.
> 2.1 Recall the nature of the changes in behaviour brought about by maturation.
> 2.2 Recall the nature of the changes in behaviour brought about by learning.
> 2.3 Recall the distinctions made between learning and performance.
> 2.4 Recall the difference between learned and unlearned behaviour.

3 Recall the essential characteristics of adaptive behaviour.
> 3.1 Recall the essential characteristics of morphological adaptation.
> 3.2 Recall the essential characteristics of behavioural adaptation at the species and individual levels.
> 3.3 Recall the differences between the characteristics of morphological and behavioural adaptation.
> 3.4 Recall the distinctions between adaptive and maladaptive behaviour.
> 3.5 Recall the learner characteristics which are prone to lead to maladaptive behaviour.
> 3.6 Recall the situational characteristics which are prone to lead to maladaptive behaviour.

4 Recall the essential characteristics of cybernetic mechanisms as they apply to human behaviour.
> 4.1 Recall the essential characteristics of homeostatic mechanisms.
> 4.2 Recall the essential characteristics of the concept of dynamic equilibrium.

119

4.3 Recall the essential characteristics of the concept of static equilibrium.

4.4 Recall the essential characteristics of feedback.

4.5 Recall the main points of the proposed 'movement towards equilibrium' as a motivator of learning.

5 Recall the essential features of classical conditioning.

5.1 Recall the main characteristics and functions of the unconditional stimulus in classical conditioning.

5.2 Recall the main characteristics and functions of the unconditional response in classical conditioning.

5.3 Recall the main characteristics and functions of the conditional stimulus in classical conditioning.

5.4 Recall the main characteristics and functions of the conditional response in classical conditioning.

5.5 Recall the propositions on the need for contiguity (in space and time) in classical conditioning.

5.6 Recall the essential features and functions of stimulus and response generalization in classical conditioning.

5.7 Recall the essential features and functions of stimulus and response discrimination in classical conditioning.

5.8 Recall the key propositions on the contribution of classical conditioning to human learning generally.

6 Recall the essential features of instrumental conditioning.

6.1 Recall the main characteristics and functions of the unconditional stimulus in instrumental conditioning.

6.2 Recall the main characteristics and functions of the unconditional response in instrumental conditioning.

6.3 Recall the main characteristics and functions of the conditional stimulus in instrumental conditioning.

6.4 Recall the main characteristics and functions of the conditional response in instrumental conditioning.

6.5 Recall the propositions on the need for contiguity (in space and time) in instrumental conditioning.

6.6 Recall the essential features and functions of stimulus and response generalization in instrumental conditioning.

6.7 Recall the essential characteristics and functions of stimulus and response discrimination in instrumental conditioning.

6.8 Recall the key propositions on the contribution of instrumental conditioning to human learning generally.

7 Recall the differences between classical and instrumental conditioning.

7.1 Recall the differences in form and functions of the unconditional stimulus, the unconditional response, the conditional stimulus and the conditional response between classical and instrumental conditioning.

7.2 Recall the differences in functions of reinforcement between classical and instrumental conditioning.

8 Recall the essential features of response chaining.

8.1 Recall the functions of simpler forms of learning in chaining.

8.2 Recall the functions of contiguity in chaining.

8.3 Recall the nature and functions of cueing in chaining.

8.4 Recall the functions of sequencing in chaining.

8.5 Recall the functions of repetition in chaining.

8.6 Recall the nature and functions of reinforcement in chaining.

8.7 Recall the essential characteristics of forward and backward chaining and the distinctions between them.

8.8 Recall the contribution of response chaining to human learning generally.

9 Recall the essential features of learning set formation.

9.1 Recall the nature and functions of the stimuli in learning set formation.

9.2 Recall the nature and functions of reinforcement in learning set formation.

9.3 Recall the functions of task variety in learning set formation.

9.4 Recall the effects of repeated presentation of a variety of related problems on task performance.

10 Recall the essential features of concept learning.
(This refers to concept attainment and concept formation)
10.1 Define a concept in terms of an abstracted class of mental experiences.
10.2 Define attribute in terms of concepts.
10.3 Recall the differences between conjunctive, disjunctive and relational concepts.
10.4 Recall the prerequisite learner capabilities for concept formation.
10.5 Recall the prerequisite learner capabilities for concept attainment.
10.6 Recall the necessary situational conditions for concept formation.
10.7 Recall the necessary situational conditions for concept attainment.
10.8 Recall the distinctions made between concept formation and concept attainment.
10.9 Recall the functions of reinforcement in concept learning.
10.10 Recall the functions of language in concept learning.
10.11 Recall the effects of concept learning on the generalizability of learned behaviour.
10.12 Recall the difference between transfer of learning at conceptual level and transfer by primary stimulus generalization.
10.13 Recall the main strategies in concept attainment.
10.14 Recall the contribution of concept learning to human learning generally.

11 Recall the essential features of principle learning.
11.1 Define a principle in terms of the meaningful juxtaposition of concepts.
11.2 Recall the prerequisite capabilities for principle learning.
11.3 Recall the necessary situational conditions for principle learning.
11.4 Recall the functions of contiguity in principle learning.
11.5 Recall the nature and functions of verbal cueing in principle learning.
11.6 Recall the nature and functions of reinforcement in principle learning.

Area   1
Type   C
Level   3

11.7 Recall the nature of the problem of 'mere verbalizing' in principle learning.

11.8 Recall the main aspects of the proposition that principle learning is 'knowledge' learning.

11.9 Recall the main propositions concerned with the hierarchical organization of principles.

11.10 Recall the contribution of principle learning to human learning generally.

12 Recall the essential features of problem solving.

12.1 Recall the nature of the prerequisite learner capabilities for problem solving.

12.2 Recall the essential situational conditions for problem solving.

12.3 Recall the main formulations on the relationship between principle learning and problem solving.

12.4 Recall the main propositions on the nature of guidance in problem solving.

12.5 Recall the main points of the distinction made between the solving of problems by 'superstitious' learning and by meaningful learning.

12.6 Recall the main propositions on the relationship between problem solving and discovery learning.

12.7 Recall the contribution of problem solving to human learning generally.

13 Recall the main influences of language on human learning.

13.1 Recall the main propositions on the labelling functions of language.

13.2 Recall the main propositions on the nature of the process functions of language (i.e. in meaningful learning).

13.3 Recall the main propositions on the function of language as a symbol system in human learning.

13.4 Recall the main propositions on the distinctions between the signal and semantic properties of words.

13.5 Recall the main propositions on the role of syntax in human learning.

13.6 Recall the main propositions on the role of language in the regulation of human behaviour.

14 Recall the main propositions of meaningful learning.

14.1 Give a definition of meaningful learning in terms of the relatability of new learning to the learner's existing cognitive structure.

14.2 Recall the propositions on the need to ensure that connections between materials to be learned are logical and substantive rather than arbitrary and verbatim.

14.3 Recall the essential learner characteristics to ensure that learning is meaningful.

14.4 Recall the main propositions on the distinctions between rote and meaningful learning.

14.5 Recall the main propositions on the role of cognitive schemas in meaningful learning.

14.6 Recall the main propositions on the importance of meaningful learning on human learning in general.

15 Recall the main propositions on the role of reinforcement of human learning.

15.1 Give a definition of reinforcement in terms of rewarded responses.

15.2 Recall the nature of the distinctions made between positive reinforcement, negative reinforcement and punishment.

15.3 Recall the conditions for bringing about extinction.

15.4 Recall the propositions linking reinforcement with cybernetic processes.

15.5 Recall the role of reinforcement in stimulus and response discrimination.

15.6 Recall the role of reinforcement in stimulus and response generalization.

15.7 Recall the role of reinforcement in shaping.

15.8 Recall the main propositions on schedules of reinforcement.

15.9 Recall the relationships between reinforcement, feedback and knowledge of results.

Area 2 : The psychology of teaching cognitive skills

LEVEL I   OBJECTIVES

Type A   Given a teaching objective involving cognitive learning, decide on the type(s) of pupil learning most appropriate to the objective and specify the teaching and learning activities most likely to optimize the pupils' learning.

Type B   Classify novel examples of teaching behaviour according to their appropriateness for different types of cognitive learning. (Given specimens of teaching behaviour a student should be able to decide what kind of learning they are intended to produce.)

Type C   Recall the key principles in teaching for efficient cognitive learning.

Notes

These objectives are closely related to areas 1 and 3, which deal with human learning and the teaching of motor skills respectively. They are dealt with separately as an aid to clarifying the concepts involved. A general point of some importance is that the objectives in this area are concerned with the way in which the teacher actively intervenes in the children's learning, whereas area 1 is concerned with a 'non-interventional' approach to learning as an object of study. The type A objective involves highly complex activity on the part of the student, mainly at levels 5 and 6 of the Bloom taxonomy and at a high level of problem solving. This objective is an important link between psychological theory and the practice of teaching.

Many of the objectives which follow refer to specific learning situations. It should be taken on all occasions that the situations will not have been encountered by the students previously.

Area 2 : The psychology of teaching cognitive skills

TYPE A   OBJECTIVES

Level 1 :   Given a teaching objective involving cognitive learning decide on the type(s) of pupil learning most appropriate to the objective and specify the teaching and learning activities most likely to optimize the pupils' learning.

Which yields the following level 2 objectives

1 Appraise a specific teaching/learning situation to determine whether there is any possibility of maladaptive learning ensuing and, if so, specify means of avoiding it.

2 Decide which, if any, of the principles of cybernetics are applicable to specific teaching/learning situations and, if any are, specify the most appropriate mode(s) of application of those principles.

3 Decide whether the learning necessary to achieve a given teaching objective involves any element of classical conditioning and, if it does, specify the optimum teaching conditions for such learning.

4 Decide whether the learning necessary to achieve a given teaching objective includes any element of instrumental conditioning and, if it does, specify the optimum teaching conditions for such learning.

5 Decide whether the learning necessary to achieve a given teaching objective involves any element of response chaining and, if it does, specify the optimum teaching conditions for such learning.

6 Decide whether the learning necessary to achieve a given teaching objective involves any element of learning set formation and, if it does, specify the optimum conditions for such learning.

7 Decide whether the learning necessary to achieve a given teaching objective involves any element of concept learning and, if it does, specify the optimum conditions for such learning.

126

8 Decide whether the learning necessary to achieve a given teaching objective involves any element of principle learning and, if it does, specify the optimum conditions for such learning.

9 Decide whether the learning necessary to achieve a given teaching objective involves any element of problem solving and, if it does, specify the optimum conditions for such learning.

10 Specify the teaching activities most likely to optimize meaningful learning in specific teaching/learning situations.

Area 2 : The psychology of teaching cognitive skills

TYPE A   OBJECTIVES

Level 3   (derived from the level 2 objectives given in **bold**)

1 **Appraise a specific teaching/learning situation to determine whether there is any possibility of maladaptive behaviour ensuing and, if so, specify means of avoiding it.**
    1.1 Appraise the learner characteristics in a given teaching/learning situation as being likely or unlikely to lead to maladaptive learning.
    1.2 Appraise the situational variables in a given teaching/learning situation as being likely or unlikely to lead to maladaptive learning.
    1.3 In the case of the learner variables in a specific teaching/learning situation being inappropriate for adaptive learning, specify appropriate remedial measures.
    1.4 In the case of the situational variables in a given teaching/learning situation being inappropriate for adaptive learning, specify the necessary adjustments to the instructional procedures.

2 **Decide which, if any, of the principles of cybernetics are applicable to specific teaching/learning situations and, if any are, specify the most appropriate mode(s) of application of those principles.**
    2.1 Appraise specific teaching/learning situations and decide on the most appropriate mode(s) of providing feedback.
    2.2 Decide whether it is appropriate to transfer feedback control from teacher to learner in specific teaching/learning situations and, if it is, specify the optimum means of arranging such feedback control.
    2.3 Specify the most appropriate method of utilizing the concepts of the 'movement towards equilibrium' in motivating learning in specific teaching/learning situations.

2.4 Compare the elements of a teaching/learning situation to the elements of a cybernetic system.

3 **Decide whether the learning necessary to achieve a given teaching objective involves any element of classical conditioning and, if it does, specify the optimum teaching conditions for such learning.**

3.1 Predict the probably differences in learning outcomes based on the use of classical conditioning in specific teaching/learning situations from outcomes based on other types of learning.

3.2 Specify the optimum conditions for stimulus presentation in specific teaching/learning situations involving classical conditioning.

3.3 Specify the optimum forms of pupil responses in specific teaching/learning situations involving classical conditioning.

3.4 Specify the optimum conditions for reinforcement in specific teaching/learning situations involving classical conditioning.

3.5 Specify the optimum conditions of stimulus presentation, response form and conditions of reinforcement in specific teaching/learning situations involving stimulus and response generalization of classically conditioned learning.

3.6 Specify the optimum conditions of stimulus presentation, response form and reinforcement in specific teaching/learning situations involving stimulus and response discrimination of classically conditioned learning.

3.7 In specific teaching/learning situations involving classical conditioning specify the optimum procedures for ensuring the extinction of learned behaviour.

3.8 Specify the most appropriate instructional material for use in specific teaching/learning situations involving classical conditioning.

3.9 Specify the appropriate use of language (if relevant) in setting up classical conditional responses in pupils.

3.10 Specify the optimum modes of evaluating pupils' learning in specific teaching/learning situations involving classical conditioning.

4 Decide whether the learning necessary to achieve a given teaching objective involves any element of instrumental conditioning and, if it does, specify the optimum teaching conditions for such learning.

4.1 Predict the probable differences in learning outcomes from specific examples of instrumental conditioning and outcomes dependent upon other types of learning.

4.2 Specify the optimum conditions for stimulus presentation in specific teaching/learning situations involving instrumental conditioning.

4.3 Specify the optimum forms of responses in specific teaching/ learning situations involving instrumental conditioning.

4.4 Specify the optimum conditions of reinforcement in teaching/ learning situations involving instrumental conditioning.

4.5 Specify the optimum conditions of stimulus presentation, response form and conditions of reinforcement in specific teaching/learning situations involving stimulus or response generalization of instrumentally conditioned responses.

4.6 Specify the optimum conditions of stimulus presentation, response form and conditions of reinforcement in specific teaching/learning situations involving stimulus or response discrimination of instrumentally conditioned responses.

4.7 Specify the optimum procedures for ensuring the extinction of instrumentally conditioned responses in specific teaching/learning situations.

4.8 Specify the optimum forms and conditions of reinforcement in specific teaching/learning situations involving the shaping of behaviour.

4.9 Specify the most appropriate instructional materials for use in specific teaching/learning situations involving instrumental conditioning.

4.10 Specify the optimum modes of evaluating pupils' learning in specific teaching/learning situations involving instrumental conditioning.

5 Decide whether the learning necessary to achieve a given teaching objective involves any element of response chaining and, if it does, specify the optimum teaching conditions for such learning.

5.1 Predict the probable differences in learning outcomes based on response chaining and outcomes based on other types of learning.

5.2 Specify the entry behaviour appropriate to specific teaching/ learning situations involving chaining.

5.3 Appraise specific teaching/learning situations and decide whether forward chaining is essential or whether backward chaining might be used.

5.4 Specify the optimum conditions of cueing, sequencing, repetition and reinforcement in specific teaching/learning situations involving chaining.

5.5 Specify the optimum forms of pupil response in specific teaching/learning situations involving chaining.

5.6 Specify the most appropriate instructional materials for use in specific teaching/learning situations involving chaining.

5.7 Specify the most appropriate use of language by teacher and pupil in specific teaching/learning situations involving chaining.

5.8 Specify the optimum modes of evaluating pupils' learning in specific teaching/learning situations involving chaining.

6 Decide whether the learning necessary to achieve a given teaching objective involves any element of learning set formation and, if it does, specify the optimum teaching conditions for such learning.

6.1 Predict the probable differences between specific learning outcomes based on learning set formation and those based on other types of learning.

6.2 Appraise a specific teaching/learning situation involving learning set formation and decide on the entry behaviour appropriate to it.

6.3 Specify the optimum conditions of stimulus presentation, reinforcement and selection of subordinate discrimination tasks in specific teaching/learning situations involving the formation of learning sets.

6.4 Specify the appropriate forms of pupil response in specific teaching/learning situations involving learning set formation.

6.5 Specify the most appropriate instructional materials for use in specific teaching/learning situations involving learning set formation.

6.6 Specify the most appropriate use of language by pupil and teacher in specific teaching/learning situations involving learning set formation.

6.7 Specify the optimum modes of evaluating pupils' learning in specific teaching/learning situations involving the formation of learning sets.

7 Decide whether the learning necessary to achieve a given teaching objective involves any element of concept learning and, if it does, specify the optimum conditions for such learning.

7.1 Predict the probable differences between specific learning outcomes based on concept learning and outcomes based on other types of learning.

7.2 Predict the probable differences between learning outcomes based on concept formation and those based on concept attainment.

7.3 Decide on the entry behaviour appropriate to a given learning situation involving concept formation.

7.4 Decide on the entry behaviour appropriate to a given learning situation involving concept attainment.

7.5 Specify the optimum conditions for the presentation of exemplars in specific teaching/learning situations involving concept learning.

7.6 Specify the optimum uses of feedback or reinforcement in specific teaching/learning situations involving concept learning.

7.7 Specify the optimum forms of pupil response in specific teaching/learning situations involving concept learning.

7.8 Specify the appropriate instructional materials for use in specific teaching/learning situations involving concept learning.

7.9 Specify the optimum modes of language usage by the teacher and the pupil in specific teaching/learning situations involving concept learning.

7.10 Specify the optimum modes of evaluating pupils' learning in specific concept learning situations.

8 Decide whether the learning necessary to achieve a given teaching objective includes any element of principle learning and, if it does, specify the optimum conditions for such learning.

8.1 Predict the probable differences between specific learning outcomes based on principle learning and those based on other types of learning.

8.2 Decide on the entry behaviour appropriate to a given teaching/learning situation involving principle learning.

8.3 Specify the optimum modes of presentation of the subordinate concepts or principles in specific teaching/learning situations involving the learning of principles.

8.4 Specify the optimum modes of deploying feedback and/or reinforcement in specific teaching/learning situations involving principle learning.

8.5 Specify the optimum forms of pupil response in specific teaching/learning situations involving principle learning.

8.6 Specify the most appropriate instructional materials for use in specific teaching/learning situations involving principle learning.

8.7 Specify the optimum modes of language usage in specific teaching/learning situations involving principle learning.

8.8 Specify the optimum modes of evaluating pupils' learning of principles in specific teaching/learning situations.

K

9 Decide whether the learning necessary to achieve a given teaching objective involves any element of problem solving and, if it does, specify the optimum conditions for such learning.

   9.1 Predict the probable differences in specific learning outcomes dependent on problem solving and outcomes dependent on other types of learning.

   9.2 Decide on the entry behaviour appropriate to a given teaching/learning situation involving the learning of principles.

   9.3 Decide on the optimum modes of structuring the learning situation for specific problem solving activities.

   9.4 Specify the optimum forms of pupil response in specific teaching/learning situations involving problem solving.

   9.5 Specify the optimum modes and extent of cueing appropriate to specific problem solving situations.

   9.6 Specify the optimum modes of deploying reinforcement or arranging for feedback in specific teaching/learning situations involving problem solving.

   9.7 Specify the optimum modes of language usage by the teacher in specific problem solving situations.

   9.8 Specify the optimum modes of language usage by the pupil in specific problem solving situations.

   9.9 Specify the most appropriate instructional materials for use in specific teaching/learning situations involving problem solving.

   9.10 Specify the optimum modes of evaluating pupils' learning in specific problem solving situations.

10 Specify the teaching activities most likely to optimize meaningful learning in specific teaching situations

   10.1 Predict the probable differences in specific learning outcomes based on meaningful learning and those based on rote learning.

   10.2 Specify the necessary conditions within the learner to ensure that new learning will be assimilated into cognitive structure meaningfully in specific learning situations.

10.3 Specify the necessary instructional procedures in specific teaching/learning situations for ensuring that new learning will be assimilated into the learner's cognitive structure meaningfully and not remembered rotely.

10.4 Specify the most appropriate modes of structuring the learning conditions in specific teaching/learning situations to optimize meaningful learning.

10.5 Specify the optimum modes of language usage to produce meaningful learning in specific teaching/learning situations.

10.6 Specify the appropriate usage of instructional materials in specific teaching/learning situations so that meaningful learning ensues.

10.7 Specify the optimum forms of pupil response for ensuring that learning is meaningful.

10.8 Specify the evaluative procedures for establishing whether learning is meaningful or rote.

Area 2 : The psychology of teaching cognitive skills

TYPE B   OBJECTIVES

Level 1 :   Classify novel examples of teaching behaviour according to their appropriateness to the different types of cognitive learning. (Given specimens of teaching behaviour a student should be able to decide what kind of pupil learning they are intended to produce.)

Which yields the following level 2 objectives

1 Distinguish between teaching/learning situations which are likely to produce adaptive behaviour in pupils and those which are not.
2 Distinguish between the different elements of entry behaviour in specific teaching/learning situations.
3 Identify the elements in specific teaching/learning situations which exemplify the principles of cybernetics.
4 Distinguish between exemplars and non-exemplars of teaching behaviour designed to produce classical conditioning.
5 Distinguish between exemplars and non-exemplars of teaching behaviour designed to produce instrumental conditioning.
6 Distinguish between exemplars and non-exemplars of teaching behaviour designed to produce response chaining.
7 Distinguish between exemplars and non-exemplars of teaching behaviour designed to produce learning set formation.
8 Distinguish between exemplars and non-exemplars of teaching behaviour designed to produce concept learning.
9 Distinguish between exemplars and non-exemplars of teaching behaviour designed to produce principle learning.
10 Distinguish between exemplars and non-exemplars of teaching behaviour designed to foster problem solving.
11 Distinguish between specific examples of teaching behaviour appropriate to rote learning and that appropriate to meaningful learning.

Area 2: The psychology of teaching cognitive skills

TYPE B   OBJECTIVES

Level 3   (derived from the level 2 objectives given in **bold**)

1 Distinguish between situations which are likely to produce adaptive behaviour in pupils and those which are not.

    1.1 Distinguish between examples of learner characteristics that are prone to lead to maladaptive learning and those that are likely to lead to adaptive learning.

    1.2 Identify the measures appropriate to the remediation of learner variables which are maladaptive in specific teaching/learning situations.

    1.3 Distinguish between situational variables that are prone to lead to maladaptive learning and those which are likely to lead to adaptive learning in specific teaching/learning situations.

    1.4 Identify the measures which are appropriate to the correction of situational variables which are likely to lead to maladaptive learning in specific teaching/learning situations.

2 Distinguish between the different elements of entry behaviour in specific teaching/learning situations.

    2.1 Distinguish between learner variables prerequisite to given learning tasks, which are dependent upon maturation and those which are dependent upon prior learning.

    2.2 Distinguish between examples of teaching approaches based on a maturational approach to the question of 'readiness' and approaches which stresses the efficacy of measures devised to develop 'readiness'.

    2.3 Identify diagnostic tests of entry behaviour appropriate to specific teaching/learning situations.

3 Identify the elements in specific teaching/learning situations which exemplify the principles of cybernetics.

    3.1 Identify different modes of providing feedback in specific teaching/learning situations.

3.2 Recognize different methods of transferring feedback control from teacher to learner in specific teaching/learning situations.

3.3 Recognize the motivating effects of cognitive disequilibrium in specific teaching/learning situations.

3.4 Distinguish between the different elements in specific teaching/learning situations considered as exemplars of cybernetic systems.

4 Distinguish between exemplars and non-exemplars of teaching behaviour designed to produce classical conditioning.

4.1 Distinguish between different modes of stimulus presentation in specific teaching/learning situations involving classical conditioning.

4.2 Distinguish between different forms of pupil response in specific teaching/learning situations involving classical conditioning.

4.3 Distinguish between different modes of reinforcement in specific teaching/learning situations involving classical conditioning.

4.4 Distinguish between different modes of stimulus presentation, response modes and conditions of reinforcement in specific teaching/learning situations involving stimulus and response generalization of classically conditioned learning.

4.5 Distinguish between different modes of stimulus presentation, response modes and conditions of reinforcement in specific teaching/learning situations involving stimulus and response discrimination in classically conditioned learning.

4.6 In specific teaching/learning situations identify the teaching procedures likely to lead to the extinction of classically conditioned responses.

4.7 Distinguish between examples of teaching materials used in setting up classically conditioned responses, and materials used in other ways.

4.8 Distinguish between language used to enhance learning involving classical conditioning and language used in other teaching approaches.

4.9 Identify the appropriate modes of evaluating pupils' learning of classically conditioned responses.

5 Distinguish between exemplars and non-exemplars of teaching behaviour designed to produce instrumental conditioning.

5.1 Distinguish between different modes of stimulus presentation in specific teaching/learning situations involving instrumental conditioning.

5.2 Distinguish between different forms of pupil response in specific teaching/learning situations involving instrumental conditioning.

5.3 Distinguish between different modes of reinforcement in specific teaching/learning situations involving instrumental conditioning.

5.4 Distinguish between different modes of stimulus presentation, response modes and conditions of reinforcement in specific teaching/learning situations involving stimulus and response generalization in instrumentally conditioned learning.

5.5 Distinguish between different modes of stimulus presentation, response modes and conditions of reinforcement in specific teaching/learning situations involving stimulus and response discrimination in instrumentally conditioned learning.

5.6 In specific teaching/learning situations identify the procedures likely to lead to the extinction of instrumentally conditioned responses.

5.7 Distinguish between examples of teaching materials used in setting up instrumentally conditioned responses and materials used in other ways.

5.8 Distinguish between language used to enhance learning involving instrumental conditioning and language used in other teaching approaches.

5.9 Identify the appropriate methods of evaluating pupils' learning of instrumentally conditioned responses.

6 Distinguish between exemplars and non-exemplars of teaching behaviour designed to produce response chaining.

6.1 Distinguish between backward chaining and forward chaining in specific teaching/learning situations.

6.2 Distinguish between those aspects of specific teaching/learning situations involving chaining which are dependent upon prior learning and those which are not.

6.3 Classify different elements of specific teaching/learning situations involving chaining as relating to cueing, sequencing, repetition and reinforcement.

6.4 Identify different modes of pupil response in specific teaching/learning situations involving chaining.

6.5 Distinguish between examples of teaching materials used in setting up response chains and materials used in other ways.

6.6 Identify language used to enhance the formation of response chains in specific teaching/learning situations.

6.7 Identify the appropriate methods of evaluating pupils' learning of response chains.

7 Distinguish between exemplars and non-examplars of teaching behaviour designed to produce learning set formation.

7.1 Identify learning outcomes dependent upon learning set formation in specific teaching/learning situations.

7.2 Identify the aspects of specific teaching/learning situations involving learning set formation which are dependent upon prior learning.

7.3 Identify the modes of stimulus presentation, reinforcement and types of subordinate learning tasks in specific teaching/learning situations involving learning set formation.

7.4 Identify different types of pupil response appropriate to learning set formation in specific teaching/learning situations.

7.5 Identify the types and modes of use of teaching materials appropriate to the formation of learning sets.

7.6 Identify different modes of language usage by pupil and teacher in establishing learning sets in specific teaching/learning situations.

7.7 Identify the appropriate methods of evaluating pupil learning of learning sets.

8 Distinguish between exemplars and non-exemplars of teaching behaviour designed to produce concept learning.

8.1 Identify examples of learning outcomes dependent upon concept learning.

8.2 Distinguish between examples of learning outcomes based on concept formation and outcomes dependent on concept attainment.

8.3 Identify the aspects of concept formation which are dependent upon prior learning, in specific teaching/learning situations.

8.4 Identify the aspects of concept attainment which are dependent upon prior learning, in specific teaching/learning situations.

8.5 Distinguish between different modes of presentation of exemplars in specific concept teaching/learning situations.

8.6 Identify different uses of feedback and reinforcement in specific teaching/learning situations involving concept learning.

8.7 Identify different forms of pupil response appropriate to specific teaching/learning situations involving concept learning.

8.8 Identify appropriate instructional materials for use in specific teaching/learning situations involving concept learning.

8.9 Identify different modes of langauge usage by teacher and pupil in specific teaching/learning situations involving concept learning.

8.10 Identify appropriate methods of evaluating concept learning in specific teaching/learning situations.

9 Distinguish between exemplars and non-exemplars of teaching designed to produce principle learning.

9.1 Identify learning outcomes dependent upon principle learning.

Area 2
Type B
Level 3

9.2 Identify the aspects of principle learning which are dependent upon prior learning in specific teaching/learning situations.

9.3 Identify different modes of presentation of the subordinate concepts and principles in specific teaching/learning situations involving the learning of principles.

9.4 Identify modes of employing feedback and reinforcement in specific teaching/learning situations involving principle learning.

9.5 Identify different forms of pupil response in specific teaching/learning situations involving principle learning.

9.6 Identify the types and modes of usage of instructional materials appropriate to specific teaching/learning situations involving principle learning.

9.7 Identify modes of language usage by pupil and teacher in specific teaching/learning situations involving principle learning.

9.8 Identify different modes of evaluating principle learning in specific teaching/learning situations.

10 Distinguish between exemplars and non-exemplars of teaching behaviour designed to foster problem solving.

10.1 Identify learning outcomes based on problem solving.

10.2 Identify aspects of problem solving which are dependent upon prior learning in specific teaching/learning situations.

10.3 Identify different modes of structuring the learning situation for specific problem solving activities.

10.4 Identify different forms of pupil response in specific teaching/learning situations involving problem solving.

10.5 Identify different methods of cueing in specific teaching/learning situations involving problem solving.

10.6 Identify appropriate modes of employing feedback and reinforcement in specific teaching/learning situations involving problem solving.

10.7 Identify appropriate modes of language usage by pupil and teacher in specific teaching/learning situations involving problem solving.

10.8 Identify the types and modes of usage of instructional materials appropriate to specific teaching/learning situations involving problem solving.

10.9 Identify appropriate modes of evaluating problem solving in specific teaching/learning situations.

11 **Distinguish between specific examples of teaching behaviour appropriate to rote learning and examples appropriate to meaningful learning.**

11.1 Distinguish between examples of learning outcomes based on meaningful learning and outcomes based on rote learning.

11.2 Identify the conditions of learner variables necessary to ensure that new learning will be assimilated into cognitive structure meaningfully in specific teaching/learning situations.

11.3 Identify different modes of structuring and presenting learning materials aimed at producing meaningful learning.

11.4 Distinguish between language usage likely to produce rote learning from language usage likely to produce meaningful learning.

11.5 Distinguish between the uses of instructional materials in ways which are likely to produce rote learning and those which are likely to produce meaningful learning.

11.6 Distinguish between pupil responses which are indicative of rote learning and those which are indicative of meaningful learning.

11.7 Distinguish between methods of evaluating rote learning and methods of evaluating meaningful learning.

Area 2 : The psychology of teaching cognitive skills

TYPE C   OBJECTIVES

Level 1 : Recall the key principles in teaching for efficient cognitive learning.

Which yields the following level 2 objectives

1 Recall the essential pedagogical considerations to ensure that pupils' learning is adaptive.
2 Recall the essential features of the concept of entry behaviour as it applies to school learning.
3 Recall the features of teaching/learning situations that exemplify cybernetic phenomena.
4 Recall the essential features of teaching behaviour designed to produce classical conditioning.
5 Recall the essential features of teaching behaviour designed to produce instrumental conditioning.
6 Recall the essential features of teaching behaviour designed to produce response chaining.
7 Recall the essential features of teaching behaviour designed to produce learning set formation.
8 Recall the essential features of teaching behaviour designed to produce concept learning.
9 Recall the essential features of teaching behaviour designed to produce principle learning.
10 Recall the essential features of teaching behaviour designed to produce problem solving.
11 Recall the teaching behaviour appropriate to pupils' rote learning and that appropriate to pupils' meaningful learning.

Area 2 : The psychology of teaching cognitive skills

TYPE C   OBJECTIVES

Level 3   (derived from the level 2 objectives given in **bold**)

1 Recall the essential pedagogical considerations to ensure that pupils' learning is adaptive.
  1.1 Recall the differences in learner characteristics that are prone to lead to adaptive and maladaptive learning.
  1.2 Recall the differences in situational variables that are prone to lead to adaptive and maladaptive learning.
  1.3 Recall the main features of measures appropriate to the remediation of maladaptive learner variables.
  1.4 Recall the main features of measures appropriate to the correction of situational variables that are prone to lead to maladaptive learning.

2 Recall the essential features of the concept of entry behaviour as it applies to school learning.
  2.1 Recall the distinctions made between learner variables prerequisite to specific learning situations which depend upon maturation and those which depend upon prior learning.
  2.2 Recall the difference in approaches to teaching based on a maturational view of 'readiness' and one based on a view which stresses the efficacy of measures to develop 'readiness'.
  2.3 Recall the essentials of diagnostic testing as a mode of evaluating entry behaviour.

3 Recall the features of teaching/learning situations that exemplify cybernetic phenomena.
  3.1 Recall the characteristics of different modes of providing feedback in teaching/learning situations.
  3.2 Recall the characteristics of different methods of transferring

145

feedback control from teacher to learner in teaching/learning situations.

3.3 Recall the key propositions on the nature of cognitive disequilibrium as a motivator of learning.

3.4 Recall the main propositions on teaching/learning situations considered as cybernetic systems.

4 Recall the essential features of teaching behaviour designed to produce classical conditioning.

4.1 Recall the characteristics of different modes of stimulus presentation in teaching/learning situations involving classical conditioning.

4.2 Recall the characteristics of different modes of pupil response in teaching/learning situations involving classical conditioning.

4.3 Recall the characteristics of different modes of reinforcement in teaching/learning situations involving classical conditioning.

4.4 Recall the characteristics of different modes of stimulus presentation, response modes and conditions of reinforcement in teaching/learning situations involving stimulus and response generalization of classically conditioned learning.

4.5 Recall the characteristics of different modes of stimulus presentation, response modes and conditions of reinforcement in teaching/learning situations involving stimulus and response discrimination of classically conditioned learning.

4.6 Recall the procedures likely to lead to the extinction of classically conditioned responses in various teaching/learning situations.

4.7 Recall the main characteristics and modes of usage of teaching materials in setting up classically conditioned responses in teaching/learning situations.

4.8 Recall the main characteristics of language used to enhance learning involving classical conditioning.

4.9 Recall the appropriate procedures for evaluating pupils' learning of classically conditioned responses.

5 Recall the essential features of teaching behaviour designed to produce instrumental conditioning.

5.1 Recall the characteristics of different modes of stimulus presentation in teaching/learning situations involving instrumental conditioning.

5.2 Recall the characteristics of different modes of pupil response in teaching/learning situations involving instrumental conditioning.

5.3 Recall the characteristics of different modes of reinforcement in teaching/learning situations involving instrumental conditioning.

5.4 Recall the characteristics of different approaches to stimulus presentation, response modes, and conditions of reinforcement in teaching/learning situations involving stimulus and response generalization of instrumentally conditioned learning.

5.5 Recall the characteristics of different approaches to stimulus presentation, response modes and conditions of reinforcement in teaching/learning situations involving stimulus and response discrimination of instrumentally conditioned learning.

5.6 Recall the procedures likely to lead to the extinction of instrumentally conditioned responses in teaching/learning situations.

5.7 Recall the main characteristics and modes of usage of teaching materials in setting up instrumentally conditioned responses in various teaching/learning situations.

5.8 Recall the main characteristics of language used to enhance learning involving instrumental conditioning.

5.9 Recall the appropriate procedures for evaluating pupils' learning of instrumentally conditioned responses.

6 Recall the essential features of teaching behaviour designed to produce response chaining.

6.1 Recall the essential characteristics of forward and backward response chaining and the distinctions between the two.

6.2 Recall the elements in response chaining which depend upon prior learning.

6.3 Recall the characteristics of cueing, sequencing, repetition and reinforcement in teaching/learning situations involving response chaining.

6.4 Recall the characteristics of different modes of pupil response in teaching/learning situations involving chaining.

6.5 Recall the main characteristics and modes of usage of teaching materials in setting up response chains in teaching/learning situations.

6.6 Recall the main modes of language usage in setting up response chains in teaching/learning situations.

6.7 Recall the characteristics of methods of evaluating pupils' learning of response chains.

7 Recall the essential features of teaching behaviour designed to produce learning set formation.

7.1 Recall the essential characteristics of learning outcomes based on learning set formation.

7.2 Recall the aspects of teaching/learning situations involving learning set formation which depend on prior learning.

7.3 Recall the characteristics of modes of stimulus presentation, reinforcement and types of subordinate learning tasks in teaching/learning situations involving learning set formation.

7.4 Recall the main characteristics of different types of pupil response in teaching/learning situations involving learning set formation.

7.5 Recall the main characteristics and modes of usage of teaching materials in teaching/learning situations involving learning set formation.

7.6 Recall the main modes of language usage in teaching/learning situations involving learning set formation.

7.7 Recall the characteristics of methods of evaluating pupils' acquisition of learning sets.

8 Recall the essential features of teaching behaviour designed to produce concept learning.

    8.1 Recall the characteristics of learning outcomes based on concept learning.

    8.2 Recall the differences between learning outcomes based on concept formation and those based on concept attainment.

    8.3 Recall the aspects of concept formation that depend upon prior learning.

    8.4 Recall the aspects of concept attainment that depend upon prior learning.

    8.5 Recall the different modes of presentation of exemplars in concept learning situations.

    8.6 Recall the characteristics of different modes of feedback and reinforcement in teaching/learning situations involving concept learning.

    8.7 Recall the characteristics of different forms of pupil response in teaching/learning situations involving concept learning.

    8.8 Recall the main modes of usage of teaching materials in teaching/learning situations involving concept learning.

    8.9 Recall the main modes of language usage by teacher and pupil in teaching/learning situations involving concept learning.

    8.10 Recall the characteristics of methods of evaluating pupils' learning of concepts.

9 Recall the essential features of teaching behaviour designed to produce principle learning.

    9.1 Recall the characteristics of learning outcomes based on principle learning.

    9.2 Recall the aspects of principle learning likely to be based on prior learning in teaching/learning situations.

    9.3 Recall the different modes of presentation of the subordinate concepts and principles in specific teaching/learning situations involving the learning of principles.

    9.4 Recall the characteristics of different modes of employing feed-

L

back in teaching/learning situations involving principle learning.

9.5 Recall the characteristics of different forms of pupil response in teaching/learning situations involving principle learning.

9.6 Recall the main characteristics modes of usage of instructional materials in teaching/learning situations involving principle learning.

9.7 Recall the main modes of language usage by teacher and pupil in teaching/learning situations involving principle learning.

9.8 Recall the characteristics of methods of evaluating pupils' learning of principles.

10 Recall the essential features of teaching behaviour designed to promote problem solving.

10.1 Recall the characteristics of learning outcomes based on problem solving.

10.2 Recall the aspects of problem solving behaviour based on prior learning in various teaching/learning situations.

10.3 Recall different modes of structuring the learning situation for problem solving activities.

10.4 Recall the characteristics of different types of pupil response in teaching/learning situations involving problem solving.

10.5 Recall the characteristics of different methods of cueing in teaching/learning situations involving problem solving.

10.6 Recall the characteristics of different modes of providing feedback and reinforcement in teaching/learning situations involving problem solving.

10.7 Recall the main characteristics and modes of usage of instructional materials in teaching/learning situations involving problem solving.

10.8 Recall the main modes of language usage by teacher and pupil in teaching/learning situations involving problem solving.

10.9 Recall the main modes of evaluating problem solving in teaching/learning situations.

11 Recall the teaching behaviour appropriate to pupils' rote learning
and that appropriate to pupils' meaningful learning.
11.1 Recall the difference between learning outcomes based on rote
learning and those based on meaningful learning.
11.2 Recall the conditions of learner variables necessary to ensure
that new learning will be assimilated into cognitive structure
meaningfully in teaching/learning situations.
11.3 Recall the characteristics of different modes of structuring and
presenting learning materials aimed at producing meaningful
learning.
11.4 Recall the difference between language usage likely to produce
rote learning and language usage likely to produce meaningful
learning.
11.5 Recall the difference between the characteristics and modes of
usage of instructional materials designed to produce rote learning
and those designed to produce meaningful learning.
11.6 Recall the differences between pupil responses which are indicative of rote learning and those which are indicative of meaningful
learning.
11.7 Recall the differences between methods of evaluating rote learning
and methods of evaluating meaningful learning.

Area 3 : The psychology of teaching motor skills

LEVEL I   OBJECTIVES

Type A   Given a teaching objective related to motor learning, decide on the type(s) of pupil learning most appropriate to the objective and specify the teaching and learning activities most likely to optimize the pupils' learning.

Type B   Classify novel examples of teaching behaviour according to their appropriateness for different types of motor learning. (Given specimens of teaching behaviour a student should be able to decide what kind of pupil behaviour they are intended to produce.)

Type C   Recall the key principles in teaching for efficient motor learning.

Notes

These objectives are closely related to those in areas 1 and 2 which deal with human learning and the teaching of cognitive skills respectively. They are dealt with separately as an aid to clarifying the concepts involved. A general point of some importance is that objectives in this area are concerned with the way the teacher actively intervenes in children's learning, whereas area 1 is concerned with a 'non-interventional' approach to learning as an object of study. The main difference between these objectives and those in area 2 is that they are chiefly concerned with simpler types of learning such as conditioning and chaining rather than with conceptual learning, although, clearly, higher levels of learning might be involved in the teaching process.

Area 4 :   The effects of cognitive variables in school learning

LEVEL I   OBJECTIVES

Type A   Given a teaching objective related to cognitive learning, decide on the cognitive variable conditions most appropriate to the learning, and specify the most suitable procedures to adopt in relating the variables to a given teaching situation.

Type B   Identify the cognitive variables related to specific learning processes and outcomes and classify their effects in specific teaching situations according to a coherent scheme.

Type C   Recall the main propositions concerning the influence of cognitive variables on school learning.

Notes

These objectives are clearly very closely related to those in area 2 and a plausible case could probably be made for subsuming them under the same general rubric. However, it seems to us helpful to consider these objectives separately in order to bring into focus the particular contribution of cognitive variables in human learning. The main points of contact with area 1 are those dealing with such things as entry behaviour and 'readiness'. They are, of course, particularly concerned with questions of individual differences *to the extent to which they impinge on the teaching/ learning process.*

Area 5 : The effects of affective variables in school learning

LEVEL I   OBJECTIVES

Type A   Given a specific teaching objective, decide on the affective variable conditions most appropriate to the learning and specify the most suitable procedures to adopt in relating the variables to a specific teaching situation.

Type B   Identify the affective variables related to specific learning processes and outcomes, and classify their effects in specific teaching situations according to a coherent scheme.

Type C   Recall the main propositions concerning the influence of affective variables on school learning.

Notes

These objectives are clearly linked with those in other areas, perhaps particularly areas 1, 2, 3 and 6. They are concerned with such things as personality, motivation and attitude *to the extent to which they impinge on the teaching/learning process.*

Area 6: The effects of social variables in school learning

LEVEL I   OBJECTIVES

Type A   Given a specific teaching objective, decide on the social variable conditions most appropriate to the learning and specify the most suitable procedures to adopt in relating the variables to a specific teaching situation.

Type B   Identify the social variables related to specific learning processes and outcomes and classify their effects according to a coherent scheme.

Type C   Recall the main propositions concerning the influence of social variables on school learning.

Notes

These objectives are particularly linked with areas 2, 5 and 7. They are concerned with such questions as group influences, social class variables, inter and intra group relationships *to the extent to which they impinge on the teaching/learning process.*

Area 7 : The effects of teacher characteristic variables in school learning

LEVEL I   OBJECTIVES

Type A   Deduce the probable effects of specific examples of teacher characteristics on pupil learning in given teaching/learning situations and specify the most suitable procedures to adopt in relating the variables to a given teaching situation.

Type B   Classify exemplars of general teacher characteristics according to their probable effects on pupil learning.

Type C   Recall the main propositions concerning the influence of teacher characteristic variables on school learning.

Notes

These objectives are particularly linked with those in area 6. They are concerned with such things as the role of the teacher, teaching styles and concepts of teacher competence.

Area   8
Types A
B
C
Level 1

Area 8 : The analysis and structuring of instructional materials

LEVEL I   OBJECTIVES

Type A   Given a specific teaching task, decide on the most effective method of structuring the instructional materials and specify the most appropriate structure for the task.

Type B   Classify specific examples of the main modes of structuring instructional materials according to a coherent scheme.

Type C   Recall the main approaches to the structuring of instructional materials.

Notes

These objectives emphasize the preparation element in teaching rather more than most of the other objectives. They are concerned with the most effective deployment of all teaching materials including those materials and methods associated with the concepts of educational technology and systems approach.

Area 9 : Evaluation and school learning

LEVEL I   OBJECTIVES

Type A   Decide on the most appropriate type of evaluatory instrument for a given teaching/learning task and devise such an instrument.

Type B   Classify examples of the main approaches to evaluation according to a coherent scheme.

Type C   Recall the key principles and methods of evaluating school learning.

Notes

The reader might look askance at objective A in view of the difficulty of constructing such instruments. However, since the alternative would almost always be no evaluation or a very crude method we consider this an important objective.

Area 10 : Children with learning difficulties

LEVEL I   OBJECTIVES

Type A   Decide on the most appropriate treatment for a specific learning difficulty and specify the optimum treatment for the remediation of the difficulty.

Type B   Classify novel examples of common learning difficulties according to the type(s) of treatment appropriate to the remediation of the difficulties.

Type C   Recall the propositions relating to learning difficulties and their treatment.

Notes

We are not proposing, here, that all students should be trained in child guidance work. However, in view of the fact that all teachers are faced with problems of learning difficulties at some time, we consider that all teachers should have some knowledge of the general principles of diagnosis and remediation of such difficulties.

Area 11 : Affective objectives

The overall aim of this area may be expressed as the developing in students of an abiding commitment to the use of psychological insights in teaching after leaving college. This general aim may be expressed (somewhat more modestly) in behavioural terms as follows:

> At the end of the course the student will be committed to an approach to teaching based on the general principles of educational psychology.

Notes

This objective cannot be compared to the objectives that have preceded it. Indeed we have sympathy with those who would see it as the overriding objective for the course. In our view it is best regarded as paralleling the other objectives taken as a group. This area cannot be broken down into the three types of objectives as we have done with the other areas, and it is clearly more global than any one of those areas. However, we believe that the objective proposed is amenable to evaluation (probably through some forms of rating scales), and indeed we are of the opinion that the monitoring of students' attitudes as they progress through a course of study could well parallel the monitoring of their cognitive learning.

6

Conclusions

Main impressions

We have referred to one of our main findings on more than one occasion. That is, the fact that by and large students have favourable attitudes towards educational psychology and we find this an encouraging augury for future work in this field. The fact that this general approval embraces a vast psychological territory does not seem to us to be a major obstacle to progress in the field if tutors and other psychologists seriously reappraise the proper boundaries of the subject as a course in teacher preparation. An important problem is still that of deciding what to leave out, but it is not the only problem. There is the equally crucial decision as to the most appropriate orientation for courses in educational psychology and our contribution to the debate on this issue can only be that of urging the close relationship of the course with the practical problems of school teaching and learning.

A second overriding impression produced by the exercise of preparing a taxonomy is the size of the problem. The conceptual difficulties of constructing a model as a guide to action are great, but even the specifying of the objectives once the model is set up are great. Apart from the conceptual problems, the sheer amount of work involved is considerable and we estimate that if our approach to a taxonomy were followed through in all areas as we have done in areas 1 and 2 we should produce a body of material of the order of about 30,000 words of objectives alone. We do not suggest that the size of the task should be taken as a reason for not carrying out the exercise, but as an indication of the nature of the problems, so that realistic provision of resources can be made by anyone wishing to adopt similar procedures in this or any other fields. We hope and believe that our first efforts reported here will make the task of anyone wishing to work in the same field somewhat less onerous and we feel confident that we shall be able to pursue our own work in this field much more adequately having gone through this exercise.

One other extremely vivid impression was borne in on us as a result of working on the taxonomy. It was the renewed conviction that the obfuscating generalities of most syllabuses were not just obstacles to the enquirer seeking to discover the objectives of courses, but were almost certainly disfunctional from the point of view of the tutor trying to operate them. It is not only a question of finishing somewhere else because you have not made up your mind where you want to go in the first place; there almost seems to be an equal danger of getting nowhere at all. This conviction was inspired by the, as it seemed to us, obvious utility of objectives stated with a measure of precision and in behavioural terms as compared with the equally obvious inutility of traditional syllabuses.

Immediate implications

The essential value of the taxonomy as it stands at present is that discussions could start among groups of tutors to see if there is any basis for consensus on the main lines of this report. If consensus can be achieved, then any group of tutors could use the existing proposals either for further development of the level 1 objectives or for devising teaching sequences based on the objectives spelled out in detail. Individual tutors could, of course, do the same, but it would seem more appropriate to begin with a group approach and follow by individual excursions once a degree of consensus has been reached. For our own part, we shall be able to use the taxonomy as it stands to continue our work on different approaches to teaching the subject in colleges of education.

We believe that the approach we have proposed has a utility outside the sphere of educational psychology. Tutors working on objectives in other aspects of the education course found early versions of the taxonomy useful and we think it probable that the model could reasonably be used as an approach of broad application.

Possible problems

The most obvious problem is that the theoretical basis of the model might be invalid. Naturally in our view it has merits but the important point is, it seems to us, that we have here a starting point for discussion.

Even if it is accepted that the main lines of the proposal are reasonable, there is still room for difficulties and weaknesses. The derivation of subordinate from superordinate objectives could be faulty. Objectives could be placed at incorrect levels of generality, or relations between different types of objectives could be spurious. These are not, of course, weaknesses in the model, but concomitants of the complexity of the problem. It is conceivable, however, that a more elegant and parsimonious model could reduce these difficulties.

Possible developments

We have already touched on the major possible developments when we referred to such things as working for consensus on parts of the taxonomy so far produced. Apart from this, the taxonomy may form the basis for a continuing examination of the objectives of educational psychology. It could also form the basis of work aimed at producing the more elegant model referred to above.

One thing could certainly be given very serious thought even within the model as it stands, and that is the question of the affective domain. It will be recalled that the objective in this domain was of a very general nature and that it did not seem to lend itself to analysis in quite the same way as the rest of the objectives. The problem could probably be approached along the lines of the Krathwohl taxonomy in one dimension and possibly this would be the most fruitful way of proceeding. We consider, however, that this objective is closely related to the cognitive ones and, as we have suggested earlier, it is quite likely that commitment will be increased by increasing the relevance of the cognitive objectives to the practice of teaching.

Some perspectives

As we said before, this is not the place to conduct a discussion on the means by which the objectives we have suggested can be achieved. That is an exercise that will build on the taxonomy. But there are some general comments, which we consider not out of place.

One intriguing possibility springs to mind. The predominant mode of instruction in college at the moment is almost certainly the formal lecture (Stones, 1969b). This mode of instruction is almost certainly inefficient (McLeish, 1968). On the other hand Mager and Clark (1963) have found that, by giving students detailed statements of objectives and no formal instruction, they have learned better than by being tutored in the conventional way. Were students to be presented with a taxonomy of the degree of detail that can be derived from the model we propose, together with notes of necessary sources and texts and access to a tutor when necessary, it is not inconceivable that some interesting learning economies would result.

Whether experiments such as the Mager–Clark investigations are ever mounted in colleges or not, it is quite certain that some movement towards a more independent form of study is inevitable. If this development is to be in line with the view of educational psychology we have presented here, we need to devise sets of carefully planned activities involving the student himself directly in the use and evaluation of psychological knowledge (Herbert and Williams, 1969). The great problem here, of course, is the very great demands which the development of such techniques makes on teaching staff, not to mention the provision of adequate instructional materials. Herbert and Williams suggest that these problems can be tackled by the sharing of resources among colleges and school districts. Tutors in the Birmingham Colleges of Education Research Group are tackling these problems by co-operative work in reappraising the content and methods of teaching and learning in various aspects of the education course.

The relationship between the taxonomy and practical teaching

Throughout our discussion of the proper concerns of educational psychology, we have stressed the need for it to be concerned with the problems of human learning and teaching in the school situation. Our model taxonomy has taken this as a guiding principle for the derivation of objectives in what is traditionally a theoretical study with its own, strong, claims on time in the theoretical component of college courses. However, the most important consequence of adopting the approach we have is that the question of the relationship between theory and practice is very sharply posed. Scrutiny of type A objectives at the lower levels of generality reveals objectives that constitute prescriptions for classroom procedures. For example, objective 8.6 from area 2 reads: 'Specify the optimum uses of feedback or reinforcement in specific teaching/learning situations involving concept learning.' This is a random choice; almost any type A objective at the same level of generality will make similar demands on the student. The objective as it stands calls for the application of general principles to a specific classroom or school situation, but the behaviour required is not necessarily practical teaching activity. The tutor concerned will make his own decision as to how best to evaluate the student's learning and, if this follows traditional lines, it will be some form of pencil and paper test. We take the view that a large variety of different approaches to the evaluation of student learning needs to be developed and some of these will necessarily be of the pencil and paper type. However, we should like to propose that the key element in any system of evaluation of a course in educational psychology should be the ability to apply the principles in classroom conditions as far as is possible in the current state of knowledge. To attempt to adopt such an approach as from now would, of course, be very difficult, but we believe that its spirit should inform approaches to evaluation in this field.

It seems to us that such an approach flows of necessity from the decision to adopt the idea of educational psychology as a theory of teaching (in so far as it can be made such). If a tutor rejects this approach, as he is perfectly at liberty to do, then he is likely to have little interest in our ideas on evaluation. But if our approach is accepted, then the acid test of a course must be the practical application of learned principles.

If this point is accepted, important implications flow both for the teaching of educational psychology and the methods of conducting the practical teaching element in teacher training courses. The concepts of educational psychology must be integrated with the practical experience of the student in the teaching situation. It thus becomes possible to conceive of a course in educational psychology with practical applications and of practical teaching experiences informed with the theoretical insights of educational psychology.

Some interesting steps in this direction have been made at the Stanford Centre for Research and Development in Teaching. Berliner (1969) reports on work using micro-teaching techniques in conjunction with a careful analysis of the technical skills involved in specific teaching situations. In the micro-teaching situation a teacher presents a brief, well planned lesson, usually five to ten minutes in duration, to a small group of pupils. As Berliner explains: 'The situation is essentially a scaled-down classroom within which real teaching takes place. It is not a simulated classroom, but merely a classroom with fewer pupils, usually four or five, and requires lessons of shorter duration than usual.' This arrangement reduces the complexity of the situation and enables the teacher to focus on specific elements in the teaching transaction. This technique is often supplemented by the use of television recording on a videotape recorder, so that the micro-lessons can be given, recorded and played back at once for the teacher to see himself in action and to examine the different elements of the lesson under scrutiny. When the methods of micro-teaching are allied to the detailed analysis of the constituent skills of a given teaching task, we have a situation that closely approximates to the conditions one might envisage in bringing together the theory of educational psychology and the practice of practical teaching. In a more extensive exposition of developments in and applications of micro-teaching, Allen and Ryan (1969) discuss some of the specific skills that have been developed in micro-teaching situations. Among these skills are reinforcing appropriately, inducing appropriate set for learning in pupils, cueing, providing feedback, and developing higher order questioning techniques (an

M

important element in concept formation). Clearly, there is great potential for developing the technical skills/micro-teaching approach as the practical manifestation of much of the theory of educational psychology.

In applying such an approach to our proposed taxonomy, we would envisage the lowest level type A objectives as providing the objectives for specific micro-lessons. An objective would be analysed in terms of its relevance to the teaching of a specific subject. The students would learn the conceptual content related to the objective and this would involve the mastery of the facts and principles in the field. They would also need to master the prerequisite skills of types B and C. Having mastered the theoretical basis for the proposed procedures and the prerequisite skills, they could then attempt to implement their skills (embodied in behaviour designed to achieve type A objectives) in a micro-teaching situation. In a scheme such as this the taxonomy produces the behavioural aim of the micro-lesson and a micro-lesson *different from the training one* provides the means of evaluation whether or not the objective has been achieved.

Clearly, spelling out the suggested approach in this way gives a distorted impression of the way in which the theory and practice would be articulated and it is possible to conceive of one micro-lesson being related to more than one low level objective. It is also possible to envisage different areas of the taxonomy contributing to the same micro-lesson. The contribution of the tutor is brought clearly into relief here as the integrator and the one who guards against fragmentation.

Bibliography

ALLEN, D. and RYAN, K. (1969) *Micro-teaching*. Reading, Mass.: Addison-Wesley.

AMERICAN COUNCIL ON EDUCATION (1946) *The Improvement of Teacher Education*. Washington, D.C.: Commission on Teacher Education.

AMERICAN EDUCATIONAL RESEARCH ASSOCIATION (1969) *Encyclopedia of Educational Research*. New York: Crowell Collier & Macmillan.

AMERICAN PSYCHOLOGICAL ASSOCIATION (1965) (DELLA-PIANA, G. *et al.*, eds.) *A Handbook for Instructors of Educational Psychology*. Urbana, Illinois: College of Education, University of Illinois.

AMMONS, M. (1964) An experimental study of process and product in curriculum development. *Journal of Educational Research*, 451–87.

ANDERSON, G. L. (1948) Theories of behaviour and some curriculum issues. *Journal of Educational Psychology*, 39, 133–9.

ANDERSON, G. L. (1949) Educational psychology and teacher education. *Journal of Educational Psychology*, 40, 275–84.

ANDERSON, G. L. (1950) What the psychology of learning has to contribute to the education of the teacher. *Journal of Educational Psychology*, 41, 362–5.

ANDERSON, R. C. (1967) Educational psychology. *Annual Review of Psychology*, 18, 127–64.

ANDERSON, R. C., FAUST, G. W., RODERICK, M. C., CUNNINGHAM, D. J., and ANDRE, T. (eds.) (1969) *Current Research on Instruction*. Englewood Cliffs, N.J.: Prentice-Hall.

ASPY, D. N. (1970) Educational psychology: challenged or challenging? *Journal of Teacher Education*, 21 (1), 5–13.

ATKIN, J. M. (1968) Behavioural objectives in curriculum design: a cautionary note. *The Science Teacher*, May 1968, 27–30. Reprinted in ANDERSON, R. C., FAUST, G. W., RODERICK, M. C., CUNNINGHAM, D. J., and ANDRE, T. (eds.) *Current Research on Instruction*. Englewood Cliffs, N.J.: Prentice-Hall.

AUSUBEL, D. P. (1967) A cognitive structure theory of school learning. In SIEGEL, L. (ed.) *Instruction: Some Contemporary Viewpoints*. San Francisco: Chandler.

AUSUBEL, D. P. (1968) *Educational Psychology: A Cognitive View*. New York: Holt, Rinehart & Winston.

Bibliography

AUSUBEL, D. P. (1969) Is there a discipline of educational psychology? In HERBERT, J. H., and AUSUBEL, D. P. *Psychology in Teacher Preparation.* Toronto, Ontario Institute for Studies in Education, Monograph No. 5. Reprinted on pp. 257–77 of this volume.

AUSUBEL, D. P., and ROBINSON, F. G. (1969) *School Learning.* New York: Holt, Rinehart and Winston.

BEARD, R. M. (1968) Changing objectives in higher education. In BEARD, R. M., HEALEY, F. G., and HOLLOWAY, P. J. *Objectives in Higher Education.* London: Society for Research into Higher Education.

BERLINER, D. C. (1969) *Micro-teaching and the Technical Skills Approach to Teacher Training.* Stanford University, Stanford Center for Research and Development in Teaching, Technical Report No. 8 (mimeographed).

BIGELOW, K. W. (1958) New directions in teacher education appraised. *Teachers College Record,* **59**, 350–6.

BIRCH, L. B. (ed.) (1962) *Teaching Educational Psychology in Training Colleges.* Report of joint working party of British Psychological Society and Association of Teachers in Colleges and Departments of Education, London. Appendix 3 is reprinted on pp. 254–6 of this volume.

BLAIR, G. M. (1941) A vocabulary of educational psychology. *Journal of Educational Psychology,* **32**, 365–61.

BLOOM, B. S. (ed.) et al. (1956) *A Taxonomy of Educational Objectives: Handbook I: The Cognitive Domain.* New York: Longmans Green.

BOARD OF EDUCATION (1909) *Regulations for the Training of Teachers in Elementary Schools.* London: H.M.S.O.

BOARD OF EDUCATION (1918) *Syllabus for Teachers in Elementary Schools.* London: H.M.S.O.

BREARLEY, M. (1957) The student's understanding of children. *Education for Teaching,* **42**, 13–18.

BRITISH PSYCHOLOGICAL SOCIETY and the ASSOCIATION OF TEACHERS IN COLLEGES AND DEPARTMENTS OF EDUCATION (1962) (BIRCH, L. B., ed.) *Teaching Educational Psychology in Training Colleges.* London. Appendix 3 is reprinted on pp. 254–6 of this volume.

BROUDY, H. S. (1967) The role of foundation studies in the preparation of teachers. In ELAM, S. M. (ed.) *Improving Teacher Education in the United States.* Stanford University, Phi Delta Kappa.

BROWNE, J. D. et al. (1957) Teaching psychology to student teachers: some problems. *Education for Teaching,* February, 3–6.

BRUNER, J. S. (1966) *Toward a Theory of Instruction.* Cambridge, Mass.: Harvard University Press.

168

BURNHAM, B. (1967) *New Designs for Learning.* Toronto: Ontario Institute for Studies in Education.

BUSH, R. N. (1961) Professional content of teacher education for the sixties. In *Teacher Education: Direction for the Sixties.* Washington, D.C.: American Association of Colleges for Teacher Education.

BUSH, R. N. (1966) The science and art of educating teachers. In ELAM, S. M. (ed.) *Improving Teacher Education in the United States.* Stanford University, Phi Delta Kappa.

BUTCHER, H. J. (1965) The attitudes of student teachers to education. *British Journal of Social and Clinical Psychology,* 4, 17–24.

CANE, B. (ed.) (1968) *Research into Teacher Education.* London: National Foundation for Educational Research.

CARPENTER, C. R. (1961) New conditions for learning in the sixties. In *Teacher Education: Direction for the Sixties.* Washington, D.C.: American Association of Colleges for Teacher Education.

CARROLL, J. B. (1965) School learning over the long haul. In KRUMBOLTZ, J. (ed.) *Learning and the Educational Process.* Chicago; Rand McNally.

COGAN, M. L. (1967) The academic major in the education of teachers. In ELAM, S. (ed.) *Improving Teacher Education in the United States.* Stanford University, Phi Delta Kappa.

COLADARCI, A. P. (1956) The relevancy of educational psychology. *Educational Leadership,* 13, 489–92. Reprinted in PARKER, R. K. (1968) *Readings in Educational Psychology.* Boston, Mass.: Allyn & Bacon. Reprinted on pp. 238–42 of this volume.

COLLIER, K. G. (1960) The teaching of psychology in training colleges. *British Journal of Educational Psychology,* 30, 103–8.

CONANT, J. B. (1963) *The Education of American Teachers.* New York: McGraw-Hill.

CORMAN, B. R. (1969) Technology, si – a psychology of techniques, no. In HERBERT, J., and AUSUBEL, D. P. (eds.) *Psychology in Teacher Preparation.* Toronto: Ontario Institute for Studies in Education, Monograph No. 5.

COX, R. C. (1966) *An Overview of Studies involving the Taxonomy of Educational Objectives, Cognitive Domain, during its first decade.* Paper read to American Educational Research Association, Chicago, February 1966 (mimeographed).

COX, R. C., and UNKS, N. J. (1967) *A Selected and Annotated Bibliography of Studies concerning the Taxonomy of Educational Objectives: Cognitive Domain.* University of Pittsburgh, Learning Research and Development Center.

Bibliography

DARROCH, A. (1911) *The Place of Psychology in the Training of the Teacher.* New York: Longmans Green.

DAY, H. P. (1959) Attitude changes of beginning teachers after initial teaching experience. *Journal of Teacher Education,* **10,** 326–8.

DEARDEN, R. F. (1969) in PETERS, R. (ed.) *Perspectives on Plowden.* London: Routledge & Kegan Paul.

DE CECCO (1968) *Psychology of Learning and Instruction.* Englewood Cliffs, N.J.: Prentice-Hall.

DELLA-PIANA, G. and associates (1965) *A Handbook for Instructors of Educational Psychology.* Urbana, Illinois: University of Illinois, College of Education.

DEPARTMENT OF EDUCATION AND SCIENCE (1966) *Children and Their Primary Schools* (Plowden Report). London: H.M.S.O.

DEWEY, J. (1929) *The Sources of a Science of Education.* New York: Liveright.

DREVER, J. (1935) The place of psychology in the training and work of the teacher. *British Journal of Educational Psychology,* **5,** 242–9.

EISNER, E. W. (1967) Educational objectives: help or hindrance? *School Review,* **75,** 250–60. Reprinted on pp. 214–23 of this volume.

ELAM, S. M. (ed.) (1966) *Improving Teacher Education in the United States.* Stanford University, Phi Delta Kappa.

ERICKSEN, S. C. (1967) The zig-zag curve of learning. In SIEGEL, L. (ed.) *Instruction: Some Contemporary Viewpoints.* San Francisco: Chandler.

FISHBURN, C. E. (1966) Learning the role of the teacher. *Journal of Teacher Education,* **17,** 329–31.

FLEMING, C. M. (1954) The place of psychology in the training of teachers. *British Journal of Educational Studies,* **3,** 17–23.

FREEMAN, F. S., and SNYGG, D. (1953) Content of educational psychology. In *Educational Psychology in Teacher Education.* Terra Haute, Indiana: National Society of College Teachers of Education, Monograph No. 3.

FRENCH, W. (1957) *Behavioural Goals in General Education in High Schools.* New York: Russell Sage Foundation.

FURST, E. J. (1957) *Constructing Evaluation Instruments.* London: Longmans.

GAGE, G. E., FREDERICKS, H. D., HUITEMA, B., KOHL, D., and BEAIRD, J. H. (1968) *Behavioural Objectives and Test Item Production: Boon or Bane?* Paper presented at the American Educational Research Association Conference, Washington, D.C.

GAGE, N. L. (ed.) (1962) *Handbook of Research on Teaching.* Chicago: Rand McNally.

GAGE, N. L. (1964) Theories of teaching. In *Theories of Learning and In-*

struction. Chicago: National Society for the Study of Education, 63rd Yearbook.

GAGE, N. L. (1967) Psychological conceptions of teaching. *International Journal of Educational Science*, 1, 151–61.

GAGE, N. L. (1968) An analytical approach to research on instructional materials. *Phi Delta Kappa*, 49, 601–6.

GAGNÉ, R. M. (1964) The implications of instructional objectives for learning. In LINDVALL, C. M. (ed.) *Defining Educational Objectives*. Report of the Regional Commission on Educational Coordination and the Learning Research and Development Center, University of Pittsburgh.

GAGNÉ, R. M. (1965) *The Conditions of Learning*. New York: Holt, Rinehart & Winston.

GAGNÉ, R. M. (1967) *Curriculum Research and the Promotion of Learning*. Invited address at the American Educational Research Association Annual Meeting, 1966. Reprinted in TYLER, R. W., GAGNÉ, R. M., and SCRIVEN, M. (1967) *Perspectives of Curriculum Evaluation*. Chicago: Rand McNally.

GILBERT, T. F. (1962) Mathetics: the technology of education. *Journal of Mathetics*, 1, 7–74.

GLASER, R. (1962) Psychology and instructional technology. In GLASER, R. (ed.) *Training Research and Education*. University of Pittsburgh.

HADOW, W. H. (1931) *Report of the Consultative Committee on the Primary School*. Board of Education, Great Britain. London: H.M.S.O.

HERBERT, J., and AUSUBEL, D. P. (1969) *Psychology in Teacher Preparation*. Toronto: Ontario Institute for Studies in Education, Monograph No. 5.

HERBERT, J., and WILLIAMS, D. (1969) Psychology in the teacher-preparation programme. In HERBERT, J., and AUSUBEL, D. P. (eds.) *Psychology in Teacher Preparation*. Toronto: Ontario Institute for Studies in Education, Monograph No. 5. Reprinted on pp. 278–98 of this volume.

HILGARD, E. R. (1964) A perspective on the relationship between learning theory and educational practices. In *Theories of Learning and Instruction*. Chicago: National Society for the Study of Education, 63rd Yearbook.

HOLLINS, T. H. B. (1963) Teaching educational psychology in training colleges. *British Journal of Educational Psychology*, 33 (2), 187–90.

ISAACS, S. (1924) An inquiry into the teaching of psychology in training colleges. *Forum for Education*, 2 (2), 133–40.

JOHNSON, M. E. B. (1966) Teachers' attitudes to educational research. *Educational Research*, 9 (1), 74–9.

JOINT MATRICULATION BOARD (1969) General Certificate of Education.

Bibliography

Statement of Objectives of Revised Syllabus in Chemistry (Advanced). Manchester.

KAY, B. (1970) *Participation in Learning: A Progress Report on the Training of Teachers.* London: Allen & Unwin.

KIMBLE, G. A. (1961) *Hilgard and Marquis' 'Conditioning and Learning'.* New York: Appleton-Century-Crofts.

KLAUSMEIER, H. and SWANSON, D. (1950) The development of a functional course in educational psychology for teachers. *Journal of Educational Psychology,* **41,** 449–72.

KRATHWOHL, D. R. (1964) The taxonomy of educational objectives: its use in curriculum building. In LINDVALL, C. M. (ed.) *Defining Educational Objectives.* Report of the Regional Commission on Educational Coordination and the Learning Research and Development Center, University of Pittsburgh.

KRATHWOHL, D. R. (1965) Stating objectives appropriately for program, for curriculum and for instructional materials development. *Journal of Teacher Education,* **16** (1), 83–92. Reprinted on pp. 188–206 of this volume.

KRATHWOHL, D. R., BLOOM, B. S. and MASIA, B. B. (1964) *Taxonomy of Educational Objectives. Handbook II: The Affective Domain.* New York: McKay.

KRUMBOLTZ, J. D. (1965) *Learning and the Educational Process.* Chicago: Rand McNally.

LINDVALL, C. M. (1961) *Testing and Evaluation: An Introduction.* New York: Harcourt, Brace & World.

LINDVALL, C. M. (ed.) (1964) *Defining Educational Objectives.* A Report of the Regional Commission on Educational Coordination and the Learning Research and Development Center, University of Pittsburgh.

LLOYD-EVANS, A. (1935) The place of psychology in the training of teachers. *British Journal of Educational Psychology,* **5,** 257–65.

LOVELL, K. (1958) *Educational Psychology and Children.* University of London Press.

LUNZER, E. A. (1968) Review of STONES, E., *An Introduction to Educational Psychology. Educational Review,* **20** (2), 172.

MACKENZIE, N., ERAUT, M., and JONES, H. C. (1970) *Teaching and Learning: An Introduction to New Methods and Resources in Higher Education.* Paris: UNESCO and International Association of Universities.

MCLEISH, J. (1968) *The Lecture Method.* Cambridge Institute of Education.

MACLURE, J. S. (1968) *Curriculum Innovation in Practice.* Report of 3rd International Curriculum Conference, Oxford 1967. London: H.M.S.O.

MAGER, R. F. (1962) *Preparing Objectives for Programmed Instruction.* Palo Alto, Calif.: Fearon.

MAGER, R. F. (1964) Transcript of lecture given at L.C.C. Teachers Course on Programme Writing, 28 January 1964. Quoted in RICHMOND, W. K. (1968) *Readings in Education.* London: Methuen.

MAGER, R. F., and CLARK, C. (1963) Explorations in student controlled instruction. *Psychological Reports*, 13, 71–6.

MARKLE, S. M., and TIEMANN, P. W. (1970) Problems of conceptual learning. *Journal of Educational Technology*, 1 (1), 52–62.

MARTIN, A. (1969) Towards a social psychology of education and training. *Bulletin of British Psychological Society*, 22, 22–6.

MECHNER, F. (1961) *Programming for Automated Instruction.* New York: Basic Systems (mimeographed).

MELTON, A. W. (1964) The taxonomy of human learning: overview. In MELTON, A. W. (ed.) *Categories of Human Learning.* New York: Academic Press.

METFESSEL, N. S., MICHAEL, W. B., and KIRSNER, D. A. (1969) Instrumentation of Bloom's and Krathwohl's taxonomies for the writing of educational objectives. *Psychology in the Schools*, 6 (3), 227–31. Reprinted on pp. 207–13 of this volume.

MINISTRY OF EDUCATION (1957) *The Training of Teachers: Suggestions for a Three Year Course.* London: H.M.S.O.

MORRISON, A., and MCINTYRE, D. (1969) *Teachers and Teaching.* Harmondsworth: Penguin Books.

MURPHY, L. B. (1952) Teaching procedures in educational psychology. *Journal of Educational Psychology*, 43, 16–22.

NATIONAL COUNCIL FOR EDUCATIONAL TECHNOLOGY (1968) *Towards More Effective Learning.* Report of N.C.E.T. 1967–8. London.

NATIONAL SOCIETY OF COLLEGE TEACHERS OF EDUCATION (1953) *Educational Psychology in Teacher Education.* Monograph No. 3. Terra Haute, Indiana.

NATIONAL UNION OF STUDENTS (1966) *Colleges of Education: The Three Year Course.* London.

NEWSOM, SIR JOHN (1963) *Half our Future.* Report of Central Advisory Council for Education, Ministry of Education, Great Britain. London: H.M.S.O.

NUNNEY, D. N. (1964) Trends in the content of educational psychology 1948–63. *Journal of Teacher Education*, 15, 372–7.

OESER, O. A. (1951) Psychology applied to the teaching of psychology. *American Psychologist*, 6, 172–6.

Bibliography

OLSON, W. C. (1957) *Psychological Foundations of the Curriculum.* Paris: UNESCO.

PARKER, R. K. (1968) *Readings in Educational Psychology.* Boston, Mass.: Allyn & Bacon.

PAVLOV, I. P. (1927) *Conditioned Reflexes.* Translated by G. V. ANREP. London: Oxford University Press.

PEEL, E. A. (1956) *The Psychological Bases of Education.* Edinburgh: Oliver & Boyd.

PETERS, R. (ed.) (1969) *Perspectives on Plowden.* London: Routledge & Kegan Paul.

PLOWDEN, LADY (1966) *Children and Their Primary Schools.* A Report of the Central Advisory Council of Education, England. London: H.M.S.O.

POPHAM, W. J. (1968) Probing the validity of arguments against behavioural goals. A Symposium presentation at the Annual Meeting of the American Educational Research Association, 1968. Reprinted in ANDERSON, R. C., FAUST, G. W., RODERICK, M. C., CUNNINGHAM, D. J., and ANDRE, T. *Current Research in Instruction.* Englewood Cliffs, N.J.: Prentice-Hall. Reprinted on pp. 229–37 of this volume.

POPHAM, W. J., EISNER, E. W., SULLIVAN, H. J., and TYLER, L. L. (1969) *Instructional Objectives.* Chicago: Rand McNally, for American Educational Research Association.

Quarterly Journal of Education (1835). London.

RAZRAN, G. (1965) Russian physiologists' psychology and American experimental psychology: a historical and systematic collation and a look into the future. *Psychological Bulletin,* **63** (1), 42–64.

RICHMOND, W. K. (1968) *Readings in Education.* London: Methuen.

RIVLIN, H. N. (1953) The objectives of educational psychology in the education of teachers. In *Educational Psychology in Teacher Education.* Terra Haute, Indiana: National Society of College Teachers of Education, Monograph No. 3. Reprinted on pp. 243–53 of this volume.

RUDD, W. G., and WISEMAN, S. (1962) Sources of dissatisfaction among a group of teachers. *British Journal of Educational Psychology,* **32**, 275–91.

RYANS, D. G. (1963) Teacher behaviour theory and research: implications for teacher education. *Journal of Teacher Education,* **14**, 274–93.

SCHOBEN, E. J. (1964) Psychology in the training of teachers. *Teachers College Record,* **65**, 436–40.

SCRIVEN, M. (1967) The methodology of evaluation. In TYLER, R., GAGNÉ, R. M., and SCRIVEN, M. (eds.) *Perspectives of Curriculum Evaluation.* Chicago: Rand McNally.

174

SIEGEL, L. (ed.) (1967) *Instruction: Some Contemporary Viewpoints*. San Francisco: Chandler.

SKINNER, B. F. (1938) *The Behaviour of Organisms: An Experimental Analysis*. New York: Appleton-Century-Crofts.

SKINNER, B. F. (1968) *The Technology of Teaching*. New York: Appleton-Century-Crofts.

SPENS, W. (1938) *Report of the Board of Education Consultative Committee on Secondary Education*, Great Britain. London: H.M.S.O.

STENHOUSE, L. (1969) *Behavoural Objectives in Curriculum Development: Their Limitations*. Invited paper read at British Psychological Society (Education Section) Conference, London, September 1969.

STILES, L. J. (1969) Teacher education programmes. In EBEL, R. L. (ed.) *Encyclopedia of Educational Research*. New York: Crowell Collier & Macmillan, for American Educational Research Association.

STOLUROW, L. M. (1965) Model the master teacher or master the teaching model. In KRUMBOLTZ, J. D. (ed.) *Learning and the Educational Process*. Chicago: Rand McNally.

STONES, E. (1966) *An Introduction to Educational Psychology*. London: Methuen.

STONES, E. (1967) *Survey of Statistics Taught in Colleges of Education*. University of Birmingham School of Education, Colleges of Education Research Group (mimeographed).

STONES, E. (1968) *Learning and Teaching: A Programmed Introduction*. London: Wiley.

STONES, E. (1969a) An experiment in the use of programmed learning in a university with an examination of student attitudes and the place of seminar discussion. In DUNN, W. R., and HOLROYD, C. (eds.) *Aspects of Educational Technology*, 2. London: Methuen.

STONES, E. (1969b) Students' attitudes to the size of teaching groups. *Educational Review*, 21 (2), 98–108.

STONES, E. (1970a) *Readings in Educational Psychology: Learning and Teaching*. London: Methuen.

STONES, E. (1970b) Towards evaluation: some thoughts on tests and teacher education. *Educational Review* occasional publication No. 4.

SULLIVAN, H. J. (1969) Objectives, evaluation and improved learner achievement. In POPHAM, W. J. (ed.) *Instructional Objectives*. Chicago: Rand McNally, for American Educational Research Association, 65–90.

SUMMERFIELD, A. (1968) *Teaching Educational Psychologists*. London: H.M.S.O.

Bibliography

THORNDIKE, E. L. (1903) *Educational Psychology*. New York: Columbia University, Teachers College.

THYNE, J. M. (1963) Critical comments on teaching educational psychology in colleges. *British Journal of Educational Psychology*, 33 (2), 190–1.

TRAVERS, R. M. W. (1969) Educational psychology. In EBEL, R. L. (ed.) *Encyclopedia of Educational Research*. New York: Crowell Collier & Macmillan, for American Educational Research Association.

TROW, W. M. (1948) How educational psychology and child development can contribute to the preparation of teachers. *Journal of Educational Psychology*, 39, 129–32.

TROW, W. M. (1949) Educational psychology charts a course. *Journal of Educational Psychology*, 40, 285–94.

TYLER, R. W. (1934) Constructing achievement tests. The Ohio State University. Quoted in LINDVALL, C. M. (ed.) (1964) *Defining Educational Objectives*. University of Pittsburgh Press.

TYLER, R. W. (1964) Some persistent questions in the defining of objectives. In LINDVALL, C. M. (ed.) *Defining Educational Objectives*. University of Pittsburgh Press. Reprinted on pp. 179–87 of this volume.

TYLER, R. W. (1969) *Basic Principles of Curriculum and Instruction*. University of Chicago Press (first published 1950).

TYLER, R. W., GAGNÉ, R. M., and SCRIVEN, M. (1967) *Perspectives of Curriculum Evaluation*. Chicago: Rand McNally.

VERDUIN, J. R. (1967) *Conceptual Models in Teacher Education*. Washington, D.C.: American Association of Colleges for Teacher Education.

VERNON, P. E. (1950) Postgraduate training of teachers in psychology. *Educational Research*, 20 (3), 149–52.

WEES, W. R. (1966) For whom we teach. In BURNHAM, B. (ed.) *New Designs for Learning*. Toronto: Ontario Curricula Institute.

WHEELER, D. K. (1967) *Curriculum Process*. University of London Press.

WOLTERS, A. W. (1935) Psychology in the training of teachers. *British Journal of Educational Psychology*, 5, 250–5.

WOOD, R. (1968) Objectives in the teaching of mathematics. *Educational Research*, 9 (3), 219–22.

WOODRING, P. (1957) *New Directions in Teacher Education*. New York: Fund for the Advancement of Education.

Part Two
Selected Readings

On objectives

I

Some persistent questions
on the defining of objectives

RALPH W. TYLER

In this paper I should like to comment on four questions which are often raised in a discussion of the subject of educational objectives.

The importance of a clear definition of objectives

One common question is: 'Why is it now considered important to define objectives clearly when teachers in the past have done excellent work without having a clear statement of goals?' It is certainly true that many teachers have a sense of what is important for students to learn and some of them are able to translate this notion of educational goals into relevant learning experiences for the student without ever having put down on paper what these implicit aims are. However, many others have not carried their thinking beyond the point of selecting the content to be presented. They have not considered carefully what the students are to do with the content. In such cases, students commonly believe that they are to memorize all or important parts of the content, and other objectives involving behaviour other than memorization are not developed.

This question can also be examined from the point of view of the student. When the objectives are clearly defined and understood by the student, he can perceive what he is trying to learn. What happens when the students are not informed of the learning aims? I have interviewed more than 100 students at the upper elementary and secondary school levels, asking them what they are expected to learn in each of their courses, and how they found out what they were to learn. Almost all of the students reported that they found out what they were to learn from three sources: the textbooks and work books, what the teacher did in class and the advice of other students. Unless the exercises in the work books and the textbook assignments clearly reflect the desired objectives, the student is likely to resort to memorization and mechanical completion of exercises rather than to carry on the activities which are really relevant to the desired goals.

179

Unfortunately, too, the teacher's behaviour in the classroom is not an example of the behaviour implied by the objectives of the course. For example, in several college history courses the teachers told me that their objectives were to develop understanding on the part of the students of the way in which past events, episodes and the like influenced later conditions and problems. They also said that they wanted the students to learn to draw on various sources of information about the past and to be able to explain what is happening today partly in terms of this influence of the past. But, in spite of mentioning these kinds of objectives, the teachers' performance in class consisted primarily in lecturing on what they had learned about the historical period under study and quizzing students on the lecture and related reading. The result was that the student, watching the performance of the teacher, thought that what was expected of him was to be able to do the same thing. He felt that he should memorize what people knew about this period rather than develop any of the desired abilities and skills. It is this kind of experience that leads me to believe that when objectives are identified and defined only casually, if at all, the students are likely to get the wrong image of what the teacher is trying to teach and what the student is expected to be able to do. He is misguided rather than helpfully steered in his learning efforts.

Two aspects of a clear definition

A second common question is: 'What should be included in a clear definition of an educational objective?' The Conference papers [i.e. in Lindvall, 1964, from which this paper is taken] have emphasized the requirement that the definition should describe behaviour, that is, *what it is that the student should be able to do, or how he should be able to think or feel*. For example, he may be expected to write clearly or he should be able to observe the results of experiments and draw reasonable inferences from them, or he should be able to perceive and respond to aesthetic qualities in music. I believe the papers have given less attention to the other aspect of the definition of an objective, and that is the content involved. Using the previous examples, the definition should not only indicate that in this English class the student is expected to learn to write clearly but also there should be an indication of the kinds of things he should be able to write. The statement that he is expected to be able to write a clear letter of application for a job would include the content part as well as the behaviour. Correspondingly, in the second example, above, the objective should indicate what kinds of experiments he should be able to observe and draw inferences from the results, and in the third example, the definition should state the aesthetic qualities and the kinds of music involved. To specify the kind of behaviour to be developed is not enough to guide the selection of learning experiences and the appraisal of results. We must also specify the kinds of content involved.

The level of specificity of the definition

Recognizing the importance of being clear about objectives, sometimes we confuse clarity with a high degree of specificity. For example, a teacher of French may state as one objective the ability to read French. Then in an effort to define what is meant, this is broken down into such specific parts as knowledge of the meaning of the most common 2500 French words, knowledge of the meaning of each of a number of common French idioms, and so on. These efforts sometimes end up with several hundred objectives for one course. This is too specific, just as the ability to read French is too general.

Here I think we need to make a distinction between the objective in terms of what repertoire we are trying to help the pupil to develop and the analysis that we may make of the objective in terms of a learning sequence. For example, in the case of a foreign language, the objective may be to be able to read the kind of material that you find in the Paris newspapers. This could be an objective, but we may have to define reading somewhat further. For example, what type of understanding is required and how far should he be able to go with respect to the possible varieties of content? Now it may be that in reaching this type of objective our foreign language teachers would use a plan in which they start from a carefully controlled vocabulary (which was the method used in the early 1930s and 1940s) or they may use patterns of oral pronunciation (as in the present-day audio-lingual methods). But specifying the various teaching procedures or learning activities is not specifying the objective. The objective should be stated at the level of generality of behaviour that you are seeking to help the student to acquire.

Now this level is largely determined by two factors. One is the level required for effective use in life. This is usually implied by a statement of behaviour that can be valued in and of itself. One can easily see the value of being able to read a French newspaper while being able to identify the subjunctive mood appears to be only a means, not an important objective in itself.

The second factor determining the desired level of generality or specificity is the probable effectiveness in teaching the students involved to generalize the learning to the level desired. Children in the primary grades can usually generalize the idea of addition so that they do not have to practise each number combination again and again as a separate objective. Hence, if this is true, it is possible to seek as objectives for these students: (1) understanding of the concept 'addition', (2) ability to add whole numbers.

In general, the first factor leads to objectives which are not highly specific. The second factor requires us to limit the generality to the level which can be learned by the students involved. This emphasizes the importance of actual experience and empirical evidence in deciding whether a given statement of objectives is too specific or too general.

Considerations involved in selecting objectives

A question continually arising in discussions of this sort concerns a step prior to that of definition: 'What considerations should be taken into account in the selection of objectives?' Realizing that there is so much to be taught, so much that it would be valuable for people to learn in a complex society such as ours, and so little time to learn, how do we decide what objectives are worth teaching? I have found it useful to keep in mind several different factors. One of these is an analysis of our culture. Other things being equal, it is important to teach those kinds of behaviour, those ways of thinking, feeling and acting that have value in our society and that help the person to become an effective human being in it. As an example of this, the question of foreign language instruction might be used. Some schools have been quite successful in teaching a foreign language at a very early age so that we know that this is something that can be done if it is desirable. But the question that faces the curriculum planner is this: How significant is this foreign language as a means for the pupil's further development? It is more important for the Englishman to learn French than it is for the average American because the Englishman usually has many more opportunities to use it. For the same reason it is more important for the people in Texas to learn Spanish than it is for the people in Illinois to learn Spanish. Where a foreign language can be used it becomes an important tool of communication.

A related question in which the facts of the culture must be considered is one of the proper grade placement for given objectives or subjects. Where possible, instruction should be planned so that the initial stages of learning will be under the supervision of the school but so that continued learning and reinforcement can and will take place outside the school. For example, if a person is going to Venezuela as a member of the Peace Corps in September, it would be most effective if he were taught Spanish in the months prior to his leaving. This would mean that as soon as he has completed some of the initial stages in learning the language he will have the opportunity to use it outside the classroom and continue to learn under the reinforcing conditions provided by this practical application.

A second factor in selecting appropriate objectives is the present status of the student. What has he already learned? What is he ready for? One of the problems here may be illustrated by developments in mathematics where many high schools are now offering advanced courses. For this reason, as reported to me by some of my college colleagues, some of the topics typically taught in college mathematics courses turn out to be 'old stuff' for students coming from the better high schools. I encountered another example of this situation in a recent conversation with a friend whose daughter is a freshman at a leading eastern college. This girl has been greatly disappointed in her first college history course. In her high school history classes use was made of a variety of interesting source materials, but the college course is using only a textbook which is read and commented on, chapter by chapter. For this student, what had been exciting about the study of history is no longer there. So a key problem in selecting objectives is that of determining the 'entering behaviour' of the student, just where he is in his educational development and what abilities he brings to the given class or learning situation. Only when this is known can we answer the question of whether or not certain objectives are appropriate for his next stage of development. This requires a procedure for finding out about the students, where they are now, and what their capabilities are.

A third factor in selecting objectives is what we know enough about to teach. It might be nice, for example, to teach a person to employ extrasensory perception, but we don't know enough about this to teach it. On the other hand, we do know enough about the art of writing to have something to teach children. And new knowledge in the various subjects is being obtained at a rapid rate. These new developments should be continually examined to see if they provide materials that can be of real value to youngsters. But these new ideas and understandings were not available to teachers at the time they were receiving their education so that we have a problem of keeping our objectives, and our ability to teach them, abreast of the most recent developments in a given field. This is a reason for the continuing effort to involve scientists and other scholars in working with teachers in the development of curricula. New subject resources are becoming available continually and these should be scrutinized by someone or some curriculum centre as a basis for making decisions as to whether or not they should be incorporated into classroom content.

Of course, a fourth basic consideration in the selection of objectives is their relevance to the schools' philosophy of education. This philosophy outlines our conception of the 'good person' we are trying to develop. It is certainly possible to teach a person as though he were an automaton, and some kinds of training programs in industry are operated pretty much in this way. We can teach him to do all the required things. He can run all of the machines without understanding them. But is this the kind of person we are trying to develop?

We have come to place an emphasis on such things as problem solving and open-endedness, that is, helping the learner to become conscious of the fact that he doesn't have the final answers in this area, that a continuing process of inquiry is involved. We also are putting an emphasis upon the values that come from aesthetic experiences in such areas as art and music. But we also have problems of conflicting values and often need to clarify our guiding philosophy. We must continuously be asking the question of what kind of young person it is that it is the responsibility of our schools and colleges to help develop. I have my own answer to the question and I suppose that each one of us does. But the clarification of our values is a basic step in curriculum planning and in the selection of objectives because we can teach in such a way that values or ends are helped, or we can teach in such a way that they are denied.

Finally, a fifth factor in selecting and stating our objectives is the consistency of these objectives with our theory of learning. As an illustration of this consideration, the question frequently arises of the possibility of meeting the demands made upon people today through the preparation provided by our present sixteen years of school. Surely, our people are required to meet problems of such range and complexity that they can't learn enough in their youth. This dilemma has resulted in a variety of suggestions for the school curriculum. One proposal is that we teach most youth to be a 'garden-variety' of citizen who will not be expected to understand much but who can be taught the skills of a particular occupation and a respect for leadership. This is the view often expressed in the English elementary schools. This proposal includes the idea that the responsibility for more adequate understanding and competence to deal with the complexities of modern life will be in the hands of the more privileged group that goes on to secondary schools and colleges.

Another proposal is based on the view that the fields of knowledge are getting so large (as the scientific fields, for example) that we can only expect to cover them rather superficially with some kind of survey. This seems to be a rather common approach.

But a proposal which is currently gaining attention is to start the student from the beginning as an inquirer, as a person who is seeking to learn, giving him the skills and the incentives that lead him to dig deeper into some sample of a content area, and then encouraging him to go on independently while he is in school, and in later life. As one example of this, the new social studies material being developed at Harvard begins at the third grade level with a study of the Eskimo and two other primitive cultures. This program says, in effect, that the culture of man is a developing thing and that its basic elements and the procedure for studying it can best be understood by starting with certain simple samples. The Eskimo is selected, not for the usual romantic reasons that have led to his inclusion in elementary school courses, but because he represents a type of culture which can be studied through the methods of the anthropologist. Then the children study a tribe from central Africa and another from Oceana. These offer the third grader the opportunity to become familiar with primitive societies. And the students begin their study, not by reading a textbook, but by bringing together a variety of materials and resources that are pertinent to the understanding of the culture and appropriate for third-graders so that, from the first, they employ the methods that are useful in beginning to understand what another culture is like. The effort is to develop persons who have the ability and the desire to be continuing inquirers.

Projects of this type are trying to attack the problem caused by the ever increasing mass of material that should be learned by producing students who have the tools and the general ability to proceed on their own. This approach views education not merely as a process of giving answers, but as a process of producing persons who can find answers on their own, can discover additional questions that need to be answered, can come up with answers to these questions and engage in an intelligent process of continual inquiry. This approach seeks to develop in students a conviction that the world is an interesting and exciting place where there is much to be seen and understood. The students are out to understand the kinds of problems that are found and the modes of inquiry that are used. They should develop an understanding of how one makes an inquiry if one were looking at a topic from the point of view of the geographer, or from the point of view of the chemist, or from the point of view of the writer of a literary document. They learn to inquire into the behaviour of people as well as the behaviour of things, of plants and of animals. This approach seeks to develop the necessary skills and the mastery of many of the pertinent concepts. The school is not expected to present all of the details or all of the specific facts or examples.

The important learning is for the pupil to understand the basic concepts such as that of social mobility, in sociology, of motivation, in psychology, or of energy transfer, in physics. Concepts of this type are basic to continued investigation in a given area. For example, the new high school physics course developed by the Physical Science Study Committee builds its work around thirty-four concepts. If the pupil masters these he has the foundation for further investigation of physical phenomena. He can learn how these concepts are related and can discover many important principles. As an example in the arts, the courses are built around concepts of form and of aesthetic values such as that of unity in literature, of the illusion of reality, etc.

The hope is, with this approach, that students really become involved in a life-long process of learning in which the school's role is to get them fairly well started. With such a view the problem of defining objectives becomes that of determining the behaviours, appropriate to the given grade level, that the pupil can carry out so that when he has done this he will have a feeling for the open-endedness of the situation, the new questions to be asked, the new knowledge to be gained and not feel that the learning is finished. For example, the fifth grade pupil in such a program will not feel that now he knows all there is to know about Egypt but will begin to see how what he knows about Egypt relates to other countries, will see, for example, the relationships between rigid social structure and economic backwardness.

What I am trying to suggest here is that, when you are formulating your objectives, it is very important that you have clearly in mind your conception of the learning process and the process of education. In this last illustrative approach, this conception included the notion that the learner is active, that he is looking at the world, and is trying to make something out of it. We are trying to guide him in his continued activity rather than trying to close the world for him by giving him all the answers. We don't want to tell him, 'You have learned what there is in this course. Everything was here in the textbook and now you have learned it all.' The student must see his learning as a constantly continuing process. To achieve this you will have to think of objectives of the sort that lead from the third grade to the fourth grade to the fifth grade and so on. It might be that in studying science in the third grade the pupils are looking at rocks and trying to make sense out of them while in the fourth grade they are looking at plants and growing flowers. But in both cases they are concerned with the same general notion of the world and how it is to be interpreted. The types of science problems involved and the kinds of skills employed can be stepping stones for continued development.

In closing I would re-state something that was touched upon by Bob Glaser in connection with his experience in producing his program [Lindvall, op. cit., pp. 47–69]. This is that as you work with objectives and with your efforts to teach them you frequently have a basis for the re-definition of your objectives. As you see what really is possible, you may see more clearly the kinds of things the pupils need in addition to those that you thought of in your original planning. The process of clarifying goals, then working towards them, then appraising progress, then re-examining the goals, modifying them and clarifying them in the light of the experience and the data is a never-ending procedure. And we hope that the carrying out of this process is one of the ways in which we are making education in 1963 better than it was in 1953.

Reprinted from C. M. Lindvall (ed.),
Defining Educational Objectives
(© 1964, University of Pittsburgh Press), pp. 77–83.

2

Stating objectives appropriately
for program, for curriculum and
for instructional materials development

DAVID R. KRATHWOHL

This article is concerned with the use of educational objectives at several levels of detail in the educational process. The most general levels of objectives are more relevant to program planning, the intermediate level to curriculum development, and the most specific level to instructional material development. The article makes two basic points:

1   Objectives at several levels of generality and specificity are needed to facilitate the process of curriculum building and instructional development.
2   A framework or taxonomy currently exists which can facilitate the development and analysis of objectives at the intermediate level, and one is at present being developed at the more detailed level.

Analysis of objectives – a powerful tool for educational improvement

The emphasis upon making educational objectives specific by defining the goals of an instructional course or program has gone through many cycles since Ralph Tyler gave the topic considerable prominence in the late thirties. For some educators, careful attention to spelling out in detail the objectives of a course has become a kind of religion. Others, interestingly enough, seem to have heard of the practice of delineating objectives but, somehow or other, have been early inoculated against the notion and have so become immune. Those of us who work as advisers to various fields of higher education, particularly with our colleagues in liberal arts, home economics, etc., are impressed with the power of this simple tool to help people structure courses and view their own process of teaching with a renewed interest and from a new perspective.

Viewed both in retrospect and contemporaneously, specifying educational objectives as student behaviours seems to be a useful and powerful approach to the analysis of the instructional process. Granted it implies a particular view of the educational process. In it, 'education' means changing the behaviour of a student so that he is able, when encountering a particular problem or situation, to display a behaviour which he did not previously exhibit. The task of the teacher is to help the student learn new or changed behaviours and determine where and when they are appropriate.

A major contribution of this approach to curriculum building is that it forces the instructor to spell out his instructional goals in terms of overt behaviour. This gives new detail; indeed it yields an operational definition of many previously general and often fuzzy and ill-defined objectives. Such goals as 'the student should become a good citizen' are spelled out in terms of the kinds of behaviours which a good citizen displays. There are then statements, such as 'the student shall be able to identify and appraise judgements and values involved in the choice of a course of political action'; 'he shall display skill in identifying different appropriate roles in a democratic group'; or 'he will be able to relate principles of civil liberties and civil rights to current events'. Thus the instructor knows what kinds of behaviour he is to try to develop in the classroom. In addition, the problem of assessing the extent to which he has achieved his goals becomes markedly simplified. He needs only to provide the student with a situation in which the kind of behaviour he is seeking to instil should be evoked and then observe to see whether indeed it appears. Spelling out the behaviours involved in an objective such as the above frequently means specifying several pages of concrete behaviours. Such specification often gives teachers a fresh perspective on their courses and new insights into ways to teach and to evaluate their teaching. This kind of analysis of objectives is clearly a step forward.

This approach to instruction fits in very well with the behaviourist school of psychology, the well-spring from which came the recent emphasis on teaching machines and programmed instruction. It is not surprising, then, that a renewed emphasis on educational objectives resulted from the development of programmed learning. The careful specification of a step-by-step procedure for the learner calls for clearly understood objectives specified at a level of detail far beyond that usually attempted. In programmed learning, such objectives have come to bear the name of 'terminal behaviours'. As psychologists, physicists, systems development specialists and others have attempted instructional programming, they have turned to education for a greater understanding of how adequately to specify educational objectives so that they concretely describe a 'terminal behaviour'.

The need for objectives at several levels of analysis

The renewed emphasis has given new insight into and perspective on the whole problem of the level of specificity needed in objectives. It is now clear that we need to analyse objectives to several levels of specificity depending upon how we intend to use them. At the first and most abstract level are the quite broad and general statements most helpful in the development of programs of instruction, for the laying out of types of courses and areas to be covered, and for the general goals towards which several years of education might be aimed or for which an entire unit such as an elementary, junior or senior high school might strive.

At a second and more concrete level, a *behavioural* objectives orientation helps to analyse broad goals into more specific ones which are useful as the building blocks for curricular instruction. These behaviourally stated objectives are helpful in specifying the goals of an instructional unit, a course or a sequence of courses.

Third and finally, there is the level needed to create instructional materials – materials which are the operational embodiment of one particular route (rarely are multiple routes included) to the achievement of a curriculum planned at the second and more abstract level, the level of detailed analysis involved in the programmed instruction movement. Just as the second level of analysis brought into concrete, detailed form the ideas of goals and purposes that were in the mind of the good teacher as he planned at the first and more abstract level, so this kind of detailed analysis brings into focus the objectives of specific lesson plans, the sequence of goals in these plans, and the level of achievement required for each goal or objective if successful accomplishment of the next goal in this sequence is to be achieved.

In realization of this, we find Gagné (1963), Mager (1962) and Miller (1961) all writing about the analysis of objectives for programmed instruction with a plea that objectives be given a great deal more specificity so that they may be more easily turned into instructional materials. They call for a description of the situation which ought to initiate the behaviour in question, a complete description of the behaviour, the object or goal of the behaviour, and a description of the level of performance of the behaviour which permits us to recognize a successful performance.

We may note in passing that even this may not be enough specification for the development of instructional materials. There is no mention in this of the characteristics of the learner and his relation to the learning situation. Thus, not all objectives or terminal behaviours will be appropriate for all kinds and types of students. Neither will the same level of proficiency be appropriate for, nor expected of, different levels of ability. Thus a successful performance cannot have a single definition. Further, those planning instructional materials need to know where the student starts, what he brings to the situation (the 'entry behaviours'). We may also need to know something about the motivation for learning (or lack of it if, for example, we are dealing with the culturally disadvantaged), and the pattern of problem solving available to us (for example, in teaching the social studies, one approach for those with rigid value patterns, another for those more flexible). While this is not a complete list, it clearly indicates that a great deal more specification is required in developing instructional materials than in laying out curricular goals.

But to return to our main theme, if we make our goals specific enough to prepare instructional materials, why use the other levels at all? Should we not, for example, discard at least the second level? Not at all! Four points need to be made.

First of all, curriculum construction requires a process of moving through descending abstractions from very general and global statements of desirable behaviours for a program, to intermediate level statements that indicate the blocks from which the program will be constructed, and finally to quite detailed statements which spell out the sub-goals, their relation to one another and the level of achievement which results in the successful attainment of the intermediate-level behavioural descriptions. All levels of specification of objectives are needed to guide the planning of the educational process. Only as each level is completed can the next be begun. The first level guides the development of the second, the second guides the third.

To return to our example of the development of citizenship, we earlier noted three objectives at the intermediate level. Once these are specified, we can begin to think at the third level of very specific goals and their teaching sequence. For example, one would specify the different possible desirable roles in a democratic group, how these roles would build on one another, to what situations each was appropriate, and how successfully each should be displayed before passing on to the next. Each level thus permits and guides the development of the next level of specification.

Second, not all objectives lend themselves to the *complete* specification at the third level. In some instances, the universe of behaviours is completely circumscribed. For example, there are only forty-five sums of two numbers o through 9 which need be learned, and we can specify that these must be mastered with perfect accuracy. But in many instances we cannot specify all the instances of behaviour. Gagné's contrasting terminology of 'mastery' objective to apply to the former and 'transfer' objective to the latter helps to illumine this difference. We cannot predict all situations the student will encounter or all the situations to which he should be able to transfer the behaviours, but we can specify a currently known sample. Nearly all our complex ability and skill objectives – application, analysis, evaluation, etc. – are 'transfer' objectives. Their specification will be inexact and confined to a known sample of relevant and typical kinds of behaviours.* Transfer objectives seem to constitute the major *ultimate* goals for the bulk of the educational process. More exact specification of mastery goals may be possible in industrial or vocational training for specific occupations than in general education. Thus the level of detail with which educational goals can be usefully specified will depend somewhat on their nature. Again we see that several levels of specificity are needed to handle different kinds of objectives.

Third, we need to have objectives at several levels of abstraction so that we can continually examine their interrelation to one another. When developing a curriculum, we try to get those involved to agree at as detailed a level as possible. But complete agreement can probably be reached only at the more abstract levels. Thus we can get general agreement that students should be good citizens, but we may get some disagreement as to what this means operationally or in behavioural terms. For some teachers this may mean that all students are taught to engage in some political action – ringing doorbells at election time, writing to congressmen, etc. To others this may be confined to voting and attempting to understand and to discuss issues with others. Further, such definitions will change as society and its pressures and fads change. It helps to have agreed-upon general and global

* Mager and others suggest that criterion performance for a successful completion be specified, e.g. 'given a human skeleton the student must be able to identify correctly by labelling at least 40 of the following bones', or 'the student must be able to reply in grammatically correct French to 95 per cent of the questions put to him in an examination' (Mager, 1962, p. 50). It is worth noting that such levels have one meaning for mastery objectives (e.g. he should be able to give the capital and lower case letters for the entire alphabet) when the universe of behaviours is known and specified. They have a different meaning when test questions of different complexity are constructed to an indeterminate universe of behaviours in a French quiz. In the latter instance, judgement of both the level of difficulty of the problems and the matter of adequacy of sampling enter the evaluation process, and both must be taken into consideration in judging a successful performance.

objectives to which all curricula can relate. These objectives can then be redefined at the less abstract level in relation to the overall goals.

Fourth, and finally, there are many routes from the intermediate level objective to the specification of instructional materials. For example, take the objective: 'The student shall be able to recognize form and pattern in literary works as a means to understanding their meaning.' This is a useful objective at the intermediate or curricular-building level of abstraction, but how does the teacher translate this into a choice of instructional materials? Does he choose those literary forms and patterns which are likely to have maximum transfer to all kinds of literary materials and teach them, or does he choose those forms and patterns that will permit the deepest penetration of meaning and concentrate on them, assuming the other forms and patterns will be picked up in the course of reading? Both approaches might be acceptable. It helps to have the objective in its original abstract form to serve as a basis for judging the routes to its achievement. The routes might be thought of as sub-objectives needing evaluation to help in learning which route best achieves the intermediate-level objective.

We do not have enough psychological knowledge for the teacher and the developer of instructional materials to move with certainty from an intermediate-level objective to a single set of very detailed and concrete objectives. In the example given above, for instance, we have little theoretical basis for judging the language forms and patterns that will permit the most complete understanding of literary material. Both the instructional material specialist and the teacher precede the psychologist into an area of most-needed research. They must make choices while the psychologist is still developing the knowledge to help them.

Thus, there are at least four reasons why objectives at various levels of analysis are useful and needed in the instructional processes:

1 Each level of analysis permits the development of the next more specific level.
2 Mastery objectives can be analysed to greater specificity than transfer objectives.
3 Curricula gain adoption by consensus that what is taught is of value. Consensus is more easily gained at the more abstract levels of analysis.
4 There are usually several alternative ways of analysing objectives at the most specific level. Objectives at the more abstract level provide a referent for evaluating these alternatives.

It seems clear then that objectives at several levels of abstraction are useful and important in the educational process. Let us turn now to some of the structures that have been constructed to aid exploration at these levels.

Frameworks to facilitate the statement of objectives

I THE TAXONOMY OF EDUCATIONAL OBJECTIVES
– A FRAMEWORK FOR CURRICULUM BUILDING

The need for objectives at various levels of abstraction has given rise to frameworks or structures that assist in the analysis and development of these objectives. One of these frameworks, the *Taxonomy of Educational Objectives* (Bloom *et al.*, 1956; Krathwohl *et al.*, 1964), appears to have proven useful in the analysis of objectives at the intermediate curriculum-building level.

Basically the taxonomy grew out of an attempt to resolve some of the confusion in communication which resulted from the translation of such general terms as 'to understand' into more specific behaviours. Thus the 'understanding' of Boyle's law might mean that the student could recall the formula, tell what it meant, interpret the particular meaning of the law in an article about it, use the formula in a new problem situation he had never met, or think up new implications of its relationships.

The problem of precisely identifying what is meant by particular terms plagues the evaluator as well as the curriculum builder. For one thing, these two must communicate with each other since the test constructor seeks accurately to translate the curriculum builders' objectives into situations where the student can display the behaviour if he knows it. Accuracy in this translation is essential. Further, evaluators working at different institutions on similar curricula know they have something in common but frequently find it difficult to communicate accurately about it. Given precise communication, they could share and compare the effectiveness of learning devices, materials and curricular organization. It was with this in mind that a group of college and university examiners, under the leadership of Dr Benjamin S. Bloom of the University of Chicago, attempted to devise a framework or taxonomy that would help to hold terms in place, provide a structure which would relate one term to another, and thus provide additional meaning for a given term through this interrelationship.

The taxonomy of educational objectives is basically a classification scheme just as the biological taxonomy is a classification scheme for animals into class, order, family, genus and species. In the educational objectives taxonomy, the kinds of behaviour we seek to have students display as a result of the learning process are classified. Every behavioural objective is composed of two parts – the behaviour the student is to display and the subject matter or content that is then used in the display. The taxonomy deals only with the behavioural part of the objective; the content or subject matter classification is left to the Library of Congress, the Dewey Decimal System, and such other similar classifications.

For purposes of convenience the taxonomy was divided into three domains, the cognitive, affective and psychomotor. Handbook I, *The Cognitive Domain* (Bloom *et al.*, 1956), has been available for about eight years. It deals with objectives having to do with thinking, knowing and problem solving. Handbook II, *The Affective Domain* (Krathwohl *et al.*, 1964), was published last year. It includes objectives dealing with attitudes, values, interest, appreciation and social-emotional adjustment. The psychomotor domain covers objectives having to do with manual and motor skills. The feasibility of developing it is being studied by a group at the University of Illinois under Dr Elizabeth Simpson.

> Basically the taxonomy is an educational–logical–psychological classification system. The terms in this order reflect the emphasis given to the organizing principles upon which it is built. It makes educational distinctions in the sense that the boundaries between categories reflect the decisions that teachers make among student behaviours in their development of curriculums, and in choosing learning situations. It is a logical system in the sense that its terms are defined precisely and are used consistently. In addition, each category permits logical subdivisions which can be clearly defined and further subdivided as necessary and useful. Finally the taxonomy seems to be consistent with our present understanding of psychological phenomena, though it does not rest on any single theory.
>
> The scheme is intended to be purely descriptive so that every type of educational goal can be represented. It does not indicate the value or quality of one class as compared to another. It is impartial with respect to views of education. One of the tests of the taxonomy has been that of inclusiveness – could one classify all kinds of educational objectives (if stated as student behaviours) in the framework? In general, it seems to have met this test. (Krathwohl, 1964)

The cognitive domain of the taxonomy

Similar to the distinctions most teachers make, the cognitive domain is divided into the acquisition of knowledge and the development of those skills and abilities necessary to use knowledge. Under the heading 'Knowledge', which is the first major category of the cognitive domain, one finds a series of subcategories, each describing the recall of a different category of knowledge. Each of the subheadings is accompanied by a definition of the behaviour classified there and by illustrative objectives taken from the educational literature. In addition, there is a summary of the kinds of test items that may be used to test for each category, a discussion of the problems which beset the individual attempting to evaluate behaviour in the category and a large number of examples of test items – mainly multiple choice but some essay type. These illustrate how items may be built to measure each of the categories.

The taxonomy is hierarchical in nature, that is, each category is assumed to involve behaviour more complex and abstract than the previous category. Thus the categories are arranged from simple to complex behaviour, and from concrete to abstract behaviour.

Perhaps the idea of the continuum is most easily gained from looking at the major headings of the cognitive domain, which include knowledge (recall of facts, principles, etc.), comprehension (ability to restate knowledge in new words), application (understanding well enough to break it apart into its parts and make the relations among ideas explicit), synthesis (the ability to produce wholes from parts, to produce a plan of operation, to derive a set of abstract relations), and evaluation (the ability to judge the value of material for given purposes).

Since the cognitive domain has been available for some time perhaps this brief summary will suffice to remind the reader of its nature or to intrigue him to look into it if it has not previously come to his attention. Since the affective domain is new let us examine it in more detail.

The affective domain of the taxonomy

Though there is confusion in communication with respect to terms in the cognitive domain, those who worked on the taxonomy found the confusion much greater when they began work on the affective domain. The state of communication with respect to a term like 'really understand' is nothing compared to the confusion that surrounds objectives dealing with attitudes, interests and appreciation. When we say that we want a child to 'appreciate' art, do we mean that he should be aware of art work? Should he be willing to give it some attention when it is around? Do we mean that he should seek it out – go to the museum on his own, for instance? Do we mean that he should regard art work as having positive values? Should he experience an emotional kick or thrill when he sees art work? Should he be able to evaluate it and to know why and how it is effective? Should he be able to compare its aesthetic impact with that of other art forms?

This list could be extended, but it is enough to suggest that the term 'appreciation' covers a wide variety of meanings. And worse, not all of these are distinct from the terms 'attitude' and 'interest'. Thus, if appreciation has the meaning that the student should like art work well enough to seek it out, how would we distinguish such behaviour from an interest in art – or are interests and appreciations, as we use these words, the same thing? If the student *values* art, does he have a favourable *attitude* towards it? Are our appreciation objectives the same as, overlapping with, or in some respects distinct from our attitude objectives?

In addition to the greater confusion of terms, the affective domain presented some special problems. For example, the hierarchical structure was most difficult to find in the affective part of the taxonomy. The principles of simple to complex and concrete to abstract were not sufficient for developing the affective domain. Something additional was needed.

By seeking the unique characteristics of the affective domain, it was hoped that the additional principles needed to structure an affective continuum would be discovered. Analysis of affective objectives showed the following characteristics which the continuum should embody: the emotional quality which is an important distinguishing feature of an affective response at certain levels of the continuum, the increasing automaticity as one progresses up the continuum, the increasing willingness to attend to a specified stimulus or stimulus type as one ascends the continuum, and the developing integration of a value pattern at the upper levels of the continuum.

A structure was first attempted by attaching certain meanings to the terms 'attitude', 'value', 'appreciation' and 'interest'. But the multitude of meanings which these terms encompassed in educational objectives showed that this was impossible. After trying a number of schemes and organizing principles, the one which appeared best to account for the affective phenomena and which best described the process of learning and growth in the affective field was the process of internalization.

Internalization refers to the inner growth that occurs as the individual becomes aware of and then adopts attitudes, principles, codes and sanctions which become inherent in forming value judgements and in guiding his conduct. It has many elements in common with the term socialization. Internalization may be best understood by looking at the categories in the taxonomy structure (Krathwohl *et al.*, 1964):

O

We begin with the individuals being aware of the stimuli which initiate the effective behaviour and which form the context in which the affective behaviour occurs. Thus, the lowest category is 1.0 *Receiving*. It is subdivided into three categories. At the 1.1 *Awareness* level, the individual merely has his attention attracted to the stimuli (e.g. he develops some consciousness of the use of shading to portray depth and lighting in a picture). The second subcategory, 1.2 *Willingness* to receive, describes the state in which he has differentiated the stimuli from others and is willing to give it his attention (e.g. he develops a tolerance for bizarre uses of shading in modern art). At 1.3 *Controlled or selected attention*, the student looks for the stimuli (e.g. he is on the alert for instances where shading has been used both to create a sense of three-dimensional depth and to indicate the lighting of the picture; or he looks for picturesque words in reading).

At the next level, 2.0 *Responding*, the individual is perceived as responding regularly to the affective stimuli. At the lowest level of responding, 2.1 *Acquiescence in responding*, he is merely complying with expectations (e.g. at the request of his teacher, he hangs reproductions of famous paintings in his dormitory room; he is obedient to traffic rules). At the next higher level 2.2 *Willingness to respond*, he responds increasingly to an inner compulsion (e.g. voluntarily looks for instances of good art where shading, perspective, colour and design have been well used, or has an interest in social problems broader than those of the local community). At 2.3 *Satisfaction in response*, he responds emotionally as well (e.g. works with clay, especially in making pottery for personal pleasure). Up to this point he has differentiated the affective stimuli; he has begun to seek them out and to attach emotional significance and value to them.

As the process unfolds, the next levels of 3.0 *Valuing* describe increasing internalization, as the person's behaviour is sufficiently consistent that he comes to hold a value: 3.1 *Acceptance of a Value* (e.g. continuing desire to develop the ability to write effectively and hold it more strongly), 3.2 *Preference for a value* (e.g. seeks out examples of good art for enjoyment of them to the level where he behaves so as to further this impression actively); and 3.3 *Commitment* (e.g. faith in the power of reason and the method of experimentation).

As the learner successively internalizes values, he encounters situations for which more than one value is relevant. This necessitates organizing the values into a system, 4.0 *Organization*. And since a prerequisite to interrelating values is their conceptualization in a form which permits organization, this level is divided in two: 4.1 *Conceptualization of a value* (e.g. desires to evaluate works of art which are appreciated, or to find out and crystallize the basic assumptions which underlie codes of ethics) and 4.2 *Organization of a value system* (e.g. acceptance of the place of art in one's life as one of dominant value, or weighs alternative social policies and practices against the standards of public welfare).

Finally, the internalization and the organization processes reach a point where the individual responds very consistently to value-laden situations with an interrelated set of values, a structure, a view of the world. The taxonomy category that describes this behaviour is 5.0 *Characterization by a value or value complex*, and it includes the categories 5.1 *Generalized set* (e.g. views all problems in terms of their aesthetic aspects, or readiness to revise judgements and to change behaviour in the light of evidence) and 5.2 *Characterization* (e.g. develops a consistent philosophy of life).

Stripped of their definitions, the category and sub-category title appear in sequence as follows:

1.0 Receiving (attending)
    1.1 Awareness
    1.2 Willingness to receive
    1.3 Controlled or selected attention

2.0 Responding
    2.1 Acquiescence in responding
    2.2 Willingness to respond
    2.3 Satisfaction in response

3.0 Valuing
    3.1 Acceptance of a value
    3.2 Preference for a value
    3.3 Commitment (conviction)

4.0 Organization
    4.1 Conceptualization of a value
    4.2 Organization of a value system

5.0 Characterization by a value or a value complex
    5.1 Generalized set
    5.2 Characterization

Uses of the taxonomy

The nature of the taxonomy should now be clear. What, however, are its uses? We have indicated that a prime use is the analysis and classification of objectives.

No longer should a teacher be faced with an objective like 'the student should understand the taxonomy of educational objectives', or 'he should appreciate the value of taxonomic frameworks'. Rather the teacher can now specify whether the first of these objectives would be at the lowest level of comprehension where he would at least expect the student to be able to translate the term 'taxonomy' into something like 'a classification system of educational goals', or perhaps at a deeper level of understanding, classified as interpretation, where the student could restate the ideas of the taxonomy in his own words. In short, the taxonomy is a relatively concise model for the analysis of education objectives.

The taxonomy, like the periodic table of elements or a check-off shopping list, provides the panorama of objectives. Comparing the range of the present curriculum with the range of possible outcomes may suggest additional goals that might be included. Further, the illustrative objectives may suggest wordings that might be adapted to the area being explored.

Frequently, when searching for ideas in building a curriculum, the work of others is most helpful. Where one's own work and that of others are built in terms of the taxonomy categories, comparison is markedly facilitated. Translation of objectives into the taxonomy framework can provide a basis for precise comparison. Further, where similarities exist, it becomes possible to trade experiences regarding the values of certain learning experiences with confidence that there is a firm basis for comparison and that the other person's experience will be truly relevant.

It is perhaps also important to note the implication of the hierarchical nature of the taxonomy for curriculum building. If the analysis of the cognitive and affective areas is correct, then a hierarchy of objectives dealing with the same subject matter concepts suggests a readiness relationship that exists between those objectives lower in the hierarchy and those higher.

The development of the affective domain has pointed up the problems of achieving objectives in this domain. For instance, a study of the relation of the cognitive and affective domains made it apparent that achievement in the affective domain is markedly underemphasized. Thus, the garden variety of objectives concentrates on specifying behaviour in only one domain at a time. No doubt this results from the typical analytic approaches to building curricula. Only occasionally do we find a statement like 'the student should learn to analyse a good argument with pleasure'. Such a statement suggests not only the cognitive behaviour but also the affective aspect that accompanies it.

In spite of the lack of explicit formulation, however, nearly all cognitive objectives have an affective component if we search for it. Most instructors hope that their students will develop a continuing interest in the subject matter taught. They hope they will have learned certain attitudes towards the phenomena dealt with or towards the way in which problems are approached. But they leave these goals unspecified. This means that many of the objectives which are classified in the cognitive domain have an implicit but unspecified affective component that could be concurrently classified in the affective domain. Where such an attitude or interest objective refers, as it most often does, to the content of the course as a whole or at least to a sizeable segment of it, it may be most convenient to specify it as a separate objective. Many such affective objectives – the interest objectives, for example – become the affective components of all or most of the cognitive objectives in the course.

The affective domain is useful in emphasizing the fact that affective components exist and in analysing their nature. Perhaps by its very existence it will encourage greater development of affective components of cognitive objectives.

Further, in the cognitive domain, we are concerned that the student shall be able to do a task when requested. In the affective domain, we are more concerned that he *does do* it when it is appropriate after he has learned that he *can do* it. Even though the whole school system rewards the student more on a *can do* than on a *does do* basis, it is the latter which every instructor seeks. By emphasizing this aspect of the affective components, the affective domain brings to light an extremely important and often missing element in cognitive objectives.

Another aspect which came to light was the extremely slow growth of some of the affective behaviours. We saw this as having implications for both the cognitive and affective domains. Thus, every teacher attempts to evaluate the changes that he has made in his students, and it is clear that it is entirely possible for him to do so successfully at the lower levels of the taxonomy. But a teacher will rarely have the same students over a sufficient period of time to make measurable changes in certain affective behaviours. Some objectives, particularly the complex ones at the top of the affective continuum, are probably attained as the product of all or at least a major portion of a student's years in school. Thus, measures of a term's or year's growth would reveal little change. This suggests that an evaluation plan covering at least several grades and involving the coordinated efforts of several teachers is probably a necessity. A plan involving all the grades in a system is likely to be even more effective. Such efforts would permit gathering longitudinal data on the same students so that gains in complex objectives would be measurable. Patterns of growth in relation to various school efforts would be revealed. Planned evaluation efforts to measure certain cognitive objectives on a longitudinal basis are to be found in some school systems, particularly where they use achievement test batteries designed to facilitate this. Similar efforts with respect to affective objectives are quite rare. If we are serious about attaining complex affective objectives, we shall have to build coordinated evaluation programs that trace the successes and failures of our efforts to achieve them.

In particular, we noted that there was a great deal of 'erosion' with respect to the affective domain objectives. When a curriculum is first conceived, affective objectives play an important part in the conceptual structure of the courses. But as time goes on, they cease to have influence on the direction of the courses or in the choice of instructional activities. In part, this results from the fact that rarely are affective objectives reflected in the grading process. Students tend to concentrate on what counts, and affective objectives rarely appear to do so. Since a part of this lack of emphasis on affective objectives in grading is due to the inadequacy of measures and ways of relating measures to objectives, it is possible that the sections of the taxonomy dealing with measurement in the affective domain may help to make these objectives more realistic parts of those courses in which affective objectives are important.

2 A FRAMEWORK TO FACILITATE CONSTRUCTION OF INSTRUCTIONAL MATERIALS

Perhaps this is enough to indicate the existence and potential usefulness of the taxonomy structure as a means of working with objectives at the curriculum-building level. What about the specification of objectives at the instructional-material-building level? Gagné (1964, p. 21) writes:

> Is it in fact possible to divide objectives into categories which differ in their implications for learning? To do this, one has to put together a selected set of learning conditions on the one hand, and an abstracted set of characteristics of human tasks on the other. This is the kind of

effort which has been called *task analysis*. Its objective is to distinguish, not the tasks themselves (which are infinitely variable), but the inferred behaviours which presumably require different conditions of learning. Such behaviour categories can be distinguished by means of several different kinds of criteria, which in an ultimate sense should be completely compatible with each other. What I should like to try to do here, however, is to use one particular set of criteria, which pertain to the question of 'What is learned?'

Gagné's categories are a blending of behaviouristic psychology and cognitive theory; the lowest four are related to the former, the upper four to the latter.

His categories also are hierarchical in the sense that having any one capability usually depends upon the previous learning of some other simpler one. Thus his two top categories of problem solving and strategy using require the pre-learning of:

Principles
    which require the pre-learning of:
Concepts
    which require the pre-learning of:
Associations
    which require the pre-learning of:
Chains
    which require the pre-learning of:
Identifications
    which require the pre-learning of:
Responses

In more detail his categories are:

Response learning. A very basic form of behaviour is called response learning, or is sometimes given other names, such as 'echoic behaviour'. The individual learns to respond to a stimulus which is essentially the same as that produced by the response itself. . . .

Identification learning (multiple discrimination). In this form of behaviour, the individual acquires the capability of making different responses to a number of different stimuli. Of course, he does this when he identifies colours, or late model cars, or numerals, or any of a great variety of specific stimuli. . . .

Chains or sequences. Long chains of responses can most readily be identified in motor acts of various sorts. But there are many kinds of *short* sequences which are very important to the individual's performance. One of the most prominent is a chain of two acts the first of which is an *observing response*. If one is concerned, for example, with getting someone to put 17 in the numerator, this act has two main parts: (1) finding the location of the numerator (an observing response), and (2) writing in that place the numeral 17.

In establishing such behaviour as part of the larger and more complex performance like simplifying fractions, one has to see to it that such a chain is learned. . . .

Association. For many years, psychologists appeared to be considering this the most basic form of learning, but such is no longer the case. It is now fairly generally agreed, and supported by a good deal of evidence, that the learning of associations involves more than an S-R connection. Instead, an association is perhaps best considered as a three-step chain, containing in order (1) an observing response which distinguishes the stimulus, (2) a *coding* response which usually is implicit and (3) the response which is to be expected as the outcome of the association. . . .

Concepts. A concept is acquired when a set of objectives or events *differing* in physical appearance is identified as a class. The class names for common objects like chairs, houses, hats, are the most familiar examples. . . . If one can assume these more basic forms as having been acquired, then the procedure of concept learning is fairly simple. It consists mainly in establishing associations in which the variety of specific stimuli that make up the class to be acquired are represented. . . .

Principles. The next more complex form of learning pertains to the acquisition of principles. One can consider these, in their basic form, as a chain of concepts of the form. If A, then B. . . . Again it is evident that the important set of conditions necessary for principle learning is previous learning, this time of the concepts which make up the principle, One either assumes that the learner already knows the concepts liquid, heating and gas, in acquiring the principle, or else they must first be learned. . . . But when one can truly assume that concept learning has previously been completed, the conditions for principle learning become clear. The proposed chain of events is presented by means of particular objects representing the concepts making up the chain.

Problem solving. Problem solving is a kind of learning by means of which principles are put together in chains to form what may be called higher-order principles. . . . Typically, the higher-order principles are induced from sets of events presented to the learner in instruction. If carried out properly, these become the generalizations which enable the student to think about an ever-broadening set of new problems. . . .

Strategies. Are there forms of behaviour which are more complex than principles, or than the higher-order principles acquired in problem solving? Some authors seem to imply another *form* of learned organization in the strategies with which an individual approaches a problem. There can be little doubt as to the existence of such strategies in problem solving. It may be that strategies are *mediating principles* which do not appear directly in the performance of the task set to the individual, but which may nevertheless affect the speed or excellence of that performance. . . . But it is possible to conceive of strategies as being principles in their fundamental nature, and of being made up of chains of concepts. . . .

(This framework is developed in further detail in Gagné's *Conditions of Learning*, published by Holt, Rinehart and Winston, 1965.)

Important needed research – how to relate the frameworks

One may question whether either or both of these frameworks are adequate to the tasks that they have set for themselves. If nothing else, however, perhaps they have heuristic value. In fact, by their very existence, they immediately raise the question, 'How are the two frameworks related?' and its derivative question, 'What instructional methods are of most value in achieving certain categories in either framework?' For example, how does Gagné's strategy development relate to the skills of the cognitive domain in applying, analysing, synthesizing, evaluating? What instructional methods most efficiently and effectively permit achievement of these goals? These are questions that should be the focus of considerable educational research.

Summary

To sum up, we have explored the necessity for developing objectives at several levels of generality and abstraction as appropriate for different stages in the process of course and instructional material development. Increasingly, the means are becoming available to do a more thorough and precise job of working with objectives at these different levels. We have explored several frameworks: the Cognitive and Affective Domains of the *Taxonomy of Educational Objectives* and the classification of capabilities developed by Gagné. We have especially examined some of the implications of the former. Hopefully, as these come to the attention of those actively concerned with course and instructional material building, their heuristic value will be tested and they may be revised to the point where the process of curriculum building and instructional material development is better structured and more researchable. As this comes about, perhaps the growth we all seek in the science of education will be at least somewhat accelerated.

References

BLOOM, B. S. (ed.) *et al.* (1956) *Taxonomy of Educational Objectives: The Classification of Educational Goals. Handbook I: The Cognitive Domain.* New York: Longmans Green.

GAGNÉ, R. M. (1963) The analysis of instructional objectives. A paper prepared for the National Symposium on Research in Programmed Instruction. Washington, D.C.: Department of Audiovisual Instruction, National Education Association.

GAGNÉ, R. M. (1964) The implications of instructional objectives for learning. In LINDVALL, C. M. (ed.) *Defining Educational Objectives.* A report of the Regional Commission on Educational Coordination and the Learning Research and Development Center, University of Pittsburgh.

KRATHWOHL, D. R. (1964) The taxonomy of educational objectives: its use in curriculum building. In LINDVALL, C. M. (ed.) *Defining Educational Objectives.* A report of the Regional Commission on Educational Coordination and the Learning Research and Development Center, University of Pittsburgh.

KRATHWOHL, D. R., BLOOM, B. S., and MASIA, B. B. (1964) *Taxonomy of Educational Objectives: The Classification of Educational Goals. Handbook II: The Affective Domain.* New York: McKay.

MAGER, R. F. (1962) *Preparing Objectives for Programmed Instruction.* Palo Alto, Calif.: Fearon.

MILLER, R. B. (1961) The newer role of the industrial psychologist. In GELMER, B. VON H. (ed.) *Industrial Psychology.* New York: McGraw-Hill.

Reprinted from *Journal of Teacher Education*,
16, March 1965, pp. 83–92.

Instrumentation of Bloom's and Krathwohl's taxonomies for the writing of educational objectives

NEWTON S. METFESSEL,
WILLIAM B. MICHAEL and DONALD A. KIRSNER

During the past six or eight years an increased amount of attention has been given to the statement of educational objectives in behavioural terms both to facilitate the evaluation of educational programs and to improve the validity of the measures and scales utilized in the evaluation process (Metfessel and Michael, 1967; Michael and Metfessel, 1967). Although set up as a programmed learning text, Mager's (1962) *Preparing Instructional Objectives* has been one of the most useful guides to teachers and specialists in curriculum who have sought help in stating the desired outcomes of instruction in behavioural language – in describing the kinds of specific and relatively terminal behaviours which the learner will be capable of exhibiting subsequent to his exposure to a program of instruction. Another useful source has been the volume edited by Lindvall (1964) who, in collaboration with Nardozza and Felton (Lindvall, Nardozza and Felton, 1964), not only prepared his own chapter concerned with the importance of specific objectives in curricular development, but also enlisted the aid of several distinguished educators, e.g. Krathwohl (1964) and Tyler (1964), with specialized interests in evaluation. Such efforts have essentially involved a fusion of curriculum design with the evaluation process in that curricular planning is described in terms of behavioural objectives that are necessary for the construction of valid tests and scales. The taxonomies provide the required model necessary to furnish meaningful evidence regarding the attainment of desired behavioural changes.

Although Krathwohl (1964) related the taxonomy of educational objectives in both the cognitive (Bloom, Englehart, Furst, Hill and Krathwohl, 1956) and the affective (Krathwohl, Bloom and Masia, 1964) domains to curriculum building, he was able to present only a limited number of concrete illustrations, some of which Mager would probably challenge because of their relative lack of specificity. Admittedly, Krathwohl has made an important and helpful start in relating objectives to a meaningful and rather well-known conceptual framework. However, the writers believe that there exists a need for an instrumentation of the taxonomy of educational objectives within both the cognitive and affective domains – that is, a more clear-cut description of how the taxonomy can be implemented in the school setting. The approach utilized was the development of *behaviourally orientated* infinitives which, when combined with given objects, would form a basis for meaningful, cohesive and operational statements.

Instrumentation

To facilitate the formulation of statements of specific behavioural objectives within the framework of Bloom's taxonomy, the writers have included a table made up of three columns. The first column contains the taxonomic classification identified by both code number and terminology employed in Bloom's (Bloom *et al.*, 1956) taxonomy. The entries in the second column consist of appropriate infinitives which the teacher or curriculum worker may consult to achieve a precise or preferred wording of the behaviour or activity desired. In the third column somewhat general terms relative to subject matter properties are stated. These direct objects, which may be expanded upon to furnish specificity at a desired level, may be permuted with one or more of the infinitive forms to yield the basic structure of an educational objective – activity (process) followed by content (subject matter property). At the discretion of the reader the words 'ability' or 'able' can be inserted in front of each of the infinitives.

TABLE I **Instrumentation of the taxonomy of educational objectives: cognitive domain**

Taxonomy classification	KEY WORDS *Examples of infinitives*	*Examples of direct objects*
1.00 Knowledge		
1.10 Knowledge of specifics		
1.11 Knowledge of terminology	to define, to distinguish, to acquire, to identify, to recall, to recognize	vocabulary, terms, terminology, meaning(s), definitions, referents, elements

TABLE I *continued*

Taxonomy classification	KEY WORDS *Examples of infinitives*	*Examples of direct objects*
1.12 Knowledge of specific facts	to recall, to recognize, to acquire, to identify	facts, factual information (sources), (names), (dates), (events), (persons), (places), (time periods), properties, examples, phenomena
1.20 Knowledge of ways and means of dealing with specifics		
1.21 Knowledge of conventions	to recall, to identify, to recognize, to acquire	form(s), conventions, uses, usage, rules, ways, devices, symbols, representations, style(s), format(s)
1.22 Knowledge of trends, sequences	to recall, to recognize, to acquire, to identify	action(s), processes, movement(s), continuity, development(s), trend(s), sequence(s), causes, relationship(s), forces, influences
1.23 Knowledge of classifications and categories	to recall, to recognize, to acquire, to identify	area(s), type(s), feature(s), class(es), set(s), division(s), arrangement(s), classification(s), category/categories
1.24 Knowledge of criteria	to recall, to recognize, to acquire, to identify	criteria, basics, elements
1.25 Knowledge of methodology	to recall, to recognize, to acquire, to identify	methods, techniques, approaches, uses, procedures, treatments
1.30 Knowledge of the universals and abstractions in a field		
1.31 Knowledge of principles, generalizations	to recall, to recognize, to acquire, to identify	principle(s), generalization(s), proposition(s), fundamentals, laws, principal elements, implication(s)
1.32 Knowledge of theories and structures	to recall, to recognize, to acquire, to identify	theories, bases, inter-relations, structure(s), organization(s), formulation(s)
2.00 Comprehension		
2.10 Translation	to translate, to transform, to give in own words, to illustrate, to prepare, to read, to represent, to change, to rephrase, to restate	meaning(s), sample(s), definitions, abstractions, representations, words, phrases

TABLE I *continued*

Taxonomy classification	KEY WORDS *Examples of infinitives*	*Examples of direct objects*
2.20 Interpretation	to interpret, to reorder, to rearrange, to differentiate, to distinguish, to make, to draw, to explain, **to demonstrate**	relevancies, relationships, essentials, aspects, new view(s), qualifications, conclusions, methods, theories, abstractions
2.30 Extrapolation	to estimate, to infer, to conclude, to predict, to differentiate, to determine, to extend, to interpolate, to extrapolate, to fill in, to draw	consequences, implications, conclusions, factors, ramifications, meanings, corollaries, effects, probabilities
3.00 Application	to apply, to generalize, to relate, to choose, to develop, to organize, to use, to employ, to transfer, to restructure, to classify	principles, laws, conclusions, effects, methods, theories, abstractions, situations, generalizations, processes, phenomena, procedures
4.00 Analysis		
4.10 Analysis of elements	to distinguish, to detect, to identify, to classify, to discriminate, to recognize, to categorize, **to deduce**	elements, hypothesis/ hypotheses, conclusions, assumptions, statements (of fact), statements (of intent), arguments, particulars
4.20 Analysis of relationships	to analyse, to contrast, to compare, to distinguish, to deduce	relationships, interrelations, relevance, relevancies, themes, evidence, fallacies, arguments, cause-effect(s), consistency/consistencies, parts, ideas, assumptions
4.30 Analysis of organizational principles	to analyse, to distinguish, to detect, to deduce	form(s), pattern(s), purpose(s), point(s) of view(s), techniques, bias(es), structure(s), theme(s), arrangement(s), organization(s)
5.00 Synthesis		
5.10 Production of a unique communication	to write, to tell, to relate, to produce, to constitute, to transmit, to originate, to modify, to document	structure(s), pattern(s), product(s), performance(s), design(s), work(s), communications, effort(s), specifics, composition(s)
5.20 Production of a plan, or proposed set of operations	to propose, to plan, to produce, to design, to modify, to specify	plan(s), objectives, specification(s), schematic(s), operations, way(s), solution(s), means

TABLE I *continued*

Taxonomy classification	KEY WORDS *Examples of infinitives*	*Examples of direct objects*
5.30 Derivation of a set of abstract relations	to produce, to derive, to develop, to combine, to organize, to synthesize, to classify, to deduce, to develop, to formulate, to modify	phenomena, taxonomies, concept(s), scheme(s), theories, relationships, abstractions, generalizations, hypothesis/hypotheses, perceptions, ways, discoveries
6.00 Evaluation		
6.10 Judgements in terms of internal evidence	to judge, to argue, to validate, to assess, to decide	accuracy/accuracies, consistency/consistencies, fallacies, reliability, flaws, errors, precision, exactness
6.20 Judgements in terms of external criteria	to judge, to argue, to consider, to compare, to contrast, to standardize, to appraise	ends, means, efficiency, economy/economies, utility, alternatives, courses of action, standards, theories, generalizations

Although within a given major process level or sublevel of the taxonomy each infinitive cannot in all instances be meaningfully or idiomatically paired with every direct object listed, many useful permutations of infinitives and direct objects that furnish entirely readable statements are possible. Certainly use of these tables should lead to a substantial gain in the clarity and speed with which teachers and curriculum specialists, as well as those involved in construction of achievement tests, may state curricular objectives. The writers have found that these tables have been of considerable help to their students, as well as to personnel in public schools who are concerned with writing objectives prior to curriculum development, constructing test items, or carrying out evaluation studies. Slight modifications can be made with the entries to meet the requirements of specific learning situations.

Instrumentation: affective domain

The instrumentation of the Affective Domain is the same as that of the Cognitive Domain, to wit, the selection of behaviourally orientated infinitives combined with selected direct objects. As in the case of the Cognitive Domain, these are to be conceptualized as examples for the stimulation of other infinitives and objects and, more important, meaningful objectives in a total framework.

TABLE 2 **Instrumentation of the taxonomy of educational objectives: affective domain**

Taxonomy classification	KEY WORDS *Examples of infinitives*	*Examples of direct objects*
1.0 Receiving		
1.1 Awareness	to differentiate, to separate, to set apart, to share	sights, sounds, events, designs, arrangements
1.2 Willingness to receive	to accumulate, to select, to combine, to accept	models, examples, shapes, sizes, meters, cadences
1.3 Controlled or selected attention	to select, to posturally respond to, to listen (for), to control	alternatives, answers, rhythms, nuances
2.0 Responding		
2.1 Acquiescence in responding	to comply (with), to follow, to commend, to approve	directions, instructions, laws, policies, demonstrations
2.2 Willingness to respond	to volunteer, to discuss, to practice, to play	instruments, games, dramatic works, charades, burlesques
2.3 Satisfaction in response	to applaud, to acclaim, to spend leisure time in, to augment	speeches, plays, presentations, writings
3.0 Valuing		
3.1 Acceptance of a value	to increase measured proficiency in, to increase numbers of, to relinquish, to specify	group membership(s), artistic production(s), musical productions, personal friendships
3.2 Preference for a value	to assist, to subsidize, to help, to support	artists, projects, viewpoints, arguments
3.3 Commitment	to deny, to protest, to debate, to argue	deceptions, irrelevancies, abdications, irrationalities
4.0 Organization		
4.1 Conceptualization of a value	to discuss, to theorize (on), to abstract, to compare	parameters, codes, standards, goals
4.2 Organization of a value system	to balance, to organize, to define, to formulate	systems, approaches, criteria, limits
5.0 Characterization by value or value complex		
5.1 Generalized set	to revise, to change, to complete, to require	plans, behaviour, methods, effort(s)
5.2 Characterization	to be rated high by peers in, to be rated high by superiors in, to be rated high by subordinates in and to avoid, to manage, to resolve, to resist	humanitarianism, ethics, integrity, maturity extravagance(s), excesses, conflicts, exorbitancy/exorbitancies

References

BLOOM, B. S. (ed.), ENGLEHART, M. D., FURST, E. J., HILL, W. H., and KRATHWOHL, D. R. (1956) *A Taxonomy of Educational Objectives: Handbook I: The Cognitive Domain*. New York: Longmans Green.

KRATHWOHL, D. R. (1964) The taxonomy of educational objectives: its use in curriculum building. In LINDVALL, C. M. (ed.) *Defining Educational Objectives*. A report of the Regional Commission on Educational Coordination and the Learning Research and Development Center, University of Pittsburgh, pp. 19–36.

KRATHWOHL, D. R., BLOOM, B. S., and MASIA, B. (1964) *Taxonomy of Educational Objectives: Handbook II: The Affective Domain*. New York: McKay.

LINDVALL, C. M. (ed.) *Defining Educational Objectives*. (1964) A report of the Regional Commission on Educational Coordination and the Learning Research and Development Center, University of Pittsburgh.

LINDVALL, C. M., NARDOZZA, S., and FELTON, M. (1964) The importance of specific objectives in curriculum development. In LINDVALL, C. M. (ed.) *Defining Educational Objectives*. A report of the Regional Commission on Educational Coordination and the Learning Research and Development Center, University of Pittsburgh. pp. 10–18.

MAGER, R. F. (1962) *Preparing Instructional Objectives*. Palo Alto, Calif.: Fearon.

METFESSEL, N. S., and MICHAEL, W. B. (1967) A paradigm involving multiple criterion measures for the evaluation of the effectiveness of school programs. *Educational and Psychological Measurement*, 27 (2), 931–43.

MICHAEL, W. B., and METFESSEL, N. S. (1967) A paradigm for developing valid measurable objectives in the evaluation of educational programs in colleges and universities. *Educational and Psychological Measurement*, 27, 373–83.

TYLER, R. W. (1964) Some persistent questions on the defining of objectives. In LINDVALL, C. M. (ed.) *Defining Educational Objectives*. A report of the Regional Commission on Educational Coordination and the Learning Research and Development Center, University of Pittsburgh.

Reprinted from *Psychology in the Schools*,
6 (3), July 1969, pp. 227–31.

4

Educational objectives:
help or hindrance ?[1]

ELLIOT W. EISNER

If one were to rank the various beliefs or assumptions in the field of curriculum that are thought most secure, the belief in the need for clarity and specificity in stating educational objectives would surely rank among the highest. Educational objectives, it is argued, need to be clearly specified for at least three reasons: first, because they provide the goals towards which the curriculum is aimed; second, because once clearly stated they facilitate the selection and organization of content; third, because when specified in both behavioural and content terms they make it possible to evaluate the outcomes of the curriculum.

It is difficult to argue with a rational approach to curriculum development – who would choose irrationality? And, if one is to build curriculum in a rational way, the clarity of premise, end or starting point would appear paramount. But I want to argue in this paper that educational objectives clearly and specifically stated can hamper as well as help the ends of instruction and that an unexamined belief in curriculum, as in other domains of human activity, can easily become dogma, which in fact may hinder the very functions the concept was originally designed to serve.

When and where did beliefs concerning the importance of educational objectives in curriculum development emerge? Who has formulated and argued their importance? What effect has this belief had upon curriculum construction? If we examine the past briefly for data necessary for answering these questions, it appears that the belief in the usefulness of clear and specific educational objectives emerged around the turn of the century with the birth of the scientific movement in education.

Before this movement gained strength, faculty psychologists viewed the brain as consisting of a variety of intellectual faculties. These faculties, they held, could be strengthened if exercised in appropriate ways with particular

214

subject matters. Once strengthened, the faculties could be used in any area of human activity to which they were applicable. Thus, if the important faculties could be identified and if methods of strengthening them developed, the school could concentrate on this task and expect general intellectual excellence as a result.

This general theoretical view of mind had been accepted for several decades by the time Thorndike, Judd and, later, Watson began, through their work, to chip away the foundations upon which it rested. Thorndike's work especially demonstrated the specificity of transfer. He argued theoretically that transfer of learning occurred if and only if elements in one situation were identical with elements in the other. His empirical work supported his theoretical views, and the enormous stature he enjoyed in education as well as in psychology influenced educators to approach curriculum development in ways consonant with his views. One of those who was caught up in the scientific movement in education was Franklin Bobbitt, often thought of as the father of curriculum theory. In 1918 Bobbitt published a signal work titled simply, *The Curriculum*.[2] In it he argued that educational theory is not so difficult to construct as commonly held and that curriculum theory is logically derivable from educational theory. Bobbitt wrote in 1918:

> The central theory is simple. Human life, however varied, consists in its performance of specific activities. Education that prepares for life is one that prepares definitely and adequately for these specific activities. However numerous and diverse they may be for any social class, they can be discovered. This requires that one go out into the world of affairs and discover the particulars of which these affairs consist. These will show the abilities, habits, appreciations, and forms of knowledge that men need. These will be the objectives of the curriculum. They will be numerous, definite, and particularized. The curriculum will then be that series of experiences which childhood and youth must have by way of attaining those objectives.[3]

In *The Curriculum*, Bobbitt approached curriculum development scientifically and theoretically: study life carefully to identify needed skills, divide these skills into specific units, organize these units into experiences, and provide these experiences to children. Six years later, in his second book, *How to Make a Curriculum*,[4] Bobbitt operationalized his theoretical assertions and demonstrated how curriculum components – especially educational objectives – were to be formulated. In this book Bobbitt listed nine areas in which educational objectives are to be specified. In these nine areas he listed

160 major educational objectives which run the gamut from 'Ability to use language in all ways required for proper and effective participation in community life' to 'Ability to entertain one's friends, and to respond to entertainment by one's friends'.[5]

Bobbitt was not alone in his belief in the importance of formulating objectives clearly and specifically. Pendleton, for example, listed 1581 social objectives for English, Guiler listed more than 300 for arithmetic in grades 1–6, and Billings prescribed 888 generalizations which were important for the social studies.

If Thorndike was right, if transfer was limited, it seemed reasonable to encourage the teacher to teach for particular outcomes and to construct curriculums only after specific objectives had been identified.

In retrospect it is not difficult to understand why this movement in curriculum collapsed under its own weight by the early 1930s. Teachers could not manage fifty highly specified objects, let alone hundreds. And, in addition, the new view of the child, not as a complex machine but as a growing organism who ought to participate in planning his own educational program, did not mesh well with the theoretical views held earlier.[6]

But, as we all know, the Progressive movement too began its decline in the forties, and by the middle fifties, as a formal organization at least it was dead.

By the late forties and during the fifties, curriculum specialists again began to remind us of the importance of specific educational objectives and began to lay down guidelines for their formulation. Rationales for constructing curriculums developed by Ralph Tyler[7] and Virgil Herrick[8] again placed great importance on the specificity of objectives. George Barton[9] identified philosophic domains which could be used to select objectives. Benjamin Bloom and his colleagues[10] operationalized theoretical assertions by building a taxonomy of educational objectives in the cognitive domain; and in 1964, Krathwohl, Bloom and Masia[11] did the same for the affective domain. Many able people for many years have spent a great deal of time and effort in identifying methods and providing prescriptions for the formulation of educational objectives, so much so that the statement 'Educational objectives should be stated in behavioural terms' has been elevated – or lowered – to almost slogan status in curriculum circles. Yet, despite these efforts, teachers seem not to take educational objectives seriously – at least as they are prescribed from above. And when teachers plan curriculum guides, their efforts first to identify overall educational aims, then specify school objectives, then identify educational objectives for specific subject matters, appear to be more like exercises to be gone through than serious efforts to build tools for curriculum planning. If educational objectives were really useful tools, teachers, I submit, would use them. If they do not, perhaps it is not because there is something wrong with the teachers but because there might be something wrong with the theory.

As I view the situation, there are several limitations to theory in curriculum regarding the functions educational objectives are to perform. These limitations I would like to identify.

Educational objectives are typically derived from curriculum theory, which assumes that it is possible to predict with a fair degree of accuracy what the outcomes of instruction will be. In a general way this is possible. If you set about to teach a student algebra, there is no reason to assume he will learn to construct sonnets instead. Yet, the outcomes of instruction are far more numerous and complex for educational objectives to encompass. The amount, type and quality of learning that occur in a classroom, especially when there is interaction among students, are only in small part predictable. The changes in pace, tempo and goals that experienced teachers employ when necessary and appropriate for maintaining classroom organization are dynamic rather than mechanistic in character. Elementary school teachers, for example, are often sensitive to the changing interests of the children they teach, and frequently attempt to capitalize on these interests, 'milking them' as it were for what is educationally valuable.[12] The teacher uses the moment in a situation that is better described as kaleidoscopic than stable. In the very process of teaching and discussing, unexpected opportunities emerge for making a valuable point, for demonstrating an interesting idea, and for teaching a significant concept. The first point I wish to make, therefore, is that the dynamic and complex process of instruction yields outcomes far too numerous to be specified in behavioural and content terms in advance.

A second limitation of theory concerning educational objectives is its failure to recognize the constraints various subject matters place upon objectives. The point here is brief. In some subject areas, such as mathematics, languages and the sciences, it is possible to specify with great precision the particular operation or behaviour the student is to perform after instruction. In other subject areas, especially the arts, such specification is frequently not possible, and when possible may not be desirable. In a class in mathematics or spelling, uniformity in response is desirable, at least in so far as it indicates that students are able to perform a particular operation adequately, that is, in accordance with accepted procedures. Effective instruction in such areas enables students to function with minimum error in these fields. In the arts and in subject matters where, for example, novel or creative responses are desired, the particular behaviours to be developed cannot easily be identified. Here curriculum and instruction should yield behaviours and products which are unpredictable. The end achieved ought to be something of a surprise to both teacher and pupil. While it could be argued that one might formulate an educational objective which specified novelty, originality or creativeness as the desired outcome, the particular referents for these terms cannot be specified in advance; one must judge after the fact whether the product produced or the behaviour displayed belongs in the 'novel' class. This is a much different procedure than is determining whether or not a particular word has been spelled correctly or a specific performance, that is, jumping a 3-foot hurdle, has been attained. Thus, the second point is that theory concerning educational objectives has not taken into account the particular relationship that holds between the subject matter being taught and the degree to which educational objectives can be predicted and specified. This, I suppose, is in part due to the fact that few curriculum specialists have high degrees of intimacy with a wide variety of subject matters and thus are unable to alter their general theoretical views to suit the demands that particular subject matters make.

The third point I wish to make deals with the belief that objectives stated in behavioural and content terms can be used as criteria by which to measure the outcomes of curriculum and instruction. Educational objectives provide, it is argued, the standard against which achievement is to be measured. Both taxonomies are built upon this assumption since their primary function is to demonstrate how objectives can be used to frame test items appropriate for evaluation. The assumption that objectives can be used as standards by which to measure achievement fails, I think, to distinguish adequately between the application of a standard and the making of a judgement. Not all – perhaps not even most – outcomes of curriculum and instruction are amenable to measurement. The application of a standard requires that some arbitrary and socially defined quantity be designated by which other qualities can be compared. By virtue of socially defined rules of grammar, syntax and logic, for example, it is possible to quantitatively compare and measure error in discursive or mathematical statement. Some fields of activity, especially those which are qualitative in character, have no comparable rules and hence are less amenable to quantitative assessment. It is here that evaluation must be made, not primarily by applying a socially defined standard, but by making a human qualitative judgement. One can specify, for example, that a student shall be expected to know how to extract a square root correctly and in an unambiguous way, through the application of a standard, determine whether this end has been achieved. But it is only in a metaphoric sense that one can measure the extent to which a student has been able to produce an aesthetic object or an expressive narrative. Here standards are unapplicable; here judgement is required. The making of a judgement in distinction to the application of a standard implies that valued qualities are not merely socially defined and arbitrary in character. The judgement by which a critic determines the value of a poem, novel or play is not achieved merely by applying standards already known to the particular product being judged; it requires that the critic – or teacher – view the product with respect to the unique properties it displays and then, in relation to his experience and sensibilities, judge its value in terms which are incapable of being reduced to quantity or rule.

This point was aptly discussed by John Dewey in his chapter on 'Perception and criticism' in *Art as Experience*.[13] Dewey was concerned with the problem of identifying the means and ends of criticism and has this to say about its proper function:

> The function of criticism is the reeducation of perception of works of art; it is an auxiliary process, a difficult process, of learning to see and hear. The conception that its business is to appraise, to judge in the legal and moral sense, arrests the perception of those who are influenced by the criticism that assumes this task.[14]

Of the distinction that Dewey makes between the application of a standard and the making of a critical judgement, he writes:

> There are three characteristics of a standard. It is a particular physical thing existing under specifiable conditions; it is *not* a value. The yard is a yard-stick, and the meter is a bar deposited in Paris. In the second place, standards are measures of things, of lengths, weights, capacities. The things measured are not values, although it is of great social value to be able to measure them, since the properties of things in the way of size, volume, weight, are important for commercial exchange. Finally, as standards of measure, standards define things with respect to *quantity*. To be able to measure quantities is a great aid to further judgments, but it is not a mode of judgment. The standard, being an external and public thing, is applied *physically*. The yard-stick is physically laid down upon things to determine their length.[15]

And I would add that what is most educationally valuable is the development of that mode of curiosity, inventiveness and insight that is capable of being described only in metaphoric or poetic terms. Indeed, the image of the educated man that has been held in highest esteem for the longest period of time in Western civilization is one which is not amenable to standard measurement. Thus, the third point I wish to make is that curriculum theory which views educational objectives as standards by which to measure educational achievement overlooks those modes of achievement incapable of measurement.

The final point I wish to make deals with the function of educational objectives in curriculum construction.

The rational approach to curriculum development not only emphasizes the importance of specificity in the formulation of educational objectives but also implies when not stated explicitly that educational objectives be stated prior to the formulation of curriculum activities. At first view, this seems to be a reasonable way to proceed with curriculum construction: one should know where he is headed before embarking on a trip. Yet, while the procedure of first identifying objectives before proceeding to identify activities is logically defensible, it is not necessarily the most psychologically efficient way to proceed. One can, and teachers often do, identify activities that seem useful, appropriate, or rich in educational opportunities, and from a consideration of what can be done in class, identify the objectives or possible consequences of using these activities. MacDonald argues this point cogently when he writes:

> Let us look, for example, at the problem of objectives. Objectives are viewed as directives in the rational approach. They are identified prior to the instruction or action and used to provide a basis for a screen for appropriate activities.
>
> There is another view, however, which has both scholarly and experiential referents. This view would state that our objectives are only known to us in any complete sense after the completion of our act of instruction. No matter what we thought we were attempting to do, we can only know what we wanted to accomplish after the fact. Objectives by this rationale are heuristic devices which provide initiating consequences which become altered in the flow of instruction.
>
> In the final analysis, it could be argued, the teacher in actuality asks a fundamentally different question from 'What am I trying to accomplish?' The teacher asks 'What am I going to do?' and out of the doing comes accomplishment.[16]

Theory in curriculum has not adequately distinguished between logical adequacy in determining the relationship of means to ends when examining the curriculum as a *product* and the psychological processes that may usefully be employed in building curriculums. The method of forming creative insights in curriculum development, as in the sciences and arts, is as yet not logically prescribable. The ways in which curriculums can be usefully and efficiently developed constitute an empirical problem; imposing logical requirements upon the process because they are desirable for assessing the product is, to my mind, an error. Thus, the final point I wish to make is that educational objectives need not precede the selection and organization of content. The means through which imaginative curriculums can be built is as open-ended as the means through which scientific and artistic inventions occur. Curriculum theory needs to allow for a variety of processes to be employed in the construction of curriculums.

I have argued in this paper that curriculum theory as it pertains to educational objectives has had four significant limitations. First, it has not sufficiently emphasized the extent to which the prediction of educational outcomes cannot be made with accuracy. Second, it has not discussed the ways in which the subject matter affects precision in stating educational objectives. Third, it has confused the use of educational objectives as a standard for measurement when in some areas it can be used only as a criterion for judgement. Fourth, it has not distinguished between the logical requirement of relating means to ends in the curriculum as a product and the psychological conditions useful for constructing curriculums.

If the arguments I have formulated about the limitations of curriculum theory concerning educational objectives have merit, one might ask: What are their educational consequences? First, it seems to me that they suggest that in large measure the construction of curriculums and the judgement of its consequences are artful tasks. The methods of curriculum development are, in principle if not in practice, no different from the making of art – be it the art of painting or the art of science. The identification of the factors in the potentially useful educational activity and the organization or construction of sequence in curriculum are in principle amenable to an infinite number of combinations. The variable teacher, student, class group, require artful blending for the educationally valuable to result.

Second, I am impressed with Dewey's view of the functions of criticism – to heighten one's perception of the art object – and believe it has implications for curriculum theory. If the child is viewed as an art product and the teacher as a critic, one task of the teacher would be to reveal the qualities of the child to himself and to others. In addition, the teacher as critic would appraise the changes occurring in the child. But because the teacher's task includes more than criticism, he would also be responsible, in part, for the improvement of the work of art. In short, in both the construction of educational means (the curriculum) and the appraisal of its consequences, the teacher would become an artist, for criticism itself when carried to its height is an art. This, it seems to me, is a dimension to which curriculum theory will someday have to speak.

Notes

[1] This is a slightly expanded version of a paper presented at the fiftieth annual meeting of the American Educational Research Association, Chicago, February 1966.

[2] BOBBITT, FRANKLIN *The Curriculum* (Boston, Houghton Mifflin, 1918).

[3] Ibid., p. 42.

[4] BOBBITT, FRANKLIN *How To Make a Curriculum* (Boston, Houghton Mifflin, 1924).

[5] Ibid., pp. 11–29.

[6] For a good example of this view of the child and curriculum development, see *The Changing Curriculum, Tenth Yearbook*, Department of Supervisors and Directors of Instruction, National Education Association and Society for Curriculum Study (New York, Appleton-Century-Crofts, 1937).

[7] TYLER, RALPH W. *Basic Principles of Curriculum and Instruction* (Chicago, University of Chicago Press, 1951).

[8] HERRICK, VIRGIL E. The concept of curriculum design, in HERRICK, VIRGIL E., and TYLER, RALPH W. (eds.) *Toward Improved Curriculum Theory* (Chicago, University of Chicago Press, 1950: Supplementary Educational Monographs No. 71), pp. 37–50.

[9] BARTON, GEORGE E. JR. Educational objectives: improvement of curriculum theory about their determination, in VIRGIL and HERRICK op. cit.

[10] BLOOM, BENJAMIN (ed.) *et al. Taxonomy of Educational Objectives. Handbook I: The Cognitive Domain* (New York, Longmans Green, 1956).

[11] KRATHWOHL, DAVID, BLOOM, BENJAMIN, and MASIA, BERTRAM, *Taxonomy of Educational Objectives. Handbook II: The Affective Domain* (New York, McKay, 1964).

[12] For an excellent paper describing educational objectives as they are viewed and used by elementary school teachers, see JACKSON, PHILIP W., and

222

BELFORD, ELIZABETH Educational objectives and the joys of teaching, *School Review*, 73, 1965, 267–91.
[13] DEWEY, JOHN *Art as Experience* (New York, Minton Balch, 1934).
[14] Ibid. p. 324.
[15] Ibid. p. 307.
[16] MACDONALD, JAMES B. Myths about instruction, *Educational Leadership*, 22 (7), May 1965, 613–14.

Reprinted from *School Review*,
75, Autumn 1967, pp. 250–60.

5

Comments on Eisner's paper

J. THOMAS HASTINGS

Elliot Eisner has put into writing a number of things which need to be said – not necessarily because they are *truth*, although truths are contained therein, but because he is expressing points of view on which other serious scholars take differing points of view. The issues involved are important in educational development; the beliefs on all sides (not two sides) are held firmly; and the open forum of professional journals is an excellent place for discussion. Let us hope that discussion may lead to better definition of terms; to clearer delineation of issues; and, therefore, to techniques and studies which encourage the weighing together of judgements based upon empirical data and pronouncements based upon personal experiences, assumptions and values whenever curriculum development is the concern.

Eisner's main message comes through beautifully in spite of some of the unintended (surely) camouflage – some historical background, little related. He wants those concerned with the evaluation end of curriculum development to desist from insisting that no progress can be made until all goals are stated in behavioural terms. At least he wants those who are saying that to quit. Excellent! They may do more harm than good. But who are these insisters? Surely not Bobbitt,[1] whose influence is not marked in today's scene. Hopefully not Thorndike (E. L., that is), who at most said that transfer is *limited* (not non-existent) and that transfer is theoretically predictable given knowledge of tasks and learning methods.[2] Tyler[3] does not, and Herrick[4] did not suggest 'Bobbittonian' specificity of outcome acts (he will add ten three-digit numbers accurately), although both have suggested that operational definition of known objectives (he will be able to apply the idea of place value to new situations) will lead to better evaluation and better teaching than will expressions in terms of covert behaviour (he will understand fundamental operations) or expressions in terms of teacher–subject intent (he will teach addition). Unfortunately, perhaps because of space limitations, Eisner's article conveys the impression that he is equating specificity of acts with specifying behaviour. It should be apparent that specific acts (Bobbitt) are not identical to behaviour which is specified; most certainly, specificity is not equal to specifying.

At the time of Tyler's (and, later, Herrick's) formulation of a model, there was a need to emphasize student outcomes in operational terms, as opposed to teachers' acts and students' covert behaviour. There are writers on evaluation and users of evaluation in developmental projects who have fixated upon the one device of stating objectives in terms of overt behaviour and looking for evidence of the existence of these. Of course, there are outcomes (with teachers and with students) which could not have been foreseen – some of which will be considered undesirable.

If one attends only to the behavioural outcomes which were intended – and only with students – he has restricted his view in a marked fashion. But Eisner seems to say that the solution is to get a different set of blinders, not to broaden the visual field. He appears to be very perceptive of the misuses of the behavioural approach in evaluation and simultaneously quite blind to the misadventures which are brought about by the handling of education as if it were solely an art. He fails to acknowledge the current writing and thinking in evaluation which is aware of both the art and the science of education (Atkin,[5] Cronbach,[6] Hastings,[7] Scriven,[8] Stake[9]).

In the past three or four years a number of writers have spoken clearly of the need to look further than at objectives which can be stated in behavioural terms. Atkin[10] made a clear statement of the danger possible in detracting the subject specialist from his main job of material development by requesting him to tackle the job of stating objectives in behavioural terms. Cronbach[11] emphasized the need for looking at more than stated objectives. I[12] stressed instructional research. Stake[13] and Scriven[14] both define evaluation far beyond the narrow setting which one must infer from Eisner's discussion. It is true that Walbesser[15] and, to an extent, Gagné[16] seem to hold that objectives defined in behavioural terms are the only way to describe or judge curricular developments. However, Eisner does not even cite these last two nor does he seem aware of the other four. He does refer to Bloom[17] and Krathwohl,[18] but with a rather narrow interpretation of their essence implied. He is, I know, speaking of curriculum-development theory; but he is treating mainly that part usually called 'evaluation'. He should make reference to some of the current thought by those engaged in that specialty.

Eisner's first point, not all outcomes can be specified in advance, is certainly one to be emphasized for those who believe that such *a priori* guesses can cover the output. Again, the current writers on evaluation (such as those mentioned above) make no such claim. Eisner would find great agreement with his statement among them. On the other hand, these evaluation specialists would not throw out the possibility of attempting to state in operational terms the objectives which are known. Let us describe all outcomes which are amenable to description – all we can locate – but surely these may include some we intended prior to the act of teaching.

The second point which Eisner makes compares the relative simplicity of specifying outcomes in science, language and mathematics with the great difficulty encountered in other subjects, especially art. Again, I refer him to Atkin,[19] who writes of science. The relative simplicity is illusory, and the illusion is held only by those who have not closely examined the new curriculum developments in mathematics and science. Surely the science and mathematics projects supported by the National Science Foundation are much more complex in intent and in outcome than Eisner suggests. Let him apply his three other points to all subject areas, not to a narrower sector.

His third point, which is essentially that some outcomes are not quantitative, implies that all evaluation is based upon quantification. This is a fairly common notion for those who equate evaluation and testing. Evaluation consists of descriptions and of judgements of those descriptions. Some descriptions can be made in quantitative terms, others are qualitative. Quantification is useful for precision (30 per cent of the children could . . . ; half of the time these pupils respond in such a fashion to this stimulus), but other forms of description are useful to the evaluator. Perhaps Eisner means not that 'educational objectives' are harmful but that the view that all description must be quantitative is the harmful element. If so, he could state it more clearly.

The fourth and last point which Eisner elaborates is that harm may come from believing that all objectives must be stated and defined *prior* to the instructional act. Even in the Eight-Year Study of the late thirties and early forties, the developers altered objectives and picked up new ones as instruction proceeded. As a matter of fact, attempts to gather evidence on stated objectives often led to delineation of new outcomes. If there are curriculum developers who do try to state objectives and then write materials or develop instruction without additions, deletions and adaptations of those objectives, they most certainly need Eisner's admonition. It does seem to me, however, that he should point out to them that curriculum projects today in science, mathematics, languages, social studies and other areas are generally following the practice of altering expectations *as* they develop instruction and that most evaluation specialists suggest that all possible outcomes be described.

In summary, Eisner's paper certainly presents some issues which should be raised. However, the paper may leave many with the impression that he has ignored current papers on evaluation. Also, many readers may feel that he has looked at subject fields of mathematics, science and language with the warped vision of the non-initiated – or perhaps that he has spoken of curriculum development without investigating current projects in these fields. It is very unfortunate that his review of the history is so irrelevant, that his charges come out (whether intended or not) as so gross, and his appeal to artistry is so overriding. Many of his colleagues who would be enthusiastic co-believers in his dictum that behavioural objectives are sometimes a hindrance (a very important point) will undoubtedly react negatively to his apparent curse on behavioural science in education.

Notes

[1] BOBBITT, FRANKLIN *How To Make A Curriculum* (Boston, Houghton Mifflin, 1924).

[2] THORNDIKE, EDWARD LEE *Educational Psychology: Briefer Course* (New York, Teachers College, Columbia University, 1914).

[3] TYLER, RALPH W. *Basic Principles of Curriculum and Instruction* (Chicago, University of Chicago Press, 1951).

[4] HERRICK, VIRGIL E. The concept of curriculum design, in HERRICK, VIRGIL E., and TYLER, RALPH W. (eds.) *Toward Improved Curriculum Theory* (Chicago, University of Chicago Press, 1950: Supplementary Educational Monograph No. 71), pp. 37–50.

[5] ATKIN, J. MYRON Some evaluation problems in a course content improvement project. *Journal of Research in Science Teaching*, 1, 1963, 129–32.

[6] CRONBACH, L. J. Evaluation for course improvement. *Teachers College Record*, 64, 1963, 672–83. Reprinted in HEATH, R. W. (ed.) *New Curricula* (New York, Harper & Row, 1964).

[7] HASTINGS, J. THOMAS Curriculum evaluation: the why of the outcomes. *Journal of Educational Measurement*, 3 (1), Spring 1966, 27–32.

[8] SCRIVEN, MICHAEL The methodology of evaluation. *AERA Monograph Series on Curriculum Evaluation*, No. 1 (Chicago, Rand McNally, 1967).

[9] STAKE, ROBERT E. The countenance of educational evaluation. *Teachers College Record*, 68, 1967, 523–40.

Selected readings

[10] ATKIN, op. cit.

[11] CRONBACH, op. cit.

[12] HASTINGS, op. cit.

[13] STAKE, op. cit.

[14] SCRIVEN, op. cit.

[15] WALBESSER, HENRY H. Evaluation as a guide to course improvement. *Science Education News*, November 1964, 1–2.

[16] GAGNÉ, ROBERT M. Elementary science: a new scheme of instruction. *Science*, 151, 7 January 1966, 49–53.

[17] BLOOM, BENJAMIN (ed.) *et al., Taxonomy of Educational Objectives. Handbook I: The Cognitive Domain* (New York, Longmans Green, 1956).

[18] KRATHWOHL, DAVID, BLOOM, BENJAMIN, and MASIA, BERTRAM *Taxonomy of Educational Objectives. Handbook II: The Affective Domain* (New York, McKay, 1964).

[19] ATKIN, op. cit.

Reprinted from *School Review*,
75, Autumn 1967, pp. 267–71.

6

Probing the validity of arguments against behavioural goals

W. JAMES POPHAM

Within the last few years a rather intense debate has developed in the field of curriculum and instruction regarding the merits of stating instructional objectives in terms of measurable learner behaviours. Because I am thoroughly committed, both rationally and viscerally, to the proposition that instructional goals should be stated behaviourally, I view this debate with some ambivalence. It is, however, probably desirable to have a dialogue of this sort among specialists in our field. We test the respective worth of opposing positions.

I am committed to the point of view that those who discourage educators from precisely explicating their instructional objectives are often permitting, if not promoting, the same kind of unclear thinking that has led in part to the generally abysmal quality of instruction in this country.

In the remainder of this paper I shall examine eleven reasons given by my colleagues in opposition to objectives stated in terms of measurable learner behaviours. I believe each of these reasons is, for the most part, invalid. There may be minor elements of truth in some, but in essence none of these reasons should be considered strong enough to deter educators from specifying all of their instructional goals in the precise form advocated by the 'good guys' in this argument.

Reason one: Trivial learner behaviours are the easiest to operationalize; hence the really important outcomes of education will be underemphasized.

This particular objection to the use of precise goals is frequently voiced by educators who have recently become acquainted with the procedures for stating explicit, behavioural objectives. Since even behavioural objectives enthusiasts admit that the easiest kinds of pupil behaviours to operationalize are usually the most pedestrian, it is not surprising to find so many examples of behavioural objectives which deal with the picayune. In spite of its overall beneficial influence, the programmed booklet by Robert Mager (1962) dealing with the preparation of instructional objectives has probably suggested to many that precise objectives are usually trivial. Almost all of Mager's examples deal with cognitive behaviours which, according to Bloom's taxonomy, would be identified at the very lowest level.

Contrary to the objection raised in reason one, however, the truth is that explicit objectives make it far *easier* for educators to attend to *important* instructional outcomes. To illustrate, if you were to ask a social science teacher what his objectives were for his government class and he responded as follows, 'I want to make my students better citizens so that they can function effectively in our nation's dynamic democracy', you would probably find little reason to fault him. His objective sounds so profound and eminently worthwhile that few could criticize it. Yet, beneath such façades of profundity, many teachers really are aiming at extremely trivial kinds of pupil behaviour changes. How often, for example, do we find 'good citizenship' measured by a trifling true–false test? Now if we'd asked for the teacher's objectives in operational terms and had discovered that, indeed, all the teacher was attempting to do was promote the learner's achievement on a true–false test, we might have rejected the aim as being unimportant. But this is possible *only* with the precision of explicitly stated goals.

In other words, there is the danger that because of their ready translation to operational statements, teachers will tend to identify too many trivial behaviours as goals. But the very fact that we can make these behaviours explicit permits the teacher and his colleagues to scrutinize them carefully and thus eliminate them as unworthy of our educational efforts. Instead of encouraging unimportant outcomes in education, the use of explicit instructional objectives makes it possible to identify and reject those objectives which are unimportant.

Reason two : Prespecification of explicit goals prevents the teacher from taking advantage of instructional opportunities unexpectedly occurring in the classroom.

When one specifies explicit *ends* for an instructional program there is no necessary implication that the *means* to achieve those ends are also specified. Serendipity in the classroom is always welcome but, and here is the important point, *it should always be justified in terms of its contribution to the learner's attainment of worthwhile objectives.* Too often teachers may believe they are capitalizing on unexpected instructional opportunities in the classroom, whereas measurement of pupil growth towards any defensible criterion would demonstrate that what has happened is merely ephemeral entertainment for the pupils, temporary diversion, or some other irrelevant classroom event.

Prespecification of explicit goals does not prevent the teacher from taking advantage of unexpectedly occurring instructional opportunities in the classroom, it only tends to make the teacher justify these spontaneous learning activities in terms of worthwhile instructional ends. There are undoubtedly gifted teachers who can capitalize magnificently on the most unexpected classroom events. These teachers should not be restricted from doing so. But the teacher who prefers to probe instructional periphery, just for the sake of its spontaneity, should be deterred by the prespecification of explicit goals.

Reason three: Besides pupil behaviour changes, there are other types of educational outcomes which are important, such as changes in parental attitudes, the professional staff, community values, etc.

There are undoubtedly some fairly strong philosophic considerations associated with this particular reason. It seems reasonable that there are desirable changes to be made in our society which might be undertaken by the schools. Certainly, we would like to bring about desirable modifications in such realms as the attitudes of parents. But as a number of educational philosophers have reminded us, the schools cannot be all things to all segments of society. It seems that the primary responsibility of the schools should be to educate effectively the youth of the society. And to the extent that this is so, all modifications of parental attitudes, professional staff attitudes, etc., should be weighed in terms of a later measurable impact on the learner himself. For example, the school administrator who tells us that he wishes to bring about new kinds of attitudes on the part of his teachers should ultimately have to demonstrate that these modified attitudes result in some kind of desirable learner changes. To stop at merely modifying the behaviour of teachers without demonstrating further effects upon the learner would be insufficient.

So while we can see that there are other types of important social outcomes to bring about, it seems that the school's primary responsibility is to its pupils. Hence, all modifications in personnel or external agencies should be justified in terms of their contribution towards the promotion of desired pupil behaviour changes.

Reason four : Measurability implies behaviour which can be objectively, mechanistically measured; hence there must be something dehumanizing about the approach.

This fourth reason is drawn from a long history of resistance to measurement on the grounds that it must, of necessity, reduce human learners to quantifiable bits of data. This resistance probably is most strong regarding earlier forms of measurement which were almost exclusively examination-based, and were frequently multiple-choice test measures at that. But a broadened conception of evaluation suggests that there are diverse and extremely sophisticated ways of securing qualitative as well as quantitative indices of learner performance.

One is constantly amazed to note the incredible agreement among a group of judges assigned to evaluate the complicated gyrations of skilled springboard divers in the televised reports of national aquatic championships. One of these athletes will perform an exotic, twisting dive, and a few seconds after he has hit the water, five or more judges raise cards reflecting their independent evaluations which can range from 0 to 10. The five ratings very frequently run as follows: 7·8, 7·6, 7·7, 7·8 and 7·5. The possibility of reliably judging something as qualitatively complicated as a springboard dive does suggest that our measurement procedures do not have to be based on a theory of reductionism. It is currently possible to assess many complicated human behaviours in a refined fashion. Developmental work is under way in those areas where we now must rely on primitive measures.

Reason five : It is somehow undemocratic to plan in advance precisely how the learner should behave after instruction.

This particular reason was raised a few years ago in a professional journal (Arnstine, 1964), suggesting that the programmed instruction movement was basically undemocratic because it spelled out in advance how the learner was supposed to behave after instruction. A brilliant refutation (Komisar and McClellan, 1965) appeared several months later, in which the rebutting authors responded that instruction is by its very nature undemocratic and to imply that freewheeling democracy is always present in the classroom would be untruthful. Teachers generally have an idea of how they wish learners to behave, and they promote these goals with more or less efficiency. Society knows what it wants its young to become, perhaps not with the precision that we would desire, but certainly in general. And if the schools were allowing students to 'democratically' deviate from societally mandated goals, one can be sure that the institutions would cease to receive society's approbation and support.

Reason six: That isn't really the way teaching is; teachers rarely specify their goals in terms of measurable learner behaviours; so let's set realistic expectations of teachers.

Jackson (1966) recently offered this argument. He observed that teachers just don't specify their objectives in terms of measurable learner behaviour and implied that, since this is the way the real world is, we ought to recognize it and live with it. Perhaps.

There is obviously a difference between identifying the *status quo* and applauding it. Most of us would readily concede that few teachers specify their instructional aims in terms of measurable learner behaviours, *but they ought to*. What we have to do is to mount a widespread campaign to modify this aspect of teacher behaviour. Instructors must begin to identify their instructional intentions in terms of measurable learner behaviours. The way teaching really is at the moment just isn't good enough.

Reason seven: In certain subject areas, e.g. fine arts and the humanities, it is more difficult to identify measurable pupil behaviours.

Sure it's tough. Yet, because it is difficult in certain subject fields to identify measurable pupil behaviours, those subject specialists should not be allowed to escape this responsibility. Teachers in the fields of art and music often claim that it is next to impossible to identify acceptable works of art in precise terms – but they do it all the time. In instance after instance the art teacher does make a judgement regarding the acceptability of pupil-produced artwork. What the art teacher is reluctant to do is put his evaluative criteria on the line. He has such criteria. He must have to make his judgements. But he is loath to describe them in terms that anyone can see.

Any English teacher, for example, will tell you how difficult it is to make a valid judgement of a pupil's essay response. Yet criteria lurk whenever this teacher does make a judgement, and these criteria must be made explicit. No one who really understands education has ever argued that instruction is a simple task. It is even more difficult in such areas as the arts and humanities. As a noted art educator observed several years ago, art educators must quickly get to the business of specifying 'tentative, but clearly defined criteria' by which they can judge their learners' artistic efforts (Munro, 1960).

Reason eight: While loose general statements of objectives may appear worthwhile to an outsider, if most educational goals were stated precisely, they would be revealed as generally innocuous.

This eighth reason contains a great deal of potential threat for school people. The unfortunate truth is that much of what is going on in the schools today is indefensible. Merely to reveal the nature of some behaviour changes we are bringing about in our schools would be embarrassing. As long as general objectives are the rule, our goals may appear worthwhile to external observers. But once we start to describe precisely what kinds of changes we are bringing about in the learner, there is the danger that the public will reject our intentions as unworthy. Yet, if what we are doing is trivial, educators would know it and those who support the educational institution should also know it. To the extent that we are achieving innocuous behaviour changes in learners, we are guilty. We must abandon the ploy of 'obfuscation by generality' and make clear exactly what we are doing. Then we are obliged to defend our choices.

Reason nine: Measurability implies accountability; teachers might be judged on their ability to produce results in learners rather than on the many bases now used as indices of competence.

This is a particularly threatening reason and serves to produce much teacher resistance to precisely stated objectives. It doesn't take too much insight on the part of the teacher to realize that if objectives are specified in terms of measurable learner behaviour, there exists the possibility that the instructor will have to become *accountable* for securing such behaviour changes. Teachers might actually be judged on their ability to bring about desirable changes in learners. They should be.

But a teacher should not be judged on the particular instructional *means* he uses to bring about desirable *ends*. At present many teachers are judged adversely simply because the instructional procedures they use do not coincide with those once used by an evaluator when 'he was a teacher'. In other words, if I'm a supervisor who has had considerable success with open-ended discussion, I may tend to view with disfavour any teachers who cleave to more directive methods. Yet, if the teacher using the more direct methods can secure learner behaviour changes which are desirable, I have no right to judge that teacher as inadequate. The possibility of assessing instructional competence in terms of the teacher's ability to bring about specified behaviour changes in learners brings with it far more assets than liabilities to the teacher. He will no longer be judged on the idiosyncratic whims of a visiting supervisor. Rather, he can amass evidence that, in terms of his pupils' actual attainments, he is able to teach efficiently.

Even though this is a striking departure from the current state of affairs, and a departure that may be threatening to the less competent, the educator must promote this kind of accountability rather than the maze of folklore and mysticism which exists at the moment regarding teacher evaluation.

Reason ten: It is far more difficult to generate such precise objectives than to talk about objectives in our customarily vague terms.

Here is a very significant objection to the development of precise goals. Teachers are, for the most part, far too busy to spend the necessary hours in stating their objectives and measurement procedures with the kind of precision implied by this discussion. It is said that we are soon nearing a time when we will have more teachers than jobs. This is the time to reduce the teacher's load to the point where he can become a professional decision maker rather than a custodian. We must reduce public school teaching loads to those of college professors. This is the time when we must give the teacher immense help in specifying his objectives. Perhaps we should *give* him objectives from which to choose, rather than force him to generate his own. Many of the federal dollars currently being used to support education would be better spent on agencies which would produce alternative behavioural objectives for all fields at all grade levels. At any rate, the difficulty of the task should not preclude its accomplishment. We can recognize how hard the job is and still allocate the necessary resources to do it.

Reason eleven: In evaluating the worth of instructional schemes, it is often the unanticipated results which are really important, but prespecified goals may make the evaluator inattentive to the unforeseen.

Some fear that if we cleave to behaviourally stated objectives which must be specified prior to designing an instructional program, we will overlook certain outcomes of the program which were not anticipated yet which may be extremely important. They point out that some of the relatively recent 'new curricula' in the sciences have had the unanticipated effect of sharply reducing pupil enrolments in those fields. In view of the possibility of such outcomes, both unexpectedly good and bad, it is suggested that we really ought not spell out objectives in advance, but should evaluate the adequacy of the instructional program after it has been implemented.

Such reasoning, while compelling at first glance, weakens under close

235

scrutiny. In the first place, really dramatic unanticipated outcomes cannot be overlooked by curriculum evaluators. They certainly should not be. We should judge an instructional sequence not only by whether it attains its prespecified objectives but also by any unforeseen consequences it produces. But what can you tell the would-be curriculum evaluator regarding this problem? 'Keep your eyes open' doesn't seem to pack the desired punch. Yet, it's about all you can say. For if there is reason to believe that a particular outcome may result from an instruction sequence, it should be built into the set of objectives for the sequence. To illustrate, if the curriculum designers fear that certain negative attitudes will be acquired by the learner as he interacts with an instructional sequence, then behavioural objectives can be devised which reveal whether the instructional sequence has effectively counteracted this affective outcome. It is probably always a good idea, for example, to identify behavioural indices of the pupil's 'subject-approaching tendencies'. We don't want to teach youngsters how to perform mathematical exercises, for example, but to learn to hate maths in the process.

Yet, it is indefensible to let an awareness of the importance of unanticipated outcomes in evaluating instructional programs lead one to the rejection of rigorous pre-planning of instructional objectives. Such objectives should be the primary, but not exclusive, focus in evaluating instruction.

While these eleven reasons are not exhaustive, they represent most of the arguments used to resist the implementation of precise instructional objectives. In spite of the very favourable overall reaction to explicit objectives during the past five to ten years, a small collection of dissident educators has arisen to oppose the quest for goal specificity. The trouble with criticisms of precise objectives isn't that they are completely without foundation. As conceded earlier, there are probably elements of truth in all of them. Yet, when we are attempting to promote the wide-scale adoption of precision in the classroom, there is the danger that many instructors will use the comments and objections of these few critics as an excuse for not thinking clearly about their goals. Any risks we run by moving to behavioural goals are miniscule in contrast with our current state of confusion regarding instructional intentions. The objections against behaviourally stated goals are not strong enough. To secure a dramatic increase in instructional effectiveness, we must abandon our customary practices of goal-stating and turn to a framework of precision.

References

ARNSTINE, D. G. (1964) The language and values of programmed instruction, part 2. *The Educational Forum*, 28.

JACKSON, P. W. (1966) *The Way Teaching Is*. Washington, D.C.: National Education Association.

KOMISAR, P. B., and MCCLELLAN, J. E. (1965) Professor Arnstine and programmed instruction. Reprint from *The Educational Forum*.

MAGER, R. F. (1962) *Preparing Objectives for Programmed Instruction*. Palo Alto, Calif.: Fearon.

MUNRO, T. (1960) The interrelation of the arts in secondary education. In MUNRO, T., and READ, H. (eds.) *The Creative Arts in American Education*. Cambridge, Mass.: Harvard University Press.

Reprinted from R. C. Anderson *et al.*,
Current Research in Instruction
(Englewood Cliffs, N.J., Prentice-Hall, 1968).
Originally a symposium presentation
at the Annual American Educational
Research Association Meeting,
Chicago, February 1968.

On educational psychology

I

The relevancy of educational psychology

ARTHUR P. COLADARCI

The relevancy of an applied area depends in part upon the definition of the process, institution or event to which it is applied. The contribution that can be made by *educational* psychology is partially a function of the particular meaning invested in 'education'. This statement is not merely the usual innocuous preface to an extended discussion. Indeed, it is our major thesis. Too many teachers and administrators have thought of educational psychology as consisting only of an ordered catalogue of educational prescriptions, which, together with those provided by the other foundational fields in education, 'tell' the teacher 'how to teach' and the administrator 'how to administer'. The fallacy lies not only in the much too complimentary respect for the status of our knowledge in these areas but, more fundamentally, in the conception of education as a collection of successful recipes – the teacher or administrator is a person who has been armed with a bag-of-tricks into which he reaches for a decision regarding any given specific professional problem. Although this unfortunate orientation becomes an increasingly less frequent one, it still exists and may be partially attributable to the turn-of-the-century efforts to make education 'scientific' by attempting to make it merely more *factual*.[1]

If one, however, thinks of the nature of the educator's role in another way, educational psychology, and education generally, become more powerful, exciting and rigorous. The conception we have in mind can be described by beginning with a rather coarse but generally acceptable definition of the educator's role: to help the learner change his behaviour in specified desirable directions. Although the definition is too ambiguous for detailed analysis, it serves to point out the two basic factors involved: a *process* ('behaviour change') and a *criterion* ('specified desirable direction'). Suppose that the educator has clearly specified what he means by 'desirable' behaviour changes in the form of operationally stated educational goals.[2] It appears, now, that the focal task for the teacher is to so interact with his pupils, and

238

to so arrange the conditions and materials, that these pupils will change in the hoped-for ways. Put in these terms, the teacher's task can be seen as one of manipulating the learning situation in such a way that the *predicted* behaviour changes actually do occur. If, at this point, the educational psychologist could say that we now know which manipulations will produce the desired changes, no problem would exist – we have only to apply the correct recipe. However, educational psychology cannot do this. Any particular combination of teacher–pupil–class–group–community-available materials, etc., is somewhat different from any other combination. There is no general prescription that can be considered to be clearly valid for particular cases. The teacher, then, *must be an active, continuous inquirer into the validity of his own procedures*. As Corey puts it:

> Most of the study of what should be kept in the schools and what should go and what should be added must be done in hundreds of thousands of classrooms and thousands of American communities. The studies must be understood by those who may have to change the way they do things as a result of the studies. Our schools cannot keep up with the life they are supposed to sustain and improve unless teachers, pupils, supervisors, administrators, and school patrons continuously examine what they are doing. Singly and in groups, they must use their imagination creatively and constructively to identify the practices that must be changed to meet the needs and demands of modern life, courageously to try out those practices that give better promise, and methodically and systematically gather evidence to test their worth.[3]

At the risk of belabouring the point, let us put it in somewhat different form before considering the relevancy of educational psychology. The educator's decisions about methods, materials and curricular procedures should be thought of as *hypotheses* regarding the way in which the desired behaviour changes can be brought about. These hypotheses must be *tested* continuously by inquiring into the degree to which the predicted behaviour changes actually occurred. This view has been referred to elsewhere by the writer[4] as 'teaching behaviour defined as the-testing-of-hypotheses behaviour'. The crucial element is *tentativeness*; ideas and decisions about method and curriculum are to be held hypothetically, continuously tested, and continuously revised if necessary.

Contribution of educational psychology

Given this conception of the educator's role, how can educational psychology be brought to bear on it in helpful ways? The contribution can be broken down into two related categories. First, educational psychology, as a body of information and an arena of research activity, can help in the generation of the educational hypotheses. Intelligent hypotheses are not chosen randomly nor are they found full-blown. An intelligent hypothesizer thinks along the lines of the following model: '*On the basis of the best information now available to me*, I hypothesize that this procedure will produce this result.' To translate this into the context of education, we might say, for instance: '*On the basis of what I now know* about individual differences and the reading process, I hypothesize that this kind of grouping-for-reading will lead to the kind of pupil progress in reading that I would like to bring about.'

Educational psychology, as a source of information, contributes to the 'on-the-basis-of-what-I-now-know' portion of the statement. It helps provide information on which to base hypotheses for particular purposes and particular children. The teacher or administrator who takes this point seriously will understand that one cannot merely 'take a course in educational psychology', but that he must constantly keep informed about those developments in this area that are most relevant to his particular educational responsibilities. The reader may also note that this conception of the interaction between educational psychology and the teacher means that every teacher can *contribute* to educational psychology in the process of testing his hypotheses.

A second kind of contribution which educational psychology can make is that of helping teachers and administrators to acquire the attitudes and skills necessary to intelligent hypothesizing and the testing of hypotheses. Limitations of space preclude an explication of this. Generally, what is involved is learning such skills as how to interpret data intelligently, how to observe accurately, how to avoid common logical fallacies in making inferences, how to make adequate decisions regarding what data should be gathered, ways in which data can be gathered and recorded, etc.

Both of these contributions of educational psychology are shared by all the fields represented in this symposium. In the writer's view, this is the *raison d'être* of any field that purports to be 'foundational' in professional education. Educational psychology, of course, has many additional and somewhat unique values for the educator. We have chosen to overlook those in this discussion since they are covered comprehensively and in detail in the available published literature. Those who are interested are invited to examine the published reports of a committee organized by the Executive Committee of the National Society of College Teachers of Education. The first report[5] discussed the ways in which educational psychology relates to curriculum development; the second[6] considers the nature of educational psychology and its general place in teacher education; the third[7] gives detailed attention to the ways in which specific areas of educational psychology can be helpful to the prospective teacher; the last report[8] describes present practices and developments in the teaching of educational psychology.

It is appropriate, in this case, that the final comment should be cautionary as well as benedictory. The writer has stated his position as though there are no responsible competing alternatives to it. Any dogmatic flavour in the statement is more a consequence of brevity than of intent. Many persons will hold that such a conception of education as we have presented here is both impractical and not valuable. Our response would be that the orientation is at least practical in the sense that many, many educators have learned to behave as inquirers; the orientation appears to be valuable in that where one finds such an educator he usually finds him to be valued by his colleagues, ego-involved in his profession, and able to criticize his procedures rationally. In short, such educators do exist and they appear to make the profession a better one by their membership in it.

References

[1] SMITH, B. OTHANEL Science of education, in MONROE, W. S. (ed.) *Encyclopedia of Educational Research* (Macmillan, 1950), pp. 1145–52.

[2] TRAVERS, ROBERT M. W. *Educational Measurement* (Macmillan, 1955), pp. 19–36.

[3] COREY, STEPHEN M. *Action Research to Improve School Practices* (Bureau of Publications, Teachers College, Columbia University, 1953), p. viii.

[4] COLADARCI, ARTHUR P. Are educational researchers prepared to do meaningful research? *California Journal of Educational Research*, 5, 1954, 3–6.

[5] The psychological basis of the modern curriculum. *Journal of Educational Psychology*, 39, 1948, 129–69.

[6] Educational psychology in the education of teachers, *Journal of Educational Psychology*, 40, 1949, 257–94.

Selected readings

[7] Educational psychology for teachers, *Journal of Educational Psychology*, 41, 1950, 321–72.
[8] Current practices and innovations in the teaching of educational psychology. *Journal of Educational Psychology*, 43, 1952, 1–30.

Reprinted from *Educational Leadership*, 13 (8), May 1956, pp. 489–92.

2

The objectives of educational psychology
in the education of teachers

HARRY N. RIVLIN

In the past twenty-five years, our schools have probably changed much more than they have in any other twenty-five years in American history. The curriculum has broadened and methods of teaching have been diversified. And as a result, the programs that were set up for preparing teachers twenty-five years ago would be quite inadequate for those in charge of modern elementary or secondary schools. Educational psychologists have an important stake in the preparation of teachers, for they have done much to help shape modern education. In the past, however, their contribution came largely as a result of their own research studies. If we now see more clearly the role that they can play in teacher education, we may speed the process of enlarging the scope of research and of translating its findings into school practices. In the light of their past attainments and present activities, what can educational psychologists contribute to the professional development of the student as a teacher?

Educational psychology in the preparation of teachers

College courses in educational psychology as conceived in the past have sometimes fallen short of being a determining influence in the professional preparation of teachers. The major reason for this failure is that we were thinking in terms of college courses rather than of a professional program. As with many college courses, the objectives of the typical educational psychology course were primarily factual. The then current explanations of learning were presented and measurement procedures were taught, but scant attention was given to the problems that students were to face later as classroom teachers. Despite what we knew about the limitations of transfer of training, we often taught as though students would automatically transfer to their own teaching the knowledge they had acquired in the markedly different setting of the college classroom. It is no wonder, then, that ther was little relationship between success in college courses in educational psychology and success in classroom teaching.

In a recent article, Trow[18] advances several additional reasons for the failure of traditional educational psychology courses to function in the improvement of the student's ability to teach. He points out that the course in educational psychology is usually set in the framework of the traditional liberal arts college with its fifty-minute periods, lectures and emphasis on subject-matter knowledge, a framework that tends to discourage those who aim at professional objectives; and that the material studied remains often on the level of mere verbalization without any real comprehension of the principles studied and their possible applications. The exhaustive and penetrating study of pre-service courses in educational psychology made by Coladarci[8] demonstrates that we cannot be content with the ways in which these courses have been organized and taught in the past. As we proceed to indicate what should be taught and how it should be taught, it is essential that we first examine the objectives we hope to attain.

What is it that we want prospective teachers to gain from educational psychology?

1 *The study of educational psychology should develop the student's interest in people, both children and adults, and help him to understand them.*

He should learn why people behave as they do, and he should see how we must proceed if we are to attempt to modify behaviour patterns. The attainment of this objective necessitates much more than a cursory survey of child psychology or adolescent psychology. The study of educational psychology should lead to insight into the dynamics of behaviour with respect to both children and adults. Such study should not be limited to an analysis of the way other people act; for the teacher needs to understand himself, as well as others. Fortunately, our typical student is himself a learner and is ordinarily either a late adolescent or a young adult not too many years away from adolescence. For this reason he should be able to apply to himself much of the insight and many of the skills he is learning. As he grows in his understanding of the dynamics of behaviour, he should gain increased insight into his own adjustment. We must aim at developing an abiding interest in children and adolescents. If the course is taught successfully, the student's interest in children should be deepened and enriched until it is far more than merely a liking for children. As the student learns how children grow and develop,

244

he should have increasing respect for them as individuals and he should want to know much more about them.

Education is a social process. The prospective teacher must learn to understand the dynamics of child adjustment as it is influenced by the various groups of which he is a member. Our understanding of motivation has been advanced by the many laboratory studies that have been conducted with children who were reacting individually to various incentives, but it is also being advanced by the numerous studies now being made of group behaviour. Since virtually all of the students will become classroom teachers rather than tutors of individual children, it is essential that they learn how to deal with children in a social setting and that they understand learning as a social as well as an individual process.

2   *The study of educational psychology as part of a teacher education program should have a favourable effect on the attitudes, behaviour and psychological understanding of students in both personal and professional relationships.*

Educational psychology is more than a body of knowledge and a set of technical skills. It promotes a point of view that sees pupils as personalities as well as learners, that regards educational procedures and values as susceptible of objective study and evaluation, and that interprets teaching as being more than a bag of tricks. Any student who feels that he is through with educational psychology when he passes in the course has obviously failed to achieve a most significant objective of the course. We must be concerned with the extent of the students' knowledge after they have studied educational psychology, but we must be concerned even more with their behaviour and with their fundamental attitudes.

Students should develop an increasing degree of insight into the applications of educational psychology to the problems of teachers and administrators. They must not only know the facts, but they must also understand the implications for their work as classroom teachers. What good will it do the beginning teacher to study the psychology of learning if it does not modify his own methods of study, and if his own teaching procedures are to be no different from those to which he was earlier subjected? We know that children can study grammar without applying it to their own writing. We sometimes do not realize that our students can study educational psychology and be equally unable to apply this knowledge in their own classroom procedures, even when the applications are as obvious to us as are the applications of grammar to an English teacher. Our prospective teachers, as

R

they study human growth, learning about both the basic patterns and the individual deviations from these patterns, and as they develop the capacity to perceive the unique world of each individual child, should become better able to determine the kind of educational environment needed for the optimum development of the children with whom they will be in daily contact.

There are many ways in which the teacher's knowledge should be reflected in improved teaching procedures. The teacher who understands and really cares about children should be able to adapt instruction to their needs, to provide them with the security and encouragement they require, and to help create the classroom climate that will challenge their best efforts. The teacher is in a key position for identifying the boys and girls whose emotional problems make it difficult for them to get along with others. Under the leadership of an understanding and sympathetic teacher, classroom activities may be an important means of developing attitudes and personality traits that persist long after many other school learnings are forgotten.

The teacher should also be able to apply to his class and to the individuals in his class many of the technical skills of the educational psychologist. The professional teacher today, for example, should be able to diagnose the learning difficulties he encounters and he should be adept at using both published materials and teacher-made instruments for this purpose. Similarly, he should be able to prepare a case study that is adequate as a basis for understanding and helping the children he teaches, and he should be skilled in organizing and evaluating the information he has gathered. Of equal importance with the ability to use some of the techniques of the professional psychologist is the classroom teacher's recognition that there are other techniques which demand a level of training to be expected only of the specialist. The classroom teacher, therefore, must be ready to refer to the clinician, rather than attempt to treat, himself, those children who need clinical tests and therapy.

3   *The study of educational psychology should enable the student to use the body of knowledge that is derived from research studies in this field and that helps explain the ways in which learning occurs.*

Viewing educational psychology as a functional part of a professional program suggests the criterion to be used in selecting the information, skills and attitudes which students should be expected to learn. No teacher can be regarded as professionally competent today unless he is intimately familiar with the psychological basis upon which our educational programs rest. This means that he must understand the fundamental facts about human growth and development, learning, personality and adjustment, measurement and evaluation, and the techniques and methods of educational psychology.

To keep this study of facts from becoming a mere collection of discrete bits of information, the student must understand the principles and the theories which explain the facts. Here, too, he must be constantly aware of the implications for classroom teaching. Of what avail is it for the young teacher or prospective teacher to know the principles that help explain the development of personality or the achievement of wholesome emotional adjustment, if his relations with children violate practically all the principles and theories he can discuss so fluently on an examination paper? As the student learns about these principles and theories, he should also understand the facts upon which they rest so that he may be prepared for keeping up with the changes that are bound to occur as new evidence is uncovered by further research. To fail to develop such an understanding is to foster a rigidity of mind that resists new developments which occur after the student has completed his teacher-education program and has started on his professional career.

The student should become familiar with the basic vocabulary which has become part of the educator's language. We are not thinking here of the clichés, worn thin by over-use before they are really understood, that have earned the contemptuous epithet of *jargon*. Instead, we are referring to such expressions as *IQ*, *mental age*, *moron*, *control group*, *grade norm*, *age norm*, *percentile* and others that have become so well defined and so widely used that any teacher who is ignorant of their meaning is professionally illiterate. As psychologists, we know that vocabulary grows best when the words are learned and used in context. The rote memorization of definitions is certainly not what is suggested. The student needs to acquire sufficient familiarity with the basic concepts in educational psychology so that he will be able to understand them when he meets them in his reading and discussions.

4   *The study of educational psychology should improve the effectiveness of the prospective teacher's ability to learn.*

Because the student in a teacher-education program is as much a learner as any of his pupils will be, he has in himself an excellent subject for demonstrating what he is studying about the improvement of learning. The prospective teacher can learn much about how people learn and what can be done to increase the efficiency of learning. His understanding of these principles and techniques will be increased as he applies them to his own study procedures.

This objective is important not only because it may make his college career more successful but also because the successful teacher is always a learner.

As part of a teacher-education program, the course in educational psychology should develop the student's ability to read professional books and the articles in this field and – even more difficult to achieve – should inculcate the habit of reading them. Developing the ability to read and the habit of reading are not exclusively our objectives, but added emphasis is required because of the technical character of this reading. Teachers of education courses are sometimes so considerate of their students' sensitivities that they hesitate to present anything that might be embarrassingly difficult for the weaker members of the class. And the concern with providing adequate first-hand experience for students sometimes blinds the teacher to the obvious benefits that follow from other sources of learning.

Without gainsaying the values of case studies, of motion pictures, of panel discussions, and of role playing, there is a very real danger that education courses may become so dependent on these learning procedures that self-directed study from books and journals is neglected. That this accusation is not without foundation is seen in the reaction of many teachers – and certification bodies, too – who apparently believe that the only way for a teacher to learn anything is to 'take a course'. Educational psychology, properly taught, should develop teachers who can read the rapidly growing professional literature with discrimination and judgement.

5   *The study of educational psychology should foster the student's appreciation and understanding of research in education.*

Educational psychology is primarily a research discipline. It has a large role in developing an objective and experimental approach to educational problems. Teachers cannot be satisfied to have educational questions decided merely by debate or emotional appeal. They should be able to penetrate beyond the rhetoric of those who call for a return to the good old days when 'children learned to read and to write'. Similarly, they should demand supporting data from some of their over-enthusiastic colleagues who apparently think that anything in education that is exciting is necessarily valuable also, and that anything which is new and untried must surely be better than current practice.

We cannot expect the undergraduate student to gain a thorough mastery of research techniques. It is more realistic to aim for respect for research, and the ability to locate and to use pertinent research studies. These aims encompass something broader than the ability to compute means, standard deviations and coefficients of correlation. Very few teachers ever have to compute more than the simplest of statistical measures. All competent teachers, however, should understand the meaning of common statistical measures and know how they are used. They should know, for example, when the coefficient of correlation is a helpful addition to a study and when its use gives a spurious dignity to an inadequate report or presents a fallacious explanation of the results. More important still, they should have at least a rudimentary understanding of research procedures so that they will not be taken in by the charlatan or the incompetent. In short, they should become intelligent consumers of educational research.

The implications of these objectives

Setting forth the objectives of a course sometimes has the advantage of clarifying our thinking about purposes and procedures, but the practice is not without its limitations, and even dangers. There is always the temptation to claim everything for the course we are describing, almost forgetting that any course is but a small part of a larger pattern. There is the danger, too, that setting forth a formidable list of objectives may give us the impression that we are achieving them all.

Objectives are formulated far too often, moreover, for ideal classes that never really exist. We may question whether any general list of objectives from outside is of optimum value in a specific institution which has its own problems of staff and student personnel, of established curriculum patterns and faculty prejudices, of administrative organization and financial policy with respect to libraries, laboratories and teaching personnel.

In seeking to attain objectives, each institution will have to think of the objectives of the total teacher-education pattern as well as of the objectives of a specific course. Some objectives, however important, may have to be sacrificed in specific institutions, perhaps because they are unattainable as goals or because they are relegated to other phases of the program which are better suited for the purpose. Speaking realistically, institutions sometimes find it impossible to achieve every objective, although each objective deserves attainment. As psychologists, we may find that the distinction between 'physiological limit' and 'practical limit' has its analogue in the degree to which any institution can approach its various goals.

In a sense, the path of development that educational psychology has taken in its growth as a field of research raises a major obstacle to achieving its objectives as a phase of teacher education. As research in educational psychology became more extensive, it was only natural that specialization should become essential to the prosecution of further research. No individual can master all the research techniques nor gain the thorough knowledge of the field that is essential for sound research, unless he limits the area in which he will become expert. Specialization is sometimes necessary even within specialties. The psychologist who diagnoses learning difficulties, for example, has enough to learn and to do, without ever trying to devise and to standardize a single new test for use in diagnosis.

The development of specialization in the various sub-areas of educational psychology has undoubtedly improved the quality of research, but it has sometimes impaired the closeness with which educational psychologists have worked with school people, and with other educators operating in non-school situations, in the solution of educational problems. Educational problems are rarely only measurement problems, or only guidance problems, or only learning problems. Educational psychologists whose competence is limited to a single area of educational psychology can give only meagre help in solving problems that cut across areas of specialization.

Educational psychologists have broadened their vision over what it was fifteen or twenty years ago. Several of the important educational psychologists at that time disavowed any responsibility for the values or direction of education. They assumed responsibility only for making learning more effective, regardless of its value. Today, more than ever before, we need educational psychologists with a view of the entire field of education, and we need teachers with a basic understanding of educational psychology. Those who are working with teachers in the public schools know that the problems faced by teachers and children – or by those engaged in any phase of education, however formal or informal – are not respecters of areas of specialization. Educators need psychologists who can see the problems in their entirety, and who can draw upon all the resources that are needed in order to solve them.

The role of educational psychology in the education of teachers is defined much too narrowly if we limit it to the preparation of prospective teachers. Educational psychologists have a responsibility for seeing that the good intentions which prospective teachers develop as undergraduates lead to the even better intentions – and achievements – of teachers who deserve to be called professionals. Those who work in applied as contrasted with theoretic areas of study must assume at least a share of the responsibility if their findings are not generally accepted and applied. To be sure, educational psychologists should not bear the sole responsibility for the failure of the schools to apply what psychologists and other students of human relations have discovered, for there are schools which cling to procedures of questionable value and there are teachers who regard their initial teaching certificate as a permanent testimonial to their competence.

Intelligent and alert teachers, eager for help in their professional activities, are disappointed when their specific questions are answered only in generalities. It is the teachers' need for guidance that has led to a change in the way educational psychology is presented, both in university classes and in textbooks. To help teachers, we must illustrate in our own teaching the points of view we wish to develop in others. Teachers need educational psychologists who understand education as well as psychology and who can help educators to use the resources and the findings of psychology in solving the problems which confront the school. We must be able to conduct research studies to validate the applications of psychology to education and we must explore more thoroughly than do other psychologists the psychological questions that arise from education. We shall have to be familiar with many areas of psychology and with related studies in human relations, even though our own research is confined to one area.

If educational psychology is to attain its objectives, we shall have to modify both the way in which our courses are organized and the methods by which they are taught. Educational psychology makes its greatest contribution to teacher education when it becomes an integral part of the whole program instead of being a discrete entity. Some of our applications are taught more effectively as part of other courses; for example, courses in methods of teaching, which afford a direct application of a principle. There is certainly no justification for the condition that obtains when educators, who urge the elementary and secondary schools to break down the rigid compartmentalization of the traditional curriculum, erect equally uncompromising barriers among the subjects they include in their teacher-education program. To be most effective, the courses in educational psychology must find their problems and their applications in all phases of the teacher-education program. Courses on the curriculum and methods of teaching, and even the student-teaching experience, should build on and develop the principles treated in the educational psychology course.

Our methods of teaching, too, will have to be modified. Students expect that those who are as well trained in educational psychology as their professors of that subject presumably are, will be very effective teachers. The class in educational psychology can be a demonstration, on the level of professional preparation of the ways in which an understanding of the learning process leads to the creation of situations in which learning and growth occur.

These objectives are difficult of realization, but we cannot accept less if we truly have faith in educational psychology as an important force in education today. A clearer recognition of our goals should increase the number of classroom teachers who will be better equipped to become practising educational psychologists, and for this reason, more understanding and more effective teachers in their elementary and secondary school classrooms. Unquestionably these objectives will tax the ingenuity of our teachers of educational psychology, but the children in the schools, the ultimate beneficiaries of such a program, merit our greatest efforts to help them get the kind of teachers they deserve and need.

Bibliography

1 AMERICAN ASSOCIATION OF TEACHERS COLLEGES *Child Growth and Development Emphasis in Teacher Education.* The Association, 1944.

2 ANDERSON, G. LESTER Educational psychology and teacher education. *Journal of Educational Psychology*, 40, May 1949, 275–84.

3 ANDERSON, G. LESTER What the psychology of learning has to contribute to the education of the teacher. *Journal of Educational Psychology*, 41, October 1959, 362–5.

4 BLAIR, GLENN M. What teachers should know about the psychology of adolescence. *Journal of Educational Psychology*, 41, October 1950, 356–61.

5 BOARDMAN, CHARLES W. An experimental approach to the integration of professional courses at the University of Minnesota. *Journal of Educational Research*, 34, May 1941, 672–8.

6 BRUCE, WILLIAM F. How can the psychology of development in infancy and childhood help teachers? *Journal of Educational Psychology*, 41, October 1950, 348–55.

7 CHARTERS, W. W., and WAPLES, DOUGLAS *Commonwealth Teacher-Training Study.* University of Chicago Press, 1929.

8 COLADARCI, ARTHUR P. Professional experiences in educational psychology: a review of opinion and a critical note. *Bulletin of the School of Education, Indiana University*, 27 (5), September 1951.

9 COOK, WALTER W. What educational measurement in the education of teachers? *Journal of Educational Psychology*, 41, October 1950, 339–47.

10 COOPER, R. M. *Better Colleges – Better Teachers.* New York: Macmillan, 1944.

11 FREEMAN, FRANK N. Courses in educational psychology in colleges, uni-

versities and normal schools. pp. 43–62 in the *Eighth Yearbook of the National Society of College Teachers of Education*, 1919.

[12] FREEMAN, FRANK S. The need to define and re-orient educational psychology. *Journal of Educational Psychology*, 40, May 1949, 257–60.

[13] GATES, ARTHUR I. The place of educational psychology in the curriculum for the education of teachers. pp. 21–35 in the *Twentieth Yearbook of the National Society of College Teachers of Education*, 1932.

[14] KLAUSMEIER, HERBERT, and SWANSON, DONOVAN Evaluation a course in educational psychology. *Journal of Educational Research*, 43, May 1950, 678–87.

[15] MACDONALD, MANLEY E. A catalog study of courses in psychology in state normal schools and teachers colleges. *Educational Administration and Supervision*, 13, April 1927, 272–82.

[16] NOLL, VICTOR H. and others, Functions of the division of educational psychology of the American Psychological Association: A Committee Report. *Journal of Educational Psychology*, 40, October 1949, 361–70.

[17] RIVLIN, HARRY N. and others *The Contributions of Educational Psychology to Education*. The Committee on the Contributions of Psychology to Educational Psychology Division, American Psychological Association, September 1948.

[18] TROW, WM CLARK Educational psychology and teaching. *Michigan Education Journal*, 29, February 1952, 369–70.

[19] TROW, WM CLARK Educational psychology charts a course. *Journal of Educational Psychology*, 40, May 1949, 285–94.

[20] WOLFLE, DAEL The sensible organization of courses in psychology. *American Psychologist*, 2, October 1947, 437–45.

Reprinted from the National Society
of College Teachers of Education
Monograph No. 3, 1953, pp. 1–11.

3

A suggested outline of topics
for inclusion in a course of educational psychology

British Psychological Society and Association
for Teachers in Colleges and Departments of Education

I: Learning

A FUNDAMENTALS OF THE LEARNING PROCESS

1 *Motivation*

Concepts of need and drive.
Classroom motivation – social relationships in the classroom, incentives, attitudes, interests, personal involvement, the creative
effect of mild emotional tension.

2 *Goal-directed activity*

Form of activity – trial and error behaviour, insight, reasoning,
imagining, thinking, problem solving.
The teacher's role in directing activity and organizing the total
learning situation so as to facilitate learning.

3 *Reinforcement*

Satisfactions of needs – social approval, satisfaction from success.

B FACTORS INFLUENCING LEARNING AND RETENTION

1 *The nature of the material to be learned*

Level of difficulty, length, relevance for the learner, meaningfulness,
interference with previous learning.

2 *Method of presentation*

Adequacy of motivation.
Teacher's technique – rapport with class, method of organization

254

of lesson, audiovisual aids, distribution and types of practice, degree of involvement of the learner.
Teaching for transfer to other situations.

3 *Individual differences of learners*

Age, sex, developmental level, experiential background, intellectual capacity, structure of the mind, motivational differences.
Emotional factors in learning.
The concept of readiness.

C LEARNING DIFFICULTIES IN SCHOOL

The characteristic attitudes of failing children.
Main causes of failure.
Value of early recognition of failing children.
Readjustment of failing children to the school learning situation.
Remedial teaching.

II: Developmental psychology

A THE NATURE OF DEVELOPMENT

Underlying principles of development – the interaction of nature and nurture, maturation and learning in development of children's behaviour. Development in emotional, social, cognitive, symbolic and aesthetic fields.

B FACTORS INFLUENCING DEVELOPMENT OF PERSONALITY

1 *Biological factors*

Physique, glandular balance, temperament.

2 *Differences in abilities*

3 *Social factors*

The home background. Early upbringing, discipline, effect of deprivation.
Attitudes, values, aspirations of parents, and members of the community. Relations with other children, with school and with other groups.

255

4 *Frustration and development*

Adjustment and maladjustment, the meaning of the terms; the value element in the concept of adjustment.

Factors influencing the process of adjustment.

The school as an institution, its psychological structure and influence.

The contribution of school and other educational institutions towards satisfactory development.

III: Educational measurement

The nature of mental measurement – basic concepts of validity, reliability sampling.

Traditional methods of evaluating attainment in school. Their advantages and limitations. Characteristics of standardized tests. Scales, units of measurement, norms.

Uses and limitations of standardized tests in schools.

Scientific method in the social sciences.

IV: Psychology and the teacher's job

The teacher's role in relation to the children, their parents and to other members of the staff.

Personal problems associated with the job of teaching. The psychology of leadership and authority.

Note: It is not suggested that the topics listed above should be presented to students in that particular order.

Reprinted from L. B. Birch (ed.),
Teaching Educational Psychology in Training Colleges
(British Psychological Society, 1962), pp. 43–4.

4

Is there a discipline
of educational psychology?

DAVID P. AUSUBEL

'Is there such a discipline as educational psychology?' is certainly not an irrelevant or irreverent question. On the contrary, it follows very pertinently if one examines many textbooks of educational psychology that were written during the past thirty years. In fact, judging from the conception of educational psychology – as a superficial, ill digested and typically disjointed and watered-down miscellany of general psychology, learning theory, developmental psychology, social psychology, psychological measurement, psychology of adjustment, mental hygiene, client-centred counselling and child-centred education put forward by these textbooks – one would be hard put not to give a negative answer to the question raised by the title of this paper.

Definition of the field

My thesis, in brief, is that educational psychology is that special branch of psychology concerned with the nature, conditions, outcomes and evaluation of school learning and retention. As such, the subject matter of educational psychology consists primarily of the theory of meaningful learning and the retention and the influence of all significant variables – cognitive, developmental, affective, motivational, personality and social – on school learning outcomes: particularly the influence of those variables that are manipulable by the teacher, the curriculum developer, the programmed instruction specialist, the educational technologist, the school psychologist or guidance counsellor, the educational administrator or society at large.

Psychology versus educational psychology

Since both psychology and educational psychology deal with the problem of learning, how can we distinguish between the theoretical and research interests of each discipline in this area? As an applied science, educational psychology is not concerned with general laws of learning *per se*, but only with those properties of learning that can be related to efficacious ways of *deliberately* effecting stable cognitive changes that have social value (Ausubel, 1953). Education, therefore, refers to guided or manipulated learning directed towards specific practical ends. These ends may be defined as the long-term acquisition of stable bodies of knowledge and of the capacities needed for acquiring such knowledge.

The psychologist's interest in learning, on the other hand, is much more general. Many aspects of learning, other than the efficient achievement of the above-designated competencies and capacities for growth in a directed context, concern him. More typically, he investigates the nature of simple, fragmentary or short-term learning experiences, which are presumably more representative of learning in general, rather than the kinds of long-term learning involved in assimilating extensive and organized bodies of knowledge.

The following kinds of learning problems, therefore, are particularly indigenous to psychoeducational research: (*a*) discovery of the *nature* of those aspects of the learning process affecting the acquisition and long-term retention of organized bodies of knowledge in the learner; (*b*) discovery of ways to achieve long-range improvement of learning and problem-solving capacities; (*c*) discovery of which cognitive and personality characteristics of the learner, and of which interpersonal and social aspects of the learning environment affect subject-matter learning outcomes, motivation for learning, and ways of assimilating school material; and (*d*) discovery of appropriate and maximally efficient ways of organizing and presenting learning materials and of deliberately motivating and directing learning towards specific goals.

Another way of epitomizing the difference between the two disciplines is to say that general aspects of learning are a concern of the psychologist, whereas classroom learning (that is, deliberately guided learning of subject matter in a particular social context) is the special province of the educational psychologist. The subject matter of educational psychology, therefore, can be inferred directly from the problems facing the classroom teacher. The latter must generate interest in subject matter, inspire commitment to learning, motivate pupils, and help induce realistic aspirations for educational achievement. He must decide what is important for pupils to learn, ascertain what learning they are ready for, pace instruction properly, and decide on the appropriate size and difficulty level of learning tasks. He is expected to organize subject matter expeditiously, present materials clearly, simplify learning tasks at initial stages of mastery and integrate current and past learnings. It is his responsibility to arrange practice schedules and reviews, to confirm, clarify and correct, to ask critical questions, to provide suitable rewards, to evaluate learning and development and, where feasible, to promote discovery learning and problem-solving ability. Finally, since he is concerned with teaching groups of students in a social environment, he must grapple with problems of group instruction, individualization, communication and discipline.

Thus the scope of educational psychology as an applied science is exceedingly broad, and the potential rewards it offers in terms of the social value of facilitating the subject-matter learning of pupils are proportionately great.

In what sense is educational psychology an 'applied' discipline?

Few persons would take issue with the proposition that education is an applied or engineering science. It is an applied science* because it is concerned with the realization of certain practical ends that have social value. The precise nature of these ends is highly controversial in terms of both substance and relative emphasis. To some individuals the function of education is to transmit the ideology of the culture, a core of knowledge and intellectual skills. To others, education is primarily concerned with the optimal development of potentiality for growth and achievement – not only with respect to cognitive abilities, but also with respect to personality goals and adjustment. Disagreement regarding ends, however, neither removes education from the category of science nor makes it any less of an applied branch of knowledge. It might be mentioned in passing that automobile engineers are also not entirely agreed as to the characteristics of the 'ideal' car; and physicians disagree violently in their definition of health.

Regardless of the ends it chooses to adopt, an applied discipline becomes a science only when it seeks to ground proposed means to ends on propositions that can be validated empirically. The operations involved in such an undertaking are commonly subsumed under the term 'research'. The question under discussion here relates to the nature of research in applied science or, more specifically, in education. Is educational research a field in its own right, with theoretical problems and a methodology of its own, or does it

---

* The term 'applied' is used here to distinguish between sciences which are orientated towards practical ends, as opposed to 'basic' or 'parent' sciences which do not have this orientation. 'Applied' does not imply that the content of the practical disciplines consists of applications from the basic or parent disciplines. The *problems* rather than the *knowledge* of applied sciences are 'applied'.

merely involve the operation of applying knowledge from 'pure' scientific disciplines to practical problems of pedagogy?

Despite the fact that education is an applied science, educational psychologists have manifested a marked tendency to extrapolate uncritically from research findings of laboratory studies of simplified learning situations to the classroom learning environment. This tendency reflects the fascination which many research workers feel for the 'basic-science' approach to research in the applied sciences, as well as their concomitant failure to appreciate its inherent limitations. They argue that progress in educational psychology is made more rapidly by focusing indirectly on basic-science problems in general psychology than by trying to come to grips directly with the applied-science problems that are indigenous to the field. Spence (1959), for example, perceived classroom learning as much too complex to permit the discovery of general laws of learning and advocated a straightforward application of the laws of learning discovered in the laboratory to the classroom situation; he saw very little scope, however, for applying the latter laws to problems of educational practice. Melton (1959) and Hilgard (1964) take a more eclectic position. They would search for basic-science laws of learning in both laboratory and classroom contexts, and would leave to the educational technologist the task of conducting the research necessary for implementing these laws in actual classroom practice.

My position, in other words, is that the principles governing the nature and conditions of classroom learning can be discovered only through an applied type of research that actually takes into account both the kinds of learning that occur in the classroom and the salient characteristics of the learner. We cannot merely apply to classroom learning general basic-science laws that are derived from the laboratory study of qualitatively different and vastly simpler instances of learning. Most attempts to do so, as, for example, Mandler's (1962) attempt to explain complex cognitive functioning in terms of the laws of association, or Sheffield's (1961) recent explanation of the hierarchical learning of sequentially organized materials in terms of the principle of contiguous conditioning, are extremely tortuous.

Laws of classroom learning at an applied* level are needed by the educational technologist before he can hope to conduct the research preparatory to effect scientific changes in teaching practices. He can be aided further by

* These laws are just as 'basic' as basic-science laws. The terms 'basic' and 'applied' refer to the distinction between basic ('pure', 'parent') and applied ('practical') sciences made earlier. 'Basic' does not mean 'fundamental'. In the latter sense, applied research is just as basic for its distinctive domain as research in the pure sciences is for its domain.

principles of teaching which are intermediate in generality and prescriptive-
ness between laws of classroom learning and the technological problems that
confront him. Contrary to Spence's (1959) contention, the greater complexity
and number of determining variables involved in classroom learning does
not preclude the possibility of discovering precise laws with wide applicability from one educational situation to another. It simply means that such
research demands the experimental ingenuity and sophisticated use of
modern techniques of research design.

The basic science versus the applied science approach

Three different kinds of research orientations have been adopted by those
who are concerned with scientific progress in applied disciplines such as
medicine and education: (*a*) basic-science research, (*b*) extrapolated research
in the basic sciences, and (*c*) applied research (Ausubel, 1953).

The basic-science research approach is predicated on the very defensible
proposition that applied sciences are ultimately related to knowledge in the
sciences on which they are based. It can be demonstrated convincingly, for
example, that progress in medicine is intimately related to progress in general
biochemistry and bacteriology; progress in engineering to progress in physics
and chemistry; and progress in education to advances in general psychology,
statistics and sociology. However, two important sets of qualifications have
to be placed on the value of basic-science research for the applied sciences:
qualifications of purpose or relevance and qualifications of the level of
applicability.

By definition, basic-science research is concerned with the discovery of
general laws of physical, biological, psychological and sociological phenomenology as an end in itself. Researchers in these fields would not object to
having their findings applied to practical problems that have social value. In
fact, there is reason to believe that they are motivated to some extent by this
consideration. But the design of basic-science research bears no intended
relation whatsoever to problems in the applied disciplines; its aim is solely to
advance knowledge. Ultimately, of course, such knowledge is applicable in
a very broad sense to practical problems; but since the research design is
not orientated to the solution of these problems, this applicability is apt to
be quite indirect and unsystematic, and relevant only over a time span too
long to be meaningful to the immediate needs of the applied disciplines.

The second qualification has to do with the level at which findings in the
basic sciences can be applied once their relevance has been established. It
should be self-evident that such findings exhibit a much higher level of

generality than the problems to which they can be applied. At the level of application, specific ends and conditions are added that demand *additional* research to indicate the precise way in which the general law operates in the specific case. That is, the applicability of general principles to specific problems is *not given* in the statement of the general principle, but must be explicitly worked out for each individual problem. Knowledge about nuclear fission, for example, does not tell us how to make an atomic bomb or an atomic-powered airplane.

In fields such as education, the problem of generality is further complicated by the fact that practical problems often exist at higher levels of complexity (with respect to the order of phenomenology involved) than do the basic-science findings that require application. New variables are added which may *qualitatively* alter the general principles from the basic science so that at the applied level they have substrate validity but lack explanatory or predictive value. For example, antibiotic reactions that take place in test tubes do not necessarily take place in living systems, and methods of rote learning that children use in mastering lists of nonsense syllables in the laboratory do not necessarily correspond to methods of learning they use in acquiring a meaningful grasp of subject matter in the classroom.

The basic-science approach in educational research, therefore, is subject to many serious disadvantages. Its relevance is too remote and indirect because it is not orientated towards solving educational problems. Its findings, if relevant, are applicable only if much additional research is performed to translate general principles into the more specific form pertinent to the task-specialized and more complex context of pedagogy.

These limitations would not be so serious if they were acknowledged. It would be defensible for educational institutions to set aside a small portion of their research funds for basic-science research as a long-term investment. But since the limitations of this approach are *not* generally appreciated, some bureaux of educational research confidently invest their major resources in basic-science programs, and then complacently expect that the findings that emerge will be both relevant and applicable in their original form to educational problems.

Naïveté with respect to the immediate applicability of findings from the basic-science approach has led to very serious distortions in our knowledge of those pedagogical aspects of the psychology of learning. The psychology of learning that teachers study is based on findings that have been borrowed from general psychology wholesale without much attempt to test their applicability to the kinds of learning situations in classrooms. It would be a shocking situation indeed if a comparable procedure were practised in medicine; that is, if physicians employed therapeutic techniques validated only *in vitro* or by animal experimentation.

The second approach taken up by research in the applied disciplines is based on the extrapolations from the basic sciences. Unlike pure basic-science research, this approach is orientated towards the solution of practical problems. It starts out by identifying significant problems in the applied field, and designs experiments to be solved on an analogous but highly simplified basic-science level. In this way it satisfies the important criterion of relevance, but must still contend with the problem of level of applicability. The rationale of this approach is that many practical problems are so complex that they must be reduced to simpler terms, and patterned after simpler models, before anyone can develop fruitful hypotheses leading to their solution. Once the problems are simplified, control and measurement become more manageable.

Extrapolations from the basic-science research may have genuine merit provided that the resulting research findings are regarded only as 'leads' or hypotheses to be tested in the applied situation, rather than as definitive answers to problems in pedagogy. As has been noted, educational researchers have a tendency to extrapolate findings from basic science to pedagogical problems without conducting the additional research necessary to bridge the gap between the two levels of generality involved.

The third approach to educational research is the most relevant and direct of the three, yet ironically it is least used of all. When research is performed in relation to the actual problems of education, under the conditions in which they are to be found in practice, the problems of relevance and extrapolation do not arise.* Most rigorous research in applied disciplines other than education is conducted at this level. The research program of a hospital or medical school would be regarded as seriously unbalanced if most of its funds and efforts went into pure biochemical or bacteriological research instead of into applied and clinical research. The major responsibility for furthering research in those theoretical areas belongs to graduate departments of chemistry and bacteriology. On the other hand, unless medical schools undertake to solve their own applied and clinical problems, who else will? The same analogy obviously holds true for education.

Although applied research presents greater difficulties with respect to

* Applied research is also directed towards the discovery of *general* laws within the framework of its applied ends. The generalizations it discovers, therefore, exist at a different plane of generality than those of 'basic' science research.

research design, control and measurement, the rewards are correspondingly greater. Certainly these problems cannot be deliberately avoided. If other applied disciplines have been able to evolve satisfactory research methodologies, there is no reason why education cannot also do so. In fact, if any applied discipline with unique and distinctive problems of its own is to survive as a science it is obliged to do so.

Many of the better known generalizations in educational psychology – the principle of readiness, the effects of overlearning, the concrete-to-abstract trend in conceptualizing the environment – illustrate the pitfalls of the basic-science approach to educational research. They are interesting and potentially useful ideas to curriculum specialists and educational technologists, but are of little use to educational practice until they are particularized at an applied level. The prevailing lack of particularization damages the 'image' of educational psychology in so far as it induces many beginning teachers to nurture unrealistic expectations about the current usefulness of these principles. Subsequently, after undergoing acute disillusionment, they may lose whatever confidence they originally had in the value of a psychological approach to educational problems.

The need for applied research in these areas is well illustrated by the principles of readiness. At present we can only speculate as to what curriculum sequences would look like if they took into account precise and detailed (but currently unavailable) research findings on readiness for the study of different subject areas, for different sub-areas and levels of difficulty within an area, and for different methods of teaching the same material. For example, because of the unpredictable specificity of readiness, as shown by the fact that four- and five-year-olds can profit from training in pitch but not in rhythm (Jersild and Bienstock, 1931, 1935), valid answers cannot be derived from logical extrapolation; they require meticulous empirical research in a school setting. The next step involves the development of teaching methods and materials appropriate for taking optimal advantage of existing degrees of readiness, and for increasing readiness wherever necessary and desirable. But because these research data are not generally available, except perhaps in reading, we can pay only lip service to principles of readiness in curriculum planning.

The basic-science-extrapolation approach, of course, has several very attractive methodological advantages in verbal learning experiments. First, by using nonsense syllables of equal meaninglessness, it is possible to work with additive units of equal difficulty. Second, by using relatively meaningless learning tasks, such as equated nonsense syllables, it is possible to eliminate, for the most part, the indeterminable influence of meaningful antecedent experience, which naturally varies from one individual to another. But it is precisely this interaction between new learning tasks and existing knowledge in the learner that is the distinctive feature of meaningful learning.

Thus, although the use of nonsense syllables doubtlessly adds methodological rigour to the study of learning, the very nature of the material limits the applicability of experimental findings to a type of short-term, discrete learning which is rare in both everyday situations and the classroom. Nevertheless, even though there are no *a priori* grounds for supposing that meaningful and non-meaningful learning and retention occur in the same way, the findings from rote-learning experiments have been commonly applied to meaningful learning situations. One cannot have one's cake and eat it too. If one chooses the particular kind of methodological rigour associated with the use of rote materials, one must also be satisfied with applying the findings from such experiments only to rote-learning tasks.

In conclusion, therefore, educational psychology is unequivocally an applied discipline, but it is not general psychology applied to educational problems any more than mechanical engineering is general physics applied to problems of designing machinery or medicine is general biology applied to problems of diagnosing, curing and preventing human diseases. In the above applied disciplines, general laws from the parent discipline are not applied to practical problems; instead, separate bodies of applied theory exist that are just as basic as the theory underlying the parent disciplines but are stated at a lower level of generality and with more direct relevance for and applicability to the problems in their respective fields.

The particular properties of knowledge in the applied sciences have also been exaggerated. Such knowledge involves more than the technological application of generalizations from basic science to current practical problems. The applied sciences are also disciplines *in their own right*, with distinctive and relatively enduring bodies of theory and methodology that cannot be derived or extrapolated from the basic sciences to which they are related. It is simply not true that only knowledge of the basic sciences can be related to and organized around general principles. Each of the applied biological sciences (e.g. medicine and agronomy) possesses an independent body of general principles underlying the detailed knowledge in its field, in addition to being related in a more general way to basic principles in biology.

Selected readings

Theories of learning versus theories of teaching

Disillusionment regarding the relevance and usefulness of learning theory for educational practice has been responsible, in part, for the recent emergence of 'theories of teaching' that are avowedly independent of theories of learning. The justification for such theories of teaching has been advanced on both historical and logical grounds.

THE HISTORICAL ARGUMENT

Gage (1964) cites the historical record in his argument that theories of learning have had very little applicability to and influence on educational practice, whether in educational psychology textbooks, in courses devoted to teaching methods, or in the everyday operations of classroom teaching. He argues further that theories of learning are inherently irrelevant for problems of instruction, and should therefore be replaced by theories of teaching in dealing with such problems. For example, he states that:

> While theories of learning deal with the ways in which an organism learns, theories of teaching deal with the ways in which a person influences an organism to learn. . . . To satisfy the practical demands of education, theories of learning must be 'stood on their head' so as to yield theories of teaching. [pp. 268–269]

Actually, *both* of these arguments are based essentially on the historical failure of learning theory to provide a psychologically relevant basis for pedagogic practice. This undeniable shortcoming of learning theory is by no means a necessary or inherent limitation in its applicability to education. It is merely characteristic of the prevailing brand of school learning theory, which, in general, does not deal with the kind of learning that occurs in the classroom but with the extrapolations from the main body of laboratory learning theory. A realistic and scientifically viable theory of classroom learning, in contrast, would be primarily concerned with complex and meaningful types of verbal and symbolic learning that take place in school and similar learning environments, and also with giving a prominent place to those *manipulable* factors that affect it. There is, in other words, a very close relationship between knowing how a pupil learns and the manipulable variables influencing learning, on the one hand, and knowing what to do to help him learn better, on the other. By 'teaching' we mean primarily the deliberate guidance of learning processes along lines suggested by relevant classroom learning theory. It would seem reasonable, therefore, that the discovery of

266

the most effective methods of teaching would be inherently dependent upon and related to the status of learning theory.

Of course, only *general* principles of learning could be considered as part of classroom learning theory. The more applied and prescriptive aspects of pedagogy that are derived from these principles would constitute a theory of instruction and would continue to be taught in methods courses.

THE LOGICAL ARGUMENT

In contrast to Gage's historical argument, B. O. Smith (1960) presents a strictly logical rationale for formulating theories of teaching that are wholly independent of theories of learning. He bases his case on the propositions that learning and teaching are neither coextensive with nor inextricable from each other, and that a theory of learning cannot tell us how to teach.

First, Smith's insistence that learning and teaching are different and separately identifiable phenomena admittedly does more than belabour the obvious. It clears up the confusion implied in the statement that 'if the child has not learned, the teacher has not taught', or else has taught incompetently. Teaching and learning are not coextensive, for teaching is only one of the conditions, and not a necessary or sufficient one, which may influence learning. Thus pupils can learn without being taught, that is, by teaching themselves; and even if teaching is manifestly competent, it does not necessarily lead to learning if the pupils concerned are inattentive, unmotivated or cognitively unprepared.

Nevertheless, once these unwarranted inferences about the coextensiveness of learning and teaching are discarded, it is useful to focus on those aspects of teaching and learning that are related to each other. These relationships include the purposes, effects and evaluation of teaching. Thus, although it is true that teaching is logically distinct from learning, and that what pupils learn can be analysed independently of what they are taught, what would be the practical advantage of so doing? The facilitation of learning is the only proper end of teaching. We do not teach as an end in itself but only that pupils may learn; and even though the pupils' failure to learn does not necessarily indict the teacher, learning is still the only feasible measure of teaching merit. Further, as has been pointed out, teaching itself is effective only to the extent that it manipulates effectively those psychological variables that govern learning.

Second, even though a valid theory of learning cannot tell us how to teach, in a prescriptive sense, it does offer us general principles of teaching that can be formulated in terms of both intervening psychological processes and cause–effect relationships. It is largely from a theory of learning that we can develop defensible notions of how crucial factors in the learning–teaching situation can be most effectively manipulated. The only other possible approach is either to vary teaching factors at random or to rely on intuition. The latter approach is more time-consuming, and can only yield purely empirical laws that cannot be formulated in general terms with respect to the psychological conditions and relevant cognitive processes involved.

It is realized, of course, that an adequate theory of learning is necessary but does not provide a sufficient condition for the improvement of instruction. Valid principles of teaching, though necessarily based on relevant principles of learning, are not, as pointed out above, simple and direct applications of these principles. Laws of classroom learning merely provide the general direction for discovering effective teaching principles; they do not indicate *per se* what these principles are. The formulation of teaching principles requires much supplementary research that takes into account practical problems and new instructional variables not implicit in the learning principle. In other words, one can consider basic principles of teaching as applied derivatives of school learning theory; they are products of an engineering type of research and are based on such modifications of learning theory as are necessitated by the practical difficulties or the additional new variables involved in teaching.

As Smith (1960) asserts in *Critical Thinking*, simply by knowing 'the cause of a phenomenon', one does not thereby acquire control of it 'for practical ends' [p. 87]. (For example, we can know the cause of a disease without knowing how to treat it, and we can treat a disease successfully without knowing its cause.) It is undeniable that many practical and useful inventions are made accidentally without any understanding of the explanatory principles and relevant variables involved. But who would advocate this as a deliberate research strategy? Ordinarily, scientists search for practical methods of control that can be related to general statements of relationship among the relevant variables involved. The superiority of this approach lies in the fact that methods of control that are relatable to general principles are not only understandable and interpretable, but more widely transferable to other practical problems. We could, for example, discover as an empirical fact that using teaching method X facilitates learning. But the practical value of such knowledge is quite limited. Would it not be preferable to formulate the research problem so that we could ascertain in what ways method X influences relevant psychological variables and intervening cognitive states in the course of facilitating learning, retention or problem solving? It is an extreme waste of time and effort to search for more efficient methods of teaching that can be described only in terms of descriptive characteristics of the teaching act and cannot be related to laws of learning.

Finally, although knowledge of causation does not imply immediate discovery of control procedures, it does constitute a tremendous advantage in discovering them. For one thing, it narrows the field; for another, it enables one to try procedures that have proven successful in controlling related conditions. Knowing that tuberculosis was caused by a micro-organism, for example, did not provide us immediately with a cure or a preventative. But it enabled us to try approaches such as vaccines, immune sera, antisepsis, quarantine and chemotherapy that had been used successfully in treating other infectious diseases. In the same sense, knowledge of the cause of cancer would help immeasurably in discovering a cure, and knowledge of the nature and relevant variables involved in concept acquisition would be of invaluable assistance in devising effective methods of teaching concepts.

The decline of classroom learning theory

The serious decline in knowledge and theorizing about classroom learning that has taken place over the past fifty years, accompanied by the steady retreat of educational psychologists from the classroom, has not been without adequate cause. Much of this can be attributed to the scientific disrepute into which studies of classroom learning have fallen as a result of both glaring deficiencies in conceptualization and research design, and excessive concern with the improvement of narrowly conceived academic skills and techniques of instruction rather than with the discovery of more general principles affecting the improvement of classroom learning and instruction in *any* subject-matter field. The vast majority of studies in the field of classroom learning, after all, has been conducted by teachers and other non-professional research workers in education. In contrast, laboratory studies of simple learning tasks were invested with the growing glamour and prestige of the experimental sciences, and thus made possible the investigation of general learning variables under rigorously controlled conditions.

Thus the more scientifically conducted research in learning theory has been undertaken largely by psychologists unconnected with the educational enterprise who have investigated problems quite remote from the type of learning that goes on in the classroom. The focus has been on animal learning and on short-term and fragmentary rote or non-verbal forms of human learning, rather than on the learning and retention of organized bodies of meaningful material. Experimental psychologists, of course, can hardly be criticized if laboratory studies on non-verbal and rote verbal learning have had little applicability to the classroom. Like all pure research efforts in the basic sciences, these studies were designed to yield only general scientific laws as ends in themselves. The blame, if any is to be assigned, must certainly fall upon educational psychologists who, in general, have failed to conduct the necessary applied research and have succumbed to the temptation of applying the theories and findings of their experimental colleagues to problems of classroom learning.

Finally, for the past thirty years, educational psychologists have been preoccupied with measurement and evaluation, personality development, mental hygiene, group dynamics and counselling. Despite the self-evident centrality of classroom learning and the cognitive development of the psychological aspects of education, these areas were ignored (Ausubel, 1963) both theoretically and empirically.

Although the withdrawal of educational psychologists from problems of meaningful classroom learning was temporarily expedient, it was, in the long run, very unfortunate on both theoretical and research grounds. In the first place, materials for rote learning are represented and organized quite differently from those for meaningful learning. Not only are the respective learning processes very dissimilar, but the significant variables involved in the two processes are also markedly different, and, where similar, have very different effects. In the second place, it is evident that a distinction must be made between learning tasks involving the short-term acquisition (of single, somewhat contrived concepts, of solution to artificial problems, or of arbitrary associations) in a laboratory setting and the long-term acquisition and retention (of the complex network of interrelated ideas characterizing an organized body of knowledge that is presented to the learner for active incorporation into his cognitive structure) required in a classroom.

Hence the extrapolation of school learning problems from rote learning theory has had many disastrous consequences. It has perpetrated erroneous conceptions about the nature and conditions of classroom learning; it has led educational psychologists to neglect research on factors influencing meaningful learning, hence delaying the discovery of more effective techniques of verbal exposition; and, finally, it has caused some educators to question the relevance of learning theory to the educational enterprise and to formulate theories of teaching that attempt to conceptualize the nature, purposes and effects of instruction without considering its relationship to learning.

Still another reason for the decline in classroom learning theory can be found in an examination of its historical development during the twentieth century. First, E. L. Thorndike initiated a movement that separated school learning theory from its concern with the acquisition of large bodies of organized knowledge (as represented by the scholastic and humanistic philosophers and by such educational theorists as Herbart) and focused attention on a mechanistic and reductionistic concern with the acquisition of discrete units of such knowledge by rote. This mechanistic concern was reinforced later by behaviourism, neobehaviourism, Pavlovian psychology, a revival of associationism, the functionalism of the twenties and thirties, and Skinnerian psychology and the teaching-machine movement it spawned. Second, the immediate theoretical reaction to connectionism, associationism and behaviourism, namely the gestalt and field theory approaches, failed to provide a viable theoretical alternative for educational psychology. Their doctrinaire overemphasis on a perceptual model of learning and retention led to a vastly oversimplified interpretation of the actual learning task involved in the acquisition of subject matter; an overvaluation of the role of stimulus properties and stimulus organization, with a corresponding undervaluation of the role of existing cognitive structure in school learning; an emphasis on nativistic explanatory principles that was quite alien to the very spirit of education; and an unrealistic preoccupation with discovery learning and problem solving that diverted attention from the more basic reception aspects of classroom learning. Third, John Dewey and the progressive education movement derogated expository teaching, verbal learning, structured learning experience and the importance of practice and testing, and overemphasized direct, non-verbal, concrete-empirical experience and learning by discovery.

Prerequisites for a discipline of educational psychology

The foregoing historical considerations and substantive propositions regarding the definition of educational psychology, its relationships to general psychology, and its status as an applied discipline lead to the conclusion that a minimum number of crucial prerequisites must first be met before educational psychology can emerge as a viable and flourishing discipline. First, the acquisition of certain basic intellectual skills, the learning and retention of subject-matter knowledge, and the development of problem solving capabilities must be regarded as the main practical concerns of theory and research in educational psychology. Second, the attainment of these objectives must be conceptualized as products of meaningful verbal or symbolical learning and retention, and a cogent theory of such learning and retention

271

must be formulated in terms of manipulable independent variables. Third, the elaboration of this theory implies the delineation of unambiguous distinctions between meaningful learning and other forms of learning such as classical and operant conditioning, rote verbal, instrumental, perceptual-motor and simple discrimination learning. It also implies distinction between varieties of meaningful verbal learning such as representational or vocabulary learning, concept learning and propositional learning, and between reception and discovery learning. Fourth, meaningful verbal learning must be studied in the form in which it actually occurs in classrooms. In other words, it must be studied as the guided, long-term learning in a social context of large bodies of logically organized and interrelated concepts, facts and principles rather than as the short-term and fragmented learning of discrete and granulated items of information represented by short-frame teaching-machine programs.

The predicted new look in educational psychology

It is obviously difficult to separate the objective delineation of future research trends in educational psychology from a statement of personal values and preferences in this area. Nevertheless, although frankly acknowledging this serious limitation at the very outset, I still venture to predict the emergence of four major trends in the coming decade. First, I am confident that educational psychologists will return to the classroom to study the kinds of learning processes that are involved in the meaningful acquisition of subject matter, instead of continuing to apply to such processes theories and evidence derived from highly simplified instances of non-verbal or rote verbal learning in laboratory situations. Second, I think we will shortly cease pretending that meaningful classroom learning consists merely of a designated series of problem solving tasks, and will also make a serious attempt to study the learning of ideas and information presented by teachers and textual materials. Third, I feel reasonably certain that we will devise appropriate methods of investigating the effects of general variables influencing meaningful learning, both singly and in combination, instead of vainly speculating on these effects from the results of particular curriculum improvement projects (e.g. the PSSC and the UICSM) in which an indeterminate number of variables are manipulated in an uncontrolled and indeterminate fashion. Fourth, I am hopeful that we will focus our attention increasingly on the long-term learning and retention of large bodies of sequentially organized subject matter rather than on the short-term mastery of fragmentary learning tasks.

What about the product of this research activity; that is, the future shape of the discipline? I am hopeful that the educational psychology of tomorrow will be primarily concerned with the nature, conditions, outcomes and evaluation of classroom learning, and will cease to be an unstable and eclectic amalgam of rote learning theory, developmental and social psychology, the psychology of adjustment, mental hygiene, measurement and client-centred counselling. Thus, hopefully, the new discipline will not consider such topics as child development, adolescent psychology, the psychology of adjustment, mental hygiene, personality and group dynamics as ends in themselves but will consider them only as they bear on classroom learning. It will confine itself only to psychological theories, evidence, problems and issues that are of *direct* concern either to the serious student of education or to the future teacher in his role as facilitator of school learning. It will also eliminate *entirely* many topics normally covered in educational psychology courses: the nature and development of needs, general determinants of behaviour, general reactions to frustration, developmental tasks, mechanisms of adjustment, parent-child relationships, non-cognitive development during infancy and the preschool years, and physical development. While it is true that physical development during childhood affects motor coordination, writing and popularity in the peer group and that physical changes in adolescence affect the self-concept, emotional stability, peer relations and athletic skills, an educational psychology course cannot cover everything. Prospective elementary school teachers will presumably have a course in child development, and prospective secondary school teachers will presumably have a course in adolescent psychology. Certain aspects of motivation *are* obviously relevant for classroom learning, but a general discussion of needs, their nature, function, development and classification, such as would be appropriate in a course in general psychology, hardly seems necessary.

One might reasonably anticipate that the new discipline of educational psychology will be concerned principally with meaningful symbolic learning, that is, reception and discovery that take place in the classroom. Some kinds of learning, such as rote learning and motor learning, are so inconsequential in this context as to warrant no systematic treatment in a course on educational psychology. Other kinds of learning (for example, the learning of values and attitudes) are not indigenous to the primary or distinctive function of the school and should be considered only in so far as they affect or are part of the learning of subject matter. Their more general aspects may be left to such courses as general and social psychology. And still other kinds of learning: animal learning, conditioning, instrumental learning and simple discrimination learning are completely irrelevant to most learning tasks in school, despite the fact that wildly extrapolated findings in these areas commonly pad many of the educational psychology textbooks. The new discipline, also, will hopefully not be eclectic in theoretical orientation, but will proceed from a consistent theoretical framework based on a cognitive theory of meaningful verbal learning. Greater stress would be placed on cognitive development and the content would be integrated more closely with related aspects of cognitive functioning.

Finally, an effort should be made to avoid oversimplified explanations, language and presentation of ideas, and to employ a level of discourse appropriate to the teaching of educational psychology to prospective teachers and mature students of education. Educational psychology is a complex rather than a simple subject. Hence to oversimplify it is to render the beginning student a serious disservice. Clarity and incisiveness of presentation do not require reversion to a kindergarten level of writing and illustration. In fact, it is the writer's firm conviction that the thinly disguised contempt many prospective teachers exhibit for courses in pedagogy and educational psychology stems from the indefensible attempt to expose them to watered-down, repetitive content and to an unnecessarily elementary level of vocabulary, sentence structure, illustration and pedagogic device.

It is true, of course, that if educational psychologists limit their coverage of learning to meaningful verbal learning, the paucity of experimental evidence in this area becomes painfully evident. This paucity is a reflection of the tendency that has prevailed in the past three or more decades for educational psychologists to extrapolate findings from animal, rote and perceptual-motor learning experiments rather than to do research on meaningful verbal learning. In my opinion, presenting certain significant theoretical propositions to students without definitive empirical support would for the time being be preferable to leaving large gaps in theory or filling them by means of unwarranted extrapolation.

Organization of the discipline

How will the subject matter of the new discipline of educational psychology be organized? Inasmuch as classroom instruction involves the manipulation of those variables influencing learning, a rational classification of learning variables can be of considerable value in clarifying both the nature of the learning process and the conditions that affect it. Such a classification also provides an organizational framework for the field, in a sense, since any course in educational psychology must, of necessity, be organized largely around the different factors influencing classroom learning.

274

One obvious way of classifying learning variables is to divide them into two categories: intrapersonal (factors within the learner) and situational (factors in the learning situation).

The intrapersonal category includes:

a : Cognitive structure variables – substantive and organizational properties of previously acquired knowledge in a particular subject-matter field that are relevant for the assimilation of another learning task in the same field. Since subject-matter knowledge tends to be organized in sequential and hierarchical fashion, what one already knows in a given field, and how well one knows it, obviously influence one's readiness for related new learnings.

b : Developmental readiness – the particular kind of readiness that reflects the learner's stage of intellectual development and the intellectual capacities and modes of intellectual functioning characteristic of that stage. The cognitive equipment of the fifteen-year-old learner evidently makes him readier for different kinds of learning tasks than does that of the six- or ten-year-old learner.

c : Intellectual ability – the relative degree of the individual's general scholastic aptitude (general intelligence or brightness level), and his relative standing with respect to particular differentiated or specialized cognitive abilities. How well a pupil learns subject matter in science, mathematics or literature obviously depends on his general intelligence, his verbal and quantitative abilities, his problem-solving ability, and his cognitive style.

d : Motivational and attitudinal factors – desire for knowledge, need for achievement and self-enhancement and ego-involvement (interest) in a particular kind of subject matter. These general variables affect such relevant conditions of learning as alertness, attentiveness, level of effort, persistence and concentration.

e : Personality factors – individual differences in level and kind of motivation, in personal adjustment, in other personality characteristics, and in level of anxiety. Subjective factors such as these have profound effects on quantitative and qualitative aspects of the learning process.

The situational category of learning variables includes:

a : Practice – its frequency, distribution, method and general conditions (including feedback or knowledge of results).

b : Instructional materials arrangement – in terms of amount, difficulty, step size, underlying logic, sequence, pacing and use of instructional aids.

c : Group and social factors – such as classroom climate, cooperation and competition, social-class stratification, cultural deprivation and racial segregation.

d : Characteristics of the teacher – his cognitive abilities, knowledge of subject matter, pedagogic competence, personality and behaviour.

As Gagné (1967) has written, intrapersonal and situational variables:

> undoubtedly have interactive effects upon learning. . . . The external variables cannot exert their effects without the presence in the learner of certain states derived from motivation and prior learning and development. Nor can the internal capabilities of themselves generate learning without the stimulation provided by external events. As a problem for research, the learning problem is one of finding the necessary relationships which must obtain among internal and external variables in order for a change in capability to take place. Instruction may be thought of as the institution and arrangement of the *external* conditions of learning in ways which will optimally interact with the internal capabilities of the learner, so as to bring about a change in these capabilities. [p. 295]

The above is not the only meaningful and useful way of classifying this set of learning variables. Another scheme would be to group them into cognitive and affective-social categories. The cognitive category would include the relatively objective intellectual factors, whereas the affective-social category would include the subjective and interpersonal determinants of learning. This scheme of categorization may be somewhat more convenient for the researcher, and may be more familiar to the classroom teacher than is the intrapersonal-situational scheme.

References

AUSUBEL, D. P. (1953) The nature of educational research. *Educational Theory*, 3, 314–20.

AUSUBEL, D. P. (1963) *The Psychology of Meaningful Verbal Learning: An Introduction to School Learning*. New York: Grune & Stratton.

GAGE, N. L. (1964) Theories of teaching. In *Theories of Learning and Instruction*. 63rd Yearbook of the National Society for the Study of Education, Part I. Chicago, University of Chicago Press. pp. 268–85.

GAGNÉ, R. M. (1967) Instruction and the conditions of learning. In SIEGEL, L. (ed.) *Instruction: Some Contemporary Viewpoints*. San Francisco, Chandler. pp. 291–313.

HILGARD, E. R. (1964) A perspective on the relationship between learning theory and educational practices. In *Theories of Learning and Instruction.* 63rd Yearbook of the National Society for the Study of Education, Part I. Chicago, University of Chicago Press. pp. 402–15.

JERSILD, A. T., and BIENSTOCK, S. F. (1931) The influence of training on the vocal ability of three-year-old children. *Child Development*, 2, 272–91.

JERSILD, A. T. and BIENSTOCK, S. F. (1935) Development of rhythm in young children. *Child Development Monographs*, No. 22.

MANDLER, G. (1962) From association to structure. *Psychological Review*, 69, 415–27.

MELTON, A. W. (1959) The science of learning and the technology of educational methods. *Harvard Educational Review*, 29, 96–106.

SHEFFIELD, F. D. (1961) Theoretical considerations in the learning of complex sequential tasks from demonstration and practice. In LUMSDAINE, A. A. (ed.) *Student Response in Programmed Instruction.* Washington, D.C., National Academy of Sciences, National Research Council. pp. 13–32.

SMITH, B. O. (1960) Critical thinking. In *Recent Research and Developments and their Implications for Teacher Education.* 13th Yearbook of the American Association of Colleges for Teacher Education, Washington, D.C. pp. 84–96.

SPENCE, K. W. (1959) The relation of learning theory to the technology of education. *Harvard Educational Review*, 29, 84–95.

Reprinted from *Psychology in the Schools*,
6 (3), July 1969, pp. 232–44.
Originally given at a Symposium on Research Opportunities
and Coming Changes in the Teaching of Psychology
to Teachers at the Annual Meeting of the
American Educational Research Association.

T

5

*Psychology in the teacher-preparation program**

JOHN HERBERT and DONALD WILLIAMS

Should prospective teachers have to study psychology? What psychological knowledge does a teacher need? There are likely to be many different answers to these questions. To the apprentice teacher who dislikes mathematics but is required to take a statistically orientated course in educational psychology, for example, the torture he undergoes seems futile, and nothing the instructor says or does will ever influence his teaching. To the instructor, on the other hand, no subject is more relevant to teaching, for he is certain that current research in his field is producing important results that will revolutionize education.

At present almost everyone who wishes to teach in public elementary and secondary schools is required by college faculties as well as by certification laws to take some courses in psychology. Prospective teachers probably constitute by far the largest group of students enrolled in psychology courses. But what psychology, if any, ought to be offered in teacher-preparation programs, and how much? These questions have been raised by educationists, psychologists and some of the livelier students, and lately they have been explored by a number of college and university departments and by a state-wide psychological foundations study group in Oregon. The difficulty of finding a widely acceptable answer may be gauged by the fact that in 1965 the Committee to Study the Improvement of Teaching Educational Psychology, which was composed of seven distinguished psychologists,† appointed by Division Fifteen of the American Psychological Association, and worked with psychologists across the nation, found that 'a detailed specification of the content of educational psychology was a task that was neither appropriate nor possible within the limits of this project'. [p. 4]

* This paper was prepared as part of a study undertaken at the request of Reed College and partly financed by the United States Office of Education, Department of Health, Education and Welfare.
† The members of the committee were: R. Stewart Jones (chairman), Gabriel Della-Piana, Philip Jackson, Bert Y. Kersh, Herbert Klausmeier, Aileen Schoeppe, M. C. Wittrock.

278

It would be presumptuous to attempt such a task here.* In view of the openness and importance of the question, however, it seems appropriate now to state the issues which seem to be emerging and to call for further discussion. This study, then, is an attempt to sample the range of opinion, with emphasis on material which is not readily accessible in published form; to report some solutions which have been proposed; to stimulate more thorough collection of information and opinions; and, finally, to suggest some directions that might usefully be followed in planning psychology courses for teachers.

The range of opinions

First, of course, there is the question of whether psychology has any place at all in teacher education. Some would deny it. Francis Keppel (1962) gives this description of their view:

> The efforts to use scientific methods to study human behaviour seem to them ridiculous if not impious. The result, they say, is a ponderous, pseudo-scientific language which takes ten pages to explain the obvious or to dilute the wisdom long ago learned in humanistic studies. They would argue that a few pages of Bacon or Montaigne are worth more than a three-volume psychological treatise. To build an art of teaching on the basis of the 'behavioural sciences', they suggest, is to build on sand. [p. 91]

The position Keppel described seems usually to be confined to those who are not themselves responsible for the professional preparation of teachers. Even among those directly concerned with teacher education, there are some, including psychologists, who appear to maintain that teachers ought not to be required to take psychology courses. Examination of their positions, however, usually reveals instead that they favour changes in the form and content of offerings to make them more meaningful and useful to teachers. In private conversations at the University of Chicago, Columbia University, Stanford University and the University of Toronto, psychologists expressed the opinion that psychology courses *as they are currently taught* are useless or even harmful to the work of teachers. One eminent psychologist said that educational psychology courses offered at present are 'baroque and arcane'.† In the words of another educational and clinical psychologist, they are poten-

* For a summary of the topics included in educational psychology textbooks, see Derek N. Nunney, Trends in the content of educational psychology, 1948–63. *Journal of Teacher Education*, 1964, **25** (4), 372–7.
† Matthew Miles, personal communication, April 1967.

tially dangerous because 'unless the beginning teacher has help in group management problems . . . the focus on the individual child may well be some barrier rather than a help'.* The doubts of these psychologists (and of other psychologists and teacher educators) were not based on doubts about the potential importance of the behavioural sciences to teachers generally or of educational psychology in particular. All responded with interest to the question and offered suggestions about what could usefully be taught to teachers. Their views will be presented later in this paper.

Among those who do consider psychology to be actually or potentially valuable to teachers are presumably the large number of staff members of advisory bodies who assist in the setting up of certification requirements and those of university and college programs for teachers who require the study of psychology as part of their program. Although at one time there was widespread criticism of these requirements, closer examination has tended to confirm the need to retain them. James B. Conant (1963) was at first sceptical but came to accept the necessity of some work in psychology, at least for elementary school teachers:

> . . . I have been convinced, largely by the testimony of students and teachers, that for those who teach children, psychology has much to say that is so valuable as to warrant the label 'necessary', at least for elementary teachers. I believe that research will continue that will yield generalizations sufficiently wide as to be called scientific. As an introduction to the point of view of those concerned with the behaviour of animals (including man), a general course in psychology would seem essential. [p. 136]

Support for the inclusion of psychology in the teacher-training program also recently came from B. F. Skinner (1965), who comments: 'Teachers . . . need the kind of help offered by a scientific analysis of behaviour. Fortunately such an analysis is now available.' [p. 80] Herbert F. LaGrone, Director of Teacher Education and Media for the American Association of Colleges for Teacher Education, also sees psychology as a useful part of the curriculum for teacher trainees. LaGrone (1964) advocates building a new series of five courses: 'Analytical Study of Teaching', 'Structure and Uses of Knowledge', 'Concepts of Human Learning and Development', 'Designs for Teaching-Learning' and 'Demonstration and Evaluation of Teaching Competencies' [pp. 16–58]. Each of these has a psychological component. Those who are concerned with the preparation of teachers of a particular discipline in the

---

* Jacob S. Kounin, personal communication, June 1967.

secondary schools also consider psychology as a necessary part of that preparation. The Commission on English (1965), for example, recommends that '. . . study in pedagogical processes include . . . one course in the psychology of learning' [p. 11].

Questionnaire results

A substantial number of experienced and student teachers seem to agree that psychology has an important place in teacher preparation, though what little specific information is available suggests that there may be very great diversity of opinion about what aspects of psychology and what kinds of instruction in psychology are useful or interesting.

NEA survey

In a recent survey conducted by the National Education Association, about seven out of every ten teachers responding (92·7 per cent of the sample responded) were satisfied with the contribution psychology courses had made to their success in teaching (see tabulation below). Results given in the published report of the survey (Davis, 1967) are restricted to undergraduate preparation and cannot be analysed to distinguish teachers with particular graduate degrees. However, when the responses of the 547 teachers with Masters degrees or more were compared with those of the 1632 teachers with Bachelor degrees or less, the percentage of responses was almost identical, suggesting a very similar attitude towards the psychology courses (as in other recent reports – Frey and Ellis, 1966). The survey is repeated and published at five-year intervals, and the figures given below (Davis, 1967, p. 10) confirm earlier findings.

Evaluation of teacher preparation by 2344 teachers responding

Question: In terms of actual contribution to your success in teaching, how would you evaluate the amount and quality of your undergraduate teacher-preparation program in the following areas?

Subject area	AMOUNT Too little	About right	QUALITY Excellent	Satisfactory	No preparation or quality poor
Psychology of learning and teaching	22·1%	68·5	15	68	13·2
Human Growth and development[1]	19·5	72·7	15·9	66·5	13·3

[1] Unpublished information, supplied by Dr Simeon P. Taylor, Assistant Director, Research Division, National Education Association, Washington, D.C.

Surveys at Cornell and Stanford Universities

Information about the views of experienced teachers who have completed five-year programs is difficult to obtain. A number of programs follow up their students, but their graduates are scattered and the rate of response is generally low. Thus, for example, Kenneth R. Stow's (1960) study at Cornell University, in its survey of 105 graduates who earned the M.Ed. degree between 1954 and 1959, received only seventy-six replies. Stanford University has consistently attempted to obtain information about the graduate of its MAT-type program. A carefully designed questionnaire was sent out each year to all graduates of the program, from 1960, when the first group of twenty-five students completed the course, through 1968, when over one hundred students graduated. In spite of considerable effort to ensure returns, only about 40 per cent of the 400 alumni of the program completed the form. Reed has experienced similar difficulties in obtaining responses to a questionnaire which was sent out this summer. However, after some effort, 108 completed questionnaires were secured from the 115 students who graduated from the MAT program over the last five years.

Even when the rate of response is low, however, the results of these surveys are interesting. It seems significant that although Philosophy of Education was by far the most popular course among graduates of Cornell's Master of Education programs (50·5 per cent reported to have liked this course best), Educational Psychology was rated the most important course (82·6 per cent thought it should be mandatory and 71·1 per cent thought the course in Educational Measurement and Testing should be mandatory, while 66·6 per cent felt that Philosophy of Education should be required). Results of the annual Stanford survey have not been reported, but another study, Report of the Secondary Education Committee 1967, submitted for use by Stanford instructors and staff members, gives some information about the students' reactions to certain activities in the educational psychology course.

In May 1967 a questionnaire was given to intern teachers at the end of their second quarter at Stanford, and all but five of the 125 students responded. Although no direct question was asked about the usefulness of psychology to teachers, there were some questions about specific aspects of the course. The results are too detailed to be reproduced here, but it seems worth while to summarize responses to some of the questions.

The following activities are examples of those found useless by more students than found them useful: the writing of a paper on adolescents, formulation of instructional strategies, study of taxonomies and participation as subjects in educational experiments. Aspects of the course which the majority of students found useful were: the writing of programs; the formulation of behavioural objectives for a unit and a nine- to twelve-week course; the planning of student evaluation; and 'micro-teaching'.*

Every topic or activity in educational psychology was either found useful or interesting by some group of students at Stanford. Although the majority of students responding recommended that lectures in educational psychology should be limited to a single summer term, most of the students found a substantial portion of the applied part of the work both useful and interesting.

Survey of MAT graduates at Reed College

At Reed, by means of the questionnaire already referred to, we recently surveyed the opinions of our MAT graduates about the contribution they believed psychology courses had made to their teaching. Some background information may be needed to interpret results. Reed MAT students, like those at Cornell and Stanford, are typically very successful liberal arts graduates who have taken few if any undergraduate courses in psychology or education. Before 1962 the Reed program required very little work in psychology – only a brief portion of a course in the Foundations of Public School Teaching. Offerings in psychology were increased, partly because of certification requirements and partly also at the request of the teaching interns. Until 1964 students normally took two courses in psychology.

In the survey following four questions are related to the students' opinions about the value of psychology courses. The results have not yet been fully analysed, but some of the main trends are clear. Question 13 asked: 'Have you found anything you learned in the psychology courses at Reed helpful in your teaching?' Of the students in the program during the two years from 1962–4, only a few more responded favourable than unfavourable, and in the year 1964–5 the negative replies exceeded the positive ones. Taking the three years together, fewer than 50 per cent of the students found the courses helpful. But in 1965–6 the number of students who believed that the courses were useful in their teaching jumped to 85 per cent, and in 1966–7 the figure remained relatively high at 71 per cent. A similar dramatic reversal occurred in the responses to Question 15: 'Did you find the courses useful for purposes other than classroom teaching?' During the two years, 1962–4, students

* Such teaching of small groups of students under close supervision is intended to train new teachers in a particular teaching skill, such as the use of silence or the encouraging of student participation in classroom discussions.

on the whole did not find them useful, by a narrow but definite margin. From 1965–7, however, three to four times as many students found the courses useful for purposes other than classroom teaching. Answers to Question 16 were more consistent: 'Did any of the courses contribute to your general education?' Affirmative answers were given by a substantial majority of the students each year, but even here there was a considerable increase over the last three years. Answers to Question 14 also shifted, but in a somewhat different way. During the first three years more students answered affirmatively than negatively to the question: 'Have you found any aspects of psychology that were not covered in the psychology courses at Reed that would have been helpful in your teaching?' During the last two years, however, answers were more evenly divided. This suggests that, as the work in psychology became more relevant to teaching, students felt less need for additional areas to be added to the psychology courses.

Tabulation of responses to questionnaire given to Reed MAT graduates, summer 1967 *Numbers in parentheses are percentages of total respondents.*

Question 13: Have you found anything you learned in the psychology courses at Reed helpful in your teaching? When and how?

Year	No. of graduates	No. of questionnaires returned	Yes	No	Non-commital	No response
1962–3	17	17	8 (47%)	5 (29%)	3 (18%)	1 (6%)
1963–4	23	22	9 (41%)	7 (32%)	4 (18%)	2 (9%)
1964–5	21	18	6 (33%)	9 (50%)	2 (11%)	1 (6%)
1965–6	28	27	23 (85%)	4 (15%)	—	—
1966–7	26	24	17 (71%)	5 (21%)	1 (4%)	1 (4%)
Totals	115	108	63 (58%)	30 (28%)	10 (9%)	5 (5%)

The results, then, show clearly that while in all years a reasonably large number of students found psychology contributed to their teaching, to other aspects of their work, and to their general education, the feeling was much stronger among students who participated in the program during the last two or three years. Each of the questions called for qualitative answers which have not yet been analysed but which may throw light on the reasons for the changes in attitude. However, it is possible to speculate without any ready

Question 14: Have you found any aspects of psychology that were not covered in the psychology courses at Reed that would have been helpful in your teaching?

Year	No. of graduates	No. of questionnaires returned	Needed additional psych. courses	Reed courses sufficient	Non-commital	No response
1962–3	17	17	8 (47%)	3 (18%)	4 (24%)	2 (12%)
1963–4	23	22	9 (41%)	2 (9%)	6 (27%)	5 (23%)
1964–5	21	18	12 (67%)	2 (11%)	—	4 (22%)
1965–6	28	27	13 (48%)	11 (41%)	2 (7%)	1 (4%)
1966–7	26	24	8 (33%)	10 (42%)	2 (8%)	4 (17%)
Totals	115	108	50 (46%)	28 (26%)	14 (13%)	16 (15%)

Question 15: Did you find the courses useful for purposes other than classroom teaching, getting a job or certification? Yes/No. Which courses were useful and how?

Year	No. of graduates	No. of questionnaires returned	Yes	No	Non-commital	No response
1962–3	17	17	7 (41%)	8 (47%)	—	2 (12%)
1963–4	23	22	5 (23%)	9 (41%)	2 (9%)	6 (27%)
1964–5	21	18	11 (61%)	4 (22%)	1 (6%)	2 (11%)
1965–6	28	27	22 (81%)	5 (19%)	—	—
1966–7	26	24	18 (75%)	4 (17%)	—	2 (8%)
Totals	115	108	63 (58%)	30 (28%)	3 (3%)	12 (11%)

Question 16: Did any of the courses contribute to your general education? If so, how?

Year	No. of graduates	No. of questionnaires returned	Yes	No	Non-commital	No response
1962–3	17	17	9 (53%)	3 (18%)	3 (18%)	2 (12%)
1963–4	23	22	12 (55%)	4 (18%)	1 (5%)	5 (23%)
1964–5	21	18	13 (72%)	2 (11%)	—	3 (17%)
1965–6	28	27	24 (89%)	2 (7%)	—	1 (4%)
1966–7	26	24	20 (83%)	2 (8%)	—	2 (8%)
Totals	115	108	78 (72%)	13 (12%)	4 (4%)	13 (12%)

analysis that since the survey (1962–7), there have been no changes in the nature of the student body or in the manner of selecting students, and since changes in staffing were continuous over the whole period, deliberate attempts at changing the courses themselves resulted in changes in the students' reactions. From 1965 on, instructors sought to provide interns with experiences that simulated some important teaching functions and enabled them to use and examine applications of psychology to their own work.*

Course content and objectives

Assuming that psychology has a part to play in teacher-preparation programs, the question remains: what should be taught, how and when? Educational psychologists usually respond to this question by asking for the objectives to be achieved by the teaching. Recently a group of psychologists,† after a series of conferences in Oregon, reached the conclusion that courses in psychology in teacher-preparation programs ought to aim at the following outcomes. They should:

a : Enable teachers to obtain orderly information about the classroom processes, using the disciplined resources of psychology.

b : Enable teachers to take a new look at classroom events, formulate hypotheses about students and learning, and test them to arrive at professional decisions.

c : Enable the instructors to screen out from teaching, students incapable of reaching professional decisions.

d : Help students to feel positively orientated towards psychological knowledge and skills, so that they will continue to apply them and to learn about them.

e : Enable teachers to assume the role of the teacher expected by administrators, parents and fellow teachers, and to possess the knowledge commonly commanded by professionals.

f : Provide the teacher with techniques for handling individual students and groups of students, with ways of shaping their behaviour, and with knowledge of how students go about shaping the teacher's behaviour.

g : Sensitize the teacher to his own students' feelings, for example those of hostility, insecurity, altruism and helpfulness, and to the ways of considering them in the classroom.

* A report of this research will be published by Reed College, Portland, Oregon.
† Psychological Foundations Planning Group, sponsored by the Oregon State Department of Education, Salem, Oregon, under a grant from the U.S. Department of Health, Education and Welfare.

286

This list of objectives cannot, of course, be taken to represent the views of educational psychologists generally, or even of those who attended the meetings in Oregon, since each item was of primary importance to only some of the participants. For example, Richard Ripple of Cornell University, who was present as a consultant, considered only the first two objectives to be critical and regarded all the others as definitely secondary. In describing the objectives of the course he teaches at Cornell, Ripple (1967) writes:

> . . . the psychological foundations can be said to be relevant in two general, but distinct ways. First educational psychology, as a body of information, can help in the generation of hypotheses. . . . A second contribution made by educational psychology is that of helping teachers acquire the attitudes and skills necessary to intelligent hypothesizing and the testing of hypotheses. This involves, for example, such skills as how to interpret data intelligently, how to observe accurately, how to avoid fallacies in making unwarranted inferences, how to make adequate decisions regarding what data should be gathered, ways in which data can be gathered and used, etc. [p. 2]

This position is distinctly that of the research-orientated psychologist. It aims at making the teacher a scientist who looks for problems and answers objectively and rigorously.

In contrast, Philip Jackson (1966) starts not from the definition of educational psychology as a field of inquiry, but from the description of the job of the teacher as it really is. 'When students are in front of him, and the fat is on the fire,' Jackson writes, 'the teacher tends to do what he *feels* or knows is right rather than with what he *thinks* is right.' Of course thought is involved, but '. . . it is thought of quite a different order from that which occurs in an empty classroom' [p. 13].

Psychological theory enters minimally into a teacher's thinking while he is facing his class, according to Jackson,* but it can assist him in preparing lessons before the students arrive (for example, considering in advance what to do about Billy who has to go to the toilet all the time) and in evaluating students' performances after they leave the classroom. During these periods, Jackson has said, teaching assumes the appearance of a 'highly rational process' in which the teacher uses psychology as one source of information and technique. We need a separate psychology for each of the two kinds of thinking that teachers do.

* Philip Jackson, personal communication, April 1967.

During the pre-active and post-active periods, according to Jackson, teachers may make decisions and establish and examine hypotheses. What is taught in the usual educational psychology course is relevant here. It is also relevant for another part of the teacher's work, the need to establish himself in the role of teacher and face his public – command the vocabulary of psychology and display the knowledge expected of him. During the period of actual teaching, however, the teacher faces a 'social maelstrom' to which the contents of courses and textbooks are irrelevant. He has to hobble along with some advice from the therapists until the social psychologists have more to offer.

Therapists such as Carl Rogers (1964) have still another view of the work of the teacher. His task is to be 'a facilitator of significant learning' [p. 5], to help students (including prospective teachers) learn what they find re-warding and to discover what has meaning in their present experiences. This comes from facing real problems, involving others in problems real to them, accepting with empathy other people's concerns and becoming sensitive to them. Psychology courses, or better, psychological experiences provided in the teacher-preparation program should not only exemplify these abilities but also help teachers to acquire them.

Social psychologists have something of the same orientation, but with more emphasis on inter-group relationships. Thus Mathew Miles of Teachers College, Columbia University, considers the problem not to be that of pro-viding courses for teachers, but of providing experiences such as sensitivity training, the use of observation techniques, interaction recording systems, and audio and video tapes to obtain information about their own teaching. Further, teachers should be familiar with various ways of shaping behaviour and with techniques that produce changes in people's attitudes and conduct. According to Miles,* traditional textbooks and courses, for example the sections dealing with learning, are useless in helping teachers to learn to teach or to improve teaching.

Some psychologists, for example Jacob Kounin in the letter cited above, feel even more strongly that help in group management must precede or accompany any work in psychology. Their feeling is supported by the frequency with which student teachers ask for more help in their relation-ships with their pupils, especially in dealing with discipline problems.

In spite of the great diversity of opinion, psychologists, educationists, administrators, teachers and student teachers appear to identify the difficulties

* Mathew Miles, personal communication, April 1967.

in a similar way, stressing the need for a more appropriate relationship between the academic study of educational psychology as a field of inquiry and the professional study of psychology in the preparation of classroom teachers.* Virtually every psychologist whose views were sought, including some not quoted here, expressed strong faith in the potential efficacy of psychological knowledge and skill to make a contribution to the performance of teachers,† but everyone either expressed strong doubts about the adequacy of the standard lecture course as a means to that end or else totally condemned the traditional course offerings.

When Philip Jackson, Jacob Kounin and Mathew Miles talk about the kind of training that would be helpful to teachers, they have in mind a series of experiences which would enable teachers to understand better how and why people, primarily themselves and students but also parents and administrators, respond to others. They do not mean a series of talks or even demonstrations or discussions, but a set of carefully planned activities involving the student teacher directly in the use and evaluation of psychological knowledge. Ripple also recognizes the need for classroom applications, though he would prefer to consider this the field of the colleague responsible for teaching methods while the professor of educational psychology teaches teachers to invent and test psychological hypotheses.

Frederick J. McDonald of Stanford University, on the other hand, would welcome the opportunity to teach the applications as well as the theory of particular units of psychology, partly because of the greater psychological efficacy of this combination and partly because of the opportunity to obtain feedback from students for research purposes.‡

We do not have the data to make inferences about the kind of work in psychology that Conant, the Commission on English, the students at Cornell or the teachers surveyed by the NEA would like to have offered to teachers. We do know, however, that LaGrone, the fifth-year students at Stanford and the teachers who had received the Reed MAT degree responded favourably to those parts of the program which bore most directly on teaching.

Recognizing then the need to teach the classroom applications of psychological theory in new ways, one must also recognize a serious obstacle in

---

* For a similar position in the United Kingdom, see Committee on Higher Education, *Evidence*, Part I, Vol. A, p. 107. Published with *Higher education : Report of the committee appointed by the Prime Minister under the chairmanship of Lord Robbins, 1961–63*. London: Her Majesty's Stationery Office, 1963.
† This is a change from the past. See, for example, James, Symonds, Watson, etc.
‡ Frederick J. McDonald, personal communication, July 1967.

the way of improvement. Teaching by providing experiences, whether they are of group interaction, of classroom events, of evaluative techniques or of shaping student behaviour or other aspects of psychology, is very demanding of staff and time. It certainly cannot be done satisfactorily in a course which at the same time attempts to give an organized survey of the total field of educational psychology, the sources of knowledge and the techniques of research.

Possible solutions

One solution might be to select only the most useful aspects of educational psychology and teach them theoretically and practically. Thus one might select testing and measurement or developmental psychology or learning or group interaction, depending on the preferences of the department or the instructor. This selective emphasis, however, would leave untouched most of the potential contributions of psychology to teaching and so leave the student in ignorance of many resources.

Another possible solution is the one which was proposed but eventually rejected at the State University of New York at Stony Brook (Peters, 1965). Each student was to have the right to choose one behavioural science (for example, anthropology, sociology or psychology) for study in depth, taking several courses in the particular field, in the expectation that this would enable him to bring the resources of that discipline to bear on his teaching and the examination of his teaching in an organized manner. One may well wonder whether the ability to make independent pedagogical applications would necessarily result from the academic study of any discipline. One may also maintain that psychology has a contribution to make to teaching and that no prospective teacher should be deprived of it.

A third suggestion made in conversation by McDonald would substitute for the lecture course given by one instructor a course in which a number of instructors would first lecture on their own specialties and then work through the applications of the topic discussed, using classroom experiences and research as needed.* Though this might be an ideal solution, it is administratively difficult to achieve. Even a university of the distinction of Stanford might have difficulty in coordinating and staffing a course of this type. Other institutions, especially smaller ones, are not likely to have enough staff members both expert in an area of psychology and knowledgeable about classroom teaching.

* Frederick J. McDonald, private communication, July 1967.

Programs for teacher education may well want to experiment with a dual approach, offering two-function-orientated courses instead of the traditional subject-orientated courses called Testing and Measurement, Child Development, Guidance and such. One would be a theoretical course, aimed at achieving the first four objectives identified by the Oregon Committee: the ordering of data, the use of the discipline of psychology, the formulation of hypotheses and the screening out of students incapable of making professional judgements. This course would also seek to enable teachers to assume the role of the professional educator, versed in the language of psychology.

This course then could form the foundation of an analytic-applied course, aimed at the other three objectives of the Oregon Committee: to help teachers feel that psychology is helpful to them in their contact with students and in classroom decisions, to sensitize the teacher to his own and his students' feelings and (together with the methods courses and the practical experience) to provide the insight necessary to incorporate the daily teaching experience into an intellectually integrated whole.

The theoretical course might well resemble some parts of currently offered courses, using materials, tests and ideas such as those which are described in the *Handbook for Instructors of Educational Psychology* or some of the more recent textbooks. Laboratory tasks would be related to this course, as they are now in many of the more effective programs. Students, aware that direct classroom applications would be developed in the applied-analytic course, could use their academic skills without the defensive reaction which comes when professional preparation is expected within an academic teaching format.

A. W. Foshay, of Teachers College, Columbia University, foresees a possible further development:

> We could think in terms of satellite courses, around a core psychology course. The core course would be taught by a psychologist and would contain psychological theories, research, etc. The satellite courses would be designed to help teachers apply the materials, and would be taught by professionals who were specially capable in assisting teachers to apply the psychological knowledge to their work.
>
> The intention then would be to prepare teachers who practiced the profession of pedagogy. They would be trained, partly through practice, to see the reasons behind the way teachers teach, even when the experienced teachers themselves do not know. They would cease to see teaching as a bag of tricks. When experienced teachers suggest to them

that it is important to start lessons definitely, they would be aware of the psychological reasons.*

Development needed

At present there are substantial difficulties facing the establishment of such a cluster of courses. One is the problem of working out the exact relationship between theoretical and applied courses, and in particular, the relationship of the instructors to one another and to the students. Perhaps progress along those lines is more likely to occur in the smaller colleges where classes are smaller, the possibility of experimenting with different course structures and faculty relationships is greater, and the problem of providing laboratory experiences in the schools is less overwhelming.

An equally serious problem is the scarcity of generally available materials for the applied work. Unlike the instructors of the theoretical, experimental or educational psychology courses, the faculty member attempting an analytic-applied course has to improvise his own movies, tapes, cases and even tests; a time-consuming, wasteful and unreliable process. There is a great need for help for teachers of applied courses. The answer to this need potentially could come from a sharing of resources among colleges, school districts and research institutes, to develop viable applied-analytic courses for instructors to adopt and adapt. However, leadership could hardly be expected from school districts or small colleges, which are unlikely to have the resources. It is ultimately the responsibility of large universities and research institutes. Courses need to be planned, outlined and developed; materials created, tried out and evaluated – so that professors of psychology and curriculum departments could work with teacher educators in an effective formulation of a program to help teachers in their increasingly complex work.

References

AUSUBEL, D. P. (1968) *Educational Psychology: a Cognitive View.* New York: Holt, Rinehart & Winston.

BIGGE, M.L., and HUNT, M.P. (1962) *Psychological Foundations of Education: An Introduction to Human Development and Learning.* New York, Harper and Row.

BLAIR, G. M., JONES, R. S., and SIMPSON, R. S. (1962) *Educational Psychology.* 2nd ed. New York, Macmillan.

* Arthur W. Foshay, private communication, April 1967.

CARPENTER, F., and HADDAN, E. (1964) *Systematic Applications of Psychology to Education.* New York, Macmillan.

COMMISSION ON ENGLISH (1965) *Freedom and Discipline in English.* New York, College Entrance Examination Board.

COMMITTEE ON HIGHER EDUCATION (1963) *Higher Education : Report of the Committee Appointed by the Prime Minister under the Chairmanship of Lord Robbins, 1961–63.* 7 vols. London, H.M.S.O.

COMMITTEE TO STUDY THE IMPROVEMENT OF TEACHING EDUCATIONAL PSYCHOLOGY (1965) (R. Steward Jones, chairman) *Handbook for Instructors of Educational Psychology.* Urbana, University of Illinois.

CONANT, J. B. (1963) *The Education of American Teachers.* New York, McGraw-Hill.

CRONBACH, L. J., in consultation with HILGARD, E., and SPALDING, W. (1963) *Educational Psychology.* 2nd ed. New York, Harcourt, Brace & World.

CROW, L. D., and CROW, A. (1963) *Educational Psychology.* rev. ed. New York, American Book Co.

DAVIS, H. (1967) Professional preparation for teaching. In *The American Public School Teacher, 1965–1966.* Research Report 1967–R4. Washington, D.C., National Education Association of the United States.

DOLL, R. C. (1964) *Curriculum Improvement : Decision-making and Process.* Boston, Allyn & Bacon.

FRANDSEN, A. N. (1961) *Educational Psychology : The Principle of Learning in Teaching.* New York, McGraw-Hill.

FREY, S., and ELLIS, J. (1966) Educational psychology and teaching: opinions of experienced teachers. *The Teachers College Journal,* 38 (3), 88–91.

INTERN ADVISORY COMMITTEE, School of Education, Stanford University (1967) *Report to the Secondary Education Committee.* Stanford, 22 May.

JACKSON, P. (1966) The way teaching is. In HITCHCOCK, C. (ed.) *The Way Teaching Is.* Seminar on Teaching, Washington, D.C., 1965. Association for Supervision and Curriculum Development and the Center for the Study of Instruction of the National Education Association.

JAMES, W. (1914) *Talks to Teachers on Psychology and to Students on Some of Life's Ideals.* New York, H. Holt.

KEPPEL, F. (1962) The education of teachers. In CHAUNCEY, H. (ed.) *Talks on American Education.* New York, Teachers College Press, Teachers College, Columbia University. pp. 83–94.

KLAUSMEIER, H. J., and GOODWIN, W. (1966) *Learning and Human Abilities : Educational Psychology.* 2nd ed. New York, Harper & Row.

U

Selected readings

KOLESNIK, W. B. (1963) *Educational Psychology*. New York, McGraw-Hill.

LAGRONE, H. F. (1964) *A Proposal for the Revision of the Pre-service Professional Component of a Program of Teacher Education*. Washington, D.C., American Association of Colleges for Teacher Education.

LINDGREN, H. C. (1967) *Educational Psychology in the Classroom*. 3rd ed. New York, Wiley.

MCDONALD, F. J. (1965) *Educational Psychology*. 2nd ed. Belmont, Calif., Wadsworth.

MORSE, W. C., and WINGO, G. M. (1962) *Psychology and Teaching*. rev. ed. Chicago: Scott, Foresman.

MOULY, G. J. (1960) *Psychology for Effective Teaching*. New York, Holt, Rinehart & Winston.

NUNNEY, D. N. (1964) Trends in the content of educational psychology, 1948–63. *Journal of Teacher Education*, **15** (4), 372–77.

OLSON, W. C. (1957) *Psychological Foundations of the Curriculum* (UNESCO), **26**, 5–67.

PETERS, F. R. (1965) *Considerations Leading to a New Program in Education for Students who Plan to Teach*. State University of New York at Stony Brook. December (mimeographed).

PRESSEY, S. L., ROBINSON, F. P., and HORROCKS, J. E. (1959) *Psychology in Education*. New York, Harper & Row.

RIPPLE, R. E. (1967) *Education 511 : Educational Psychology*. Ithaca, N.Y., Cornell University (mimeographed).

ROGERS, C. (1964) *What Psychology has to offer Teacher Education*. Paper prepared for the Conference on Educational Foundations, Cornell University, 27–8 April (mimeographed).

ROGERS, C. (1965) *Five Fields and Teacher Education*. Ithaca, N.Y., Cornell University, Project One Publication.

SCHOBEN, E. J. (1964) Psychology in the training of teachers. *Teachers College Record*, **65**, 436–40.

SKINNER, B. F. (1965) Why teachers fail. *Saturday Review*, **48**, 16 October, 80–1, 98–102.

SKINNER, B. F. (1968) *The Technology of Teaching*. New York, Appleton Century Crofts.

STEPHENS, J. M. (1956) *Educational Psychology: The Study of Educational Growth*. rev. ed. New York: Holt, Rinehart & Winston.

STEPHENS, J. M. (1965) *The Psychology of Classroom Learning*. New York: Holt, Rinehart & Winston.

STOW, K. R. (1960) *A Study of the Master of Education Programs at*

Cornell University. Unpub. Master thesis, Cornell University (typewritten).

SYMONDS, P. M. (1960) *What Education has to Learn from Psychology*. New York: Teachers College Press, Teachers College, Columbia University.

THOMPSON, G. G., GARDNER, E. F., and DIVESTA, F. (1959) *Educational Psychology*. New York: Appleton Century Crofts.

THYNE, J. M. (1963) *The Psychology of Learning and Techniques of Teaching*. London: University of London Press.

TROW, W. C. (1960) *Psychology in Teaching and Learning*. CARMICHAEL, L. (ed.). Boston: Houghton Mifflin.

WATSON, G. (1961) *What Psychology Can We Trust?* New York, Teachers College Press, Teachers College, Columbia University.

Reprinted from J. Herbert and D. P. Ausubel (eds.),
Psychology in Teacher Preparation (Ontario Institute for Studies
in Education Monograph No. 5, 1969), pp. 24–38.

Appendices

Appendix 1

The schedule of suggested objectives
in the teaching of educational psychology

The rubric

(The instructions for completing the schedule were the same for all groups in so far as the means of expressing preferences is concerned.)

To complete the questionnaire would you please adopt the following procedure:

Opinions of instructional objectives:

  (i) Think about each item as an objective which you might expect a student to attain following a three-year course in educational psychology.
 (ii) Consider each item individually, assuming that sufficient teaching time is available to cover it adequately.
(iii) In the column headed 'A' on the questionnaire write a number to indicate your opinion of each objective according to the following key:

  1   I strongly disagree
  2   I disagree
  3   I am uncertain
  4   I agree
  5   I strongly agree

We think that the objectives given cover all the broad areas of the educational psychology course. If you feel that we have overlooked an important area of study please make your suggestions on a separate sheet of paper and enclose it when you return the questionnaire.

Please respond to every item

Appendices

(Columns for completion have been omitted)
At the end of the course it is essential that the student should:

1 be able to state the essential aspects of the physiology of the nervous system and relate them to human personality;

2 be able to describe the necessary learning conditions for classical conditioning and operant conditioning and distinguish between them;

3 be able to compute the mean, median and mode of groups of scores and know the uses of these measurements;

4 be able to analyse a teaching task, construct an appropriate teaching sequence, and devise a suitable test for it;

5 be able to explain the currently most important psychological views on the nature of intelligence;

6 be able to identify a maladjusted child and decide on the psychologically most desirable way of treating him;

7 have developed an interest in educational psychology so that he enjoys discussing the subject with others;

8 be able to describe the normal sequence of the physical growth of children during the pre-school years;

9 be able to describe the necessary conditions for building up learning sets;

10 be able to state the characteristics of the normal curve of distribution and compute the standard deviation of a group of scores;

11 be able to prepare effective instructional procedures in the teaching of reading;

12 be able to replicate some of Piaget's experiments with children;

13 be able to assess the influence of play on children's development;

14 be willing to modify his teaching methods to allow for the varying needs of individual children;

15 be able to describe the normal sequence of the physical growth of children during middle childhood;

16 be able to distinguish between rote and meaningful learning;

17 be able to translate a group of raw scores into standard scores;

18 be able to identify children who are failing at school and to propose effective remedial treatment;

19 be able to outline current views on the nature of language and its relationship to learning;

20 be able to identify the possible causes of delinquency and relate these to individual children;

At the end of the course it is essential that the student should:

21 be convinced that the solution to many professional problems may be found in the principles of psychology;

22 be able to describe some important features of development at adolescence;

23 be able to distinguish between reception and discovery learning;

24 be able to state the principles underlying test construction, test validity, test reliability, and to be able to compare standardized tests with traditional methods of evaluating school performance;

25 be able to outline the key aspects of current work in the field of classroom interaction analysis;

26 be able to list the characteristics of each phase of Piaget's model of cognitive development and relate them to classroom situations;

27 be able to interpret reports of research as presented in professional journals;

28 have the psychological insight to make professional judgements which are objective, realistic and tolerant and not fixed by dogmatic precept or emotional thinking;

29 be able to describe the concept of critical periods of development in relation to its usefulness for teachers;

30 be able to define a hierarchical model of types of learning and give examples of classroom behaviour which might be related to each type;

31 be able to administer and mark an intelligence test, compute IQs for a group of children and interpret the results taking into account the characteristics, advantages and limitations of such tests;

32 be able to list the characteristics of programmed instruction and prepare instruction in this form;

33 be able to describe the main elements in concept formation and the main strategies involved in concept attainment;

34 be able to outline the major factors which influence the emotional development of children;

35 respond naturally to children's spontaneous interests, acting as a leader in their learning experiences rather than a source of information;

36 be able to describe how the child learns to perceive the world around him;

37 be able to describe learning experiments with simple animals and relate the essential features of reinforcement to the classroom;

38 be able to describe the construction and use of attitude scales;

Appendices

At the end of the course it is essential that the student should:

39 be able to maintain order in a classroom and obtain satisfactory work from a class;

40 be able to outline the main findings of key experimental studies concerning the intellectual development of children;

41 be able to describe the development of personality and the ways in which personality can be assessed;

42 have acquired the habit of considering educational problems and practices in the light of psychological knowledge;

43 be able to distinguish between examples of normal behaviour and deviant behaviour at various ages between birth and adolescence;

44 be able to evaluate the importance of gestalt psychology in the development of learning theory;

45 be able to construct sociograms of groups of children with some practical aim in mind;

46 be able to adapt himself to a variety of teaching situations;

47 be able to outline current views on the nature of thinking;

48 be able to outline the most important social influences on children's learning;

49 be ready to use psychological knowledge to decide on the socially most appropriate of a number of different educational policies;

50 be able to state the most important features of Freudian and neo-Freudian psychology.

Appendix 2

Tables

TABLE A **Mean choice scores accorded to the objectives by different groups**

Objective	TUTORS M	S.D.	Rank	TEACHERS M	S.D.	Rank	STUDENTS M	S.D.	Rank	ALL M	Rank
1	2·92	1·09	50	3·12	1·05	48	3·14	0·99	44	3·06	48
2	3·78	1·00	37	3·51	1·0	34	3·61	0·84	27	3·63	33
3	3·69	0·96	39	3·42	0·98	38	3·39	0·96	36	3·50	39
4	4·23	0·87	21	4·26	0·81	10	4·03	0·80	16	4·17	12
5	4·48	0·64	7	3·53	0·95	33	3·63	0·96	25	3·88	23
6	3·59	1·28	45	4·28	1·00	9	4·09	1·08	9	3·98	18
7	4·38	0·78	13	3·68	0·98	28	3·44	1·09	34	3·83	25
8	3·92	1·01	31	3·91	0·87	21	3·56	1·03	28	3·79	28
9	3·94	0·80	30	3·85	0·90	23	3·65	0·87	24	3·81	27
10	3·62	0·99	42	3·37	1·03	40	3·09	1·00	41	3·36	44
11	4·59	0·75	4	4·47	0·54	6	3·96	1·02	7	4·34	6
12	3·95	0·95	28	3·19	1·10	46	3·05	1·17	47	3·39	42
13	4·37	0·73	14	4·22	0·80	12	4·11	0·79	8	4·23	10
14	4·86	0·38	1	4·79	0·64	1	4·63	0·66	1	4·76	1
15	4·08	0·90	26	4·19	0·74	14	3·67	0·95	22	3·98	18
16	4·67	0·52	2	4·49	0·70	5	4·14	0·87	7	4·43	3
17	3·45	1·00	47	3·45	1·04	37	3·06	1·05	46	3·32	45
18	4·39	0·81	12	4·54	0·70	3	4·25	0·88	4	4·39	4
19	4·45	0·68	8	3·74	1·00	25	3·77	0·88	20	3·95	21
20	3·95	0·85	28	4·26	0·78	10	4·05	0·84	11	4·08	15
21	3·61	1·04	44	3·24	1·05	45	3·07	1·08	45	3·30	47
22	4·33	0·66	15	4·14	0·67	17	3·85	0·84	17	4·10	13
23	4·29	0·66	19	4·12	0·78	18	3·79	0·80	18	4·06	17
24	3·82	0·90	36	3·69	1·00	27	3·49	0·96	30	3·66	31
25	3·62	0·85	42	3·46	0·95	36	3·39	0·88	36	3·49	40
26	4·29	0·75	19	3·13	1·09	47	3·39	1·08	36	3·60	36
27	3·86	0·88	34	3·66	1·09	29	3·39	0·89	36	3·63	33
28	4·55	0·70	5	4·22	0·84	12	4·17	0·89	6	4·31	7
29	4·10	0·78	25	3·89	0·80	22	3·97	0·75	14	3·98	18
30	3·64	0·90	40	3·29	0·99	43	3·24	0·94	43	3·39	42

TABLE A *continued*

Objective	TUTORS M	S.D.	Rank	TEACHERS M	S.D.	Rank	STUDENTS M	S.D.	Rank	ALL M	Rank
31	3·88	1·03	33	3·97	0·82	19	3·52	1·08	29	3·79	28
32	3·72	0·90	38	3·70	0·93	26	3·33	1·00	42	3·58	37
33	4·33	0·70	15	3·61	0·94	30	3·78	0·87	19	3·90	22
34	4·44	0·60	10	4·37	0·78	8	4·23	0·70	5	4·31	7
35	4·41	0·80	11	4·41	0·86	7	4·37	0·86	3	4·39	4
36	4·32	0·71	18	3·94	0·86	20	3·98	0·83	13	4·08	15
37	3·59	1·00	45	3·31	1·08	42	3·04	1·12	48	3·31	46
38	3·08	0·96	49	3·00	1·14	49	2·87	0·89	49	2·98	49
39	4·45	0·83	8	4·53	0·90	4	3·66	1·24	23	4·21	11
40	4·18	0·72	22	3·51	0·90	34	3·45	0·90	33	3·71	30
41	4·12	0·90	23	3·75	0·84	24	3·75	0·87	21	3·87	24
42	4·33	0·96	15	3·56	0·93	32	3·62	0·87	26	3·83	25
43	4·11	0·79	24	4·16	0·70	16	4·02	0·84	12	4·09	14
44	3·64	0·88	40	3·36	1·00	41	3·40	0·90	35	3·46	41
45	3·85	0·80	35	3·26	1·02	44	3·49	1·05	30	3·53	38
46	4·62	0·66	3	4·68	0·60	2	4·39	0·87	2	4·56	2
47	4·04	0·86	27	3·41	0·88	39	3·47	0·91	32	3·64	32
48	4·54	0·59	6	4·19	0·66	14	4·07	0·84	4	4·26	9
49	3·90	0·99	32	3·60	0·95	31	3·38	1·00	40	3·62	35
50	3·34	1·02	48	2·81	1·16	50	2·72	1·08	50	2·95	50

TABLE B **Students' choice of objectives by colleges**

In this table the pattern of choices of objectives made by students in each college is compared with the pattern of choices for the remainder of the colleges. In each cell the numbers in the first row represent the number of students disfavouring that objective, the centre row represents neutral choices and the third row represents choices in favour of the objective. The right-hand column in each cell contains the numbers of students choosing particular options in the college indicated in the left margin. The left column gives the number of students making the various choices in the remainder of the colleges. Totals for each objective are different since zero returns indicating that students were not familiar with the objective are omitted. The chi square value for each 2 × 3 table is given in each cell and underlined.

College	Objective									
	1	2	3	4	5	6	7	8	9	10
1	369 52 214 30 549 72 0·165	130 16 172 22 690 92 0·091	216 31 230 32 598 75 0·439	81 9 99 13 986 136 0·368	215 22 173 16 782 121 5·581	120 26 89 18 964 115 8·886	279 43 171 22 721 93 0·858	236 45 129 17 807 97 5·694	113 23 258 31 712 98 3·356	333 46 296 35 454 66 0·861
2	372 49 213 31 543 78 0·246	127 19 158 36 677 105 3·558	210 37 219 43 599 74 5·931	74 16 94 18 985 137 3·378	202 35 151 38 804 99 12·447	127 19 88 19 944 135 2·351	272 50 165 28 719 95 3·461	232 49 131 15 795 90 6·551	112 24 249 40 708 102 2·599	327 52 279 52 468 52 6·479
3	407 14 230 14 607 14 6·729	139 7 187 7 763 19 2·771	238 9 253 9 689 14 2·349	87 3 107 5 1087 35 0·588	226 11 183 6 877 26 1·811	145 1 102 5 1042 37 3·803	315 7 180 13 791 23 9·094	272 9 142 4 874 30 0·089	130 6 279 10 788 22 1·265	368 11 320 11 506 14 0·222
4	414 7 229 15 268 53 21·626	143 3 190 4 715 67 16·295	239 8 240 22 629 44 5·967	88 2 108 4 1053 69 3·406	232 5 184 5 838 65 12·816	136 10 95 12 1026 53 7·697	315 7 188 5 751 63 17·342	272 9 140 6 844 60 5·450	134 2 278 11 751 59 9·952	366 13 307 24 484 36 6·170
5	401 20 234 10 590 31 0·308	139 7 184 10 749 33 0·360	236 11 252 10 652 21 0·998	85 5 108 4 1070 52 0·455	216 21 184 5 868 35 12·516	136 10 105 2 1030 49 3·488	307 15 185 8 776 38 0·066	272 9 143 3 855 49 4·764	127 9 271 18 779 31 3·978	359 20 312 19 504 16 4·157
6	413 8 232 12 610 11 8·061	142 4 193 1 756 26 4·559	243 4 252 10 661 12 4·104	87 3 110 2 1069 26 0·537	233 4 179 10 886 17 8·466	134 12 105 2 1062 17 25·176	320 2 190 3 788 26 7·237	277 4 141 5 882 22 1·756	135 1 285 4 786 24 4·013	372 7 317 14 515 5 10·603
7	376 45 230 14 585 36 9·970	132 14 183 11 720 62 1·897	215 32 252 10 624 49 15·325	83 7 108 4 1040 82 2·259	213 24 173 16 848 55 5·154	134 12 104 3 999 80 3·403	292 30 181 12 761 53 3·015	255 26 129 17 852 52 8·967	118 18 273 16 755 55 8·780	335 44 319 12 482 38 16·084
8	403 18 235 9 604 17 1·854	142 4 189 5 745 37 2·619	241 6 256 6 645 28 2·886	89 1 108 4 1080 42 1·681	227 10 181 8 875 28 1·042	136 10 102 5 1047 32 6·008	306 16 191 2 787 27 5·694	274 7 143 3 867 37 2·622	134 2 284 5 775 35 6·046	371 8 326 5 486 34 18·231
9	401 20 238 6 602 19 3·087	134 12 189 5 758 24 10·037	234 13 257 5 645 28 4·126	87 3 108 4 1084 38 0·007	227 10 186 3 870 33 2·418	143 3 106 1 1037 42 3·460	310 12 188 5 785 29 0·503	272 9 139 7 875 29 0·966	131 5 278 11 785 25 0·338	361 18 323 8 500 20 2·657
10	373 48 222 22 546 75 1·649	137 9 172 22 712 70 2·730	222 25 237 25 587 86 2·525	82 8 100 12 991 131 0·698	215 22 172 17 791 112 3·032	143 3 102 5 936 143 21·162	290 32 173 20 715 99 1·344	261 20 134 12 785 119 9·367	128 8 251 38 720 90 4·994	339 40 294 37 466 60 0·198
11	411 10 240 4 593 28 6·131	146 0 189 5 749 33 7·161	238 9 254 8 649 24 0·171	85 5 106 6 1091 31 4·013	233 4 183 6 871 32 2·047	144 2 106 1 1040 39 3·951	309 13 186 7 792 22 1·427	272 9 139 7 878 26 1·461	133 3 285 4 775 35 6·228	366 13 315 16 507 13 3·299
12	384 37 227 17 583 38 2·705	138 8 174 20 743 39 7·911	233 14 240 22 629 44 1·630	85 5 102 10 1042 80 0·871	217 20 171 18 846 57 3·136	137 9 96 11 1004 75 1·833	285 37 177 16 772 42 14·360	251 30 134 12 851 53 7·759	125 11 258 31 761 49 6·925	351 28 306 25 489 31 1·059
13	401 20 238 6 604 17 3·871	137 9 191 3 750 32 4·908	239 8 254 8 647 26 0·447	83 7 109 3 1091 31 8·095	224 13 186 3 874 29 5·113	140 6 103 4 1043 36 0·328	311 11 188 5 785 29 0·405	268 13 143 3 875 29 2·160	130 6 277 12 787 23 1·677	370 9 324 7 492 28 8·523
14	370 51 203 41 518 103 4·529	121 25 157 37 684 98 6·563	215 32 228 34 557 116 4·055	79 11 95 17 950 172 0·627	206 31 158 31 765 138 1·010	129 17 91 16 911 168 1·535	285 37 157 36 686 128 5·402	244 37 113 33 773 131 7·472	123 13 241 48 697 118 3·709	320 59 290 41 442 78 1·636
15	399 22 231 13 592 29 0·240	137 9 188 6 737 45 2·393	239 8 244 18 641 32 3·668	85 5 109 3 1062 60 1·520	232 5 182 7 847 56 7·346	140 6 103 4 1021 58 0·835	312 10 182 11 767 47 3·494	276 5 144 2 843 61 15·612	131 5 279 10 766 44 2·206	363 11 306 25 491 29 7·543

Values of chi² for 2df

5%	2%	1%	0·1%
5·991	7·824	9·210	13·815

College	11	12	13	14	15	16	17	18	19	20
					Objective					
1	144 24	403 86	52 16	19 2	167 40	62 12	297 44	68 18	128 10	54 18
	130 20	215 24	94 10	19 6	158 22	106 22	321 45	87 14	227 17	119 25
	889 115	535 45	1027 132	1132 150	846 97	949 118	414 42	1015 127	810 131	1000 116
	1·348	25·437	9·579	3·642	13·185	5·410	3·229	7·665	12·121	18·244
2	152 16	440 49	58 10	17 4	166 41	62 12	290 51	70 16	111 27	61 11
	135 15	213 26	92 12	23 2	150 30	111 17	325 41	92 9	197 47	125 19
	863 141	488 95	1008 151	1115 167	842 101	936 131	401 55	994 148	842 99	973 143
	3·938	10·639	0·351	1·129	15·051	1·032	2·479	3·877	18·721	0·368
3	167 1	472 17	63 5	19 2	199 8	72 2	329 12	83 3	132 6	69 3
	142 8	226 13	95 9	21 4	173 7	118 10	355 11	97 4	236 8	139 5
	971 33	570 10	1130 29	1245 37	915 28	1038 29	446 10	1106 36	912 29	1081 35
	5·872	8·323	15·379	16·150	0·721	9·541	1·299	0·212	0·614	0·260
4	166 2	470 19	64 4	20 1	204 3	72 2	328 13	82 4	138 0	70 2
	144 6	226 13	99 5	25 0	173 7	127 1	347 19	94 7	243 1	132 12
	937 67	538 42	1093 66	1208 74	878 65	995 72	416 40	1078 64	867 74	1000 116
	8·951	5·610	0·128	1·564	10·651	8·745	9·180	0·476	29·382	3·139
5	149 19	457 32	66 2	21 0	204 3	72 2	329 12	83 3	125 13	71 1
	142 8	225 14	·102 2	25 0	173 7	119 9	348 18	101 0	226 18	142 2
	970 34	525 53	1102 57	1221 61	892 51	1031 36	446 6	1084 58	1029 25	1058 58
	20·682	11·393	2·363	2·294	6·289	4·507	9·066	5·720	16·697	6·600
6	159 9	478 11	65 3	21 0	205 2	73 1	336 5	81 5	137 1	68 4
	139 11	227 12	101 3	25 0	175 5	128 0	352 14	92 9	236 8	137 7
	993 11	573 7	1134 25	1251 31	919 24	1037 30	451 5	1125 17	919 22	1096 20
	29·741	10·928	1·537	1·138	2·041	4·183	8·331	27·253	2·505	0·467
7	137 31	431 58	65 3	21 0	193 14	70 4	296 45	75 11	122 16	70 2
	133 17	219 20	97 7	24 1	173 7	117 11	348 20	90 11	220 24	142 2
	961 43	564 16	1074 85	1188 94	869 74	992 75	431 25	1069 73	886 55	1025 91
	50·283	33·546	0·834	2·053	3·623	0·762	20·355	7·219	9·112	0·632
8	167 1	480 9	65 3	20 1	201 6	73 1	336 5	86 0	136 2	69 3
	149 1	235 4	102 2	24 1	175 5	126 2	357 9	98 3	241 3	139 5
	959 45	547 33	1117 42	1239 43	907 36	1024 43	424 32	1098 44	899 42	1077 39
	10·383	14·448	0·949	0·154	0·769	3·154	18·941	3·582	7·830	0·033
9	164 4	466 23	66 2	21 0	202 5	70 4	329 12	86 0	132 6	69 3
	145 5	232 7	97 7	25 0	173 7	127 1	359 7	98 3	238 6	138 6
	967 37	564 16	1122 37	1236 46	909 34	1027 40	432 24	1100 42	907 34	1079 37
	0·696	3·219	3·602	1·709	0·830	3·136	6·444	3·364	0·831	0·393
10	161 7	458 31	64 4	21 0	190 17	67 7	311 30	85 1	132 6	66 6
	143 7	224 15	97 7	25 0	162 18	116 12	316 50	94 7	230 14	129 15
	867 137	476 104	1019 140	1131 151	827 116	943 124	409 47	999 143	811 130	986 130
	20·396	42·865	4·834	6·113	3·198	0·834	4·552	12·366	20·063	0·875
11	158 10	471 18	67 1	21 0	203 4	73 1	323 18	84 2	136 2	72 0
	135 15	229 10	104 0	25 0	173 7	126 2	349 17	99 2	240 4	143 1
	989 15	566 14	1118 41	1240 42	912 31	1028 39	449 7	1104 38	905 36	1077 39
	37·785	2·199	4·537	1·556	1·382	2·505	9·457	0·759	4·505	3·310
12	158 10	444 45	62 6	17 4	191 16	67 7	318 23	76 10	120 18	67 5
	139 11	221 18	93 11	22 3	165 15	110 18	337 29	95 6	223 21	136 8
	930 74	553 27	1081 78	1194 88	879 64	1000 67	422 34	1063 79	888 53	1034 82
	0·422	8·729	2·419	5·518	0·672	10·858	0·366	2·913	11·457	0·622
13	146 22	469 20	66 2	18 3	195 12	70 4	329 12	81 5	131 7	69 3
	138 12	236 3	95 9	23 2	173 7	127 1	362 4	94 7	232 12	143 1
	993 11	558 22	1125 34	1242 40	917 26	1027 40	427 29	1111 31	916 25	1075 41
	73·849	4·208	9·538	9·523	4·961	3·736	15·264	7·177	4·537	3·613
14	157 11	431 58	61 7	17 4	175 32	61 13	291 50	79 7	116 22	64 8
	138 12	181 58	85 19	20 5	148 32	111 17	308 58	89 12	187 57	136 8
	828 176	498 82	984 175	1091 191	807 136	905 162	383 73	960 182	821 120	945 171
	20·150	20·040	2·028	0·764	1·366	0·685	0·301	4·683	17·159	0·940
15	167 1	476 13	68 0	21 0	203 4	72 2	332 9	85 1	136 2	69 3
	148 2	237 2	103 1	24 1	176 4	123 5	342 24	94 7	240 4	132 12
	939 65	527 53	1092 67	1215 67	883 60	1006 61	429 27	1082 60	879 62	1063 53
	15·192	33·860	8·413	1·226	10·415	1·831	6·387	3·498	14·005	3·520

Values of chi^2 for 2df

5%	2%	1%	0·1%
5·991	7·824	9·210	13·815

College	Objective									
	21	22	23	24	25	26	27	28	29	30
1	318 68	108 23	73 10	181 29	126 25	271 56	252 49	70 10	57 13	202 43
	382 44	136 16	196 41	266 24	330 33	195 31	211 34	112 22	149 18	365 32
	453 44	926 120	827 96	670 100	454 74	678 68	698 75	965 126	933 122	465 62
	17·400	4·429	8·586	5·150	7·124	14·702	9·896	2·670	3·295	13·177
2	345 41	110 21	72 11	189 21	130 21	288 39	265 36	71 9	55 15	217 28
	373 53	121 31	216 21	243 47	298 65	205 21	215 30	117 17	140 27	343 54
	418 79	926 120	789 134	674 96	480 48	634 112	666 107	949 142	932 123	456 71
	5·598	10·594	5·216	4·581	15·078	5·254	0·873	0·211	7·603	0·753
3	374 12	124 7	80 3	197 13	147 4	313 14	290 11	80 0	69 1	233 12
	412 14	149 3	223 14	281 9	348 15	218 8	234 11	126 8	156 11	383 14
	481 16	1013 33	898 25	752 18	515 13	729 17	753 20	1056 35	1024 31	511 16
	0·013	2·654	5·924	7·971	2·116	3·368	2·522	5·761	6·740	1·681
4	375 11	126 5	82 1	202 8	148 3	324 3	299 2	79 1	69 1	241 4
	394 32	148 4	231 6	268 22	338 25	215 11	237 8	131 3	164 3	373 24
	467 30	980 66	861 62	727 43	499 29	685 61	709 64	1020 71	984 71	482 45
	8·639	4·282	9·505	3·303	4·953	22·401	26·821	7·174	8·984	13·635
5	367 19	127 4	78 5	201 9	143 8	299 28	286 15	78 2	67 3	235 10
	411 15	150 2	227 10	279 11	344 19	209 17	235 10	130 4	160 7	383 14
	471 26	991 55	882 41	732 38	508 20	734 12	737 36	1036 55	1004 51	508 19
	1·677	0·406	0·498	0·675	1·298	32·578	0·253	1·307	0·163	0·146
6	379 7	130 1	82 1	205 5	149 2	324 3	299 2	80 0	68 2	243 2
	418 8	151 1	234 3	288 2	356 7	219 7	242 3	132 2	167 0	387 10
	481 16	1017 29	896 27	746 24	508 20	725 21	749 24	1062 29	1027 28	510 17
	2·506	4·175	2·743	5·215	4·137	4·043	7·272	2·772	4·571	4·017
7	358 28	127 4	76 7	183 27	141 10	284 43	267 34	73 7	66 4	218 27
	391 35	147 5	220 17	274 16	340 23	213 13	231 14	127 7	160 7	369 28
	468 29	960 86	856 67	722 48	491 37	708 38	727 46	1013 78	973 82	493 34
	2·029	8·514	0·164	12·395	0·157	22·849	10·243	1·051	3·011	5·231
8	375 11	126 5	81 2	207 3	147 4	322 5	292 9	77 3	70 0	242 3
	412 14	145 7	230 7	287 3	347 16	220 6	235 10	129 5	159 8	383 14
	476 21	1011 35	887 36	732 38	510 18	710 36	745 28	1054 37	1016 39	500 27
	1·309	0·650	0·858	12·701	1·110	7·783	0·487	0·064	3·285	7·063
9	376 10	127 4	78 5	202 8	142 9	323 4	292 9	77 3	66 4	237 8
	414 12	146 6	231 6	282 8	354 9	209 17	238 7	131 3	162 5	386 11
	474 23	1010 36	889 34	740 30	505 23	708 38	743 30	1051 40	1018 37	503 24
	3·449	0·173	2·190	3·265	3·921	12·413	0·866	0·727	1·110	2·181
10	354 32	114 17	76 7	188 22	137 14	307 20	253 48	69 11	68 2	221 24
	367 59	134 18	206 31	254 36	333 30	206 20	215 30	118 16	155 12	348 49
	444 53	931 115	823 100	682 88	457 71	633 113	701 72	974 117	925 130	474 53
	6·464	0·510	1·605	0·458	6·437	22·478	9·669	0·819	8·960	0·975
11	381 5	129 2	80 3	201 9	146 5	321 6	298 3	76 4	70 0	241 4
	410 16	149 3	226 11	280 10	355 8	220 6	234 11	133 1	164 3	388 9
	476 21	1009 37	896 27	748 22	503 25	716 30	746 27	1055 36	1016 39	499 28
	6·549	2·327	1·768	1·136	3·978	3·739	6·326	3·524	4·142	9·396
12	346 40	124 7	75 8	192 18	133 18	292 35	272 29	70 10	64 6	218 27
	397 29	140 12	218 19	271 19	320 23	206 20	227 18	120 14	151 16	373 24
	473 24	970 76	859 64	716 54	488 40	710 36	726 47	1021 70	987 68	496 31
	10·145	0·792	1·030	0·815	4·090	13·463	4·157	6·464	2·477	7·605
13	366 20	128 3	77 6	204 6	148 3	313 14	289 12	77 3	66 4	237 8
	417 9	148 4	227 10	282 8	350 13	209 17	236 9	127 7	162 5	380 17
	481 16	1008 38	899 24	743 27	416 12	720 26	751 22	1057 34	1021 34	512 15
	5·859	0·895	6·125	0·488	1·017	1·708	1·056	1·664	1·333	1·431
14	319 67	106 25	70 13	183 27	131 20	274 53	267 34	66 14	58 12	208 37
	364 62	126 26	206 31	239 51	301 62	174 52	205 40	116 18	129 38	319 78
	426 71	897 149	786 137	661 109	455 73	662 84	648 125	928 163	913 142	471 56
	1·840	1·302	0·557	2·672	2·169	20·213	4·379	0·651	10·136	14·791
15	371 15	128 3	82 1	205 5	146 5	323 4	293 8	77 3	67 3	237 8
	402 24	138 14	227 10	266 24	348 15	218 8	235 10	127 7	160 7	378 19
	469 28	995 51	874 49	735 35	503 25	692 54	723 50	1033 58	997 58	498 29
	1·712	7·491	3·027	9·816	0·622	18·364	7·123	0·370	0·643	1·834

Values of chi² for 2df

5%	2%	1%	0·1%
5·991	7·824	9·210	13·815

College	Objective									
	31	32	33	34	35	36	37	38	39	40
1	236 41	252 38	113 19	38 7	60 20	82 19	374 66	259 53	242 57	194 45
	180 20	287 36	184 24	59 8	52 12	114 27	267 31	393 44	110 17	265 24
	755 97	600 84	816 113	1073 143	1056 126	972 112	520 59	211 27	815 83	694 86
	3·129	0·559	0·645	0·595	17·668	14·180	6·298	8·351	21·000	15·117
2	248 29	242 48	112 20	34 11	66 14	85 16	377 63	266 46	255 44	196 43
	179 21	269 54	192 16	54 13	57 7	123 18	251 47	377 60	105 22	247 42
	730 122	622 62	794 135	1068 148	1032 150	946 138	518 61	211 27	792 106	696 84
	3·995	16·774	7·156	8·389	1·762	0·781	5·799	1·371	4·003	9·326
3	271 6	282 8	127 5	43 2	78 2	99 2	428 12	299 13	291 8	233 6
	188 12	308 15	197 11	63 4	59 5	138 3	284 14	424 13	119 8	279 10
	827 25	664 20	905 24	179 37	1146 36	1046 38	568 16	235 3	871 27	753 27
	6·091	2·377	4·263	1·949	4·511	1·260	2·804	3·924	4·183	0·514
4	267 10	281 9	130 2	45 0	77 3	101 0	438 2	305 7	294 5	236 3
	190 10	306 17	204 4	66 1	61 3	137 4	290 8	400 37	117 10	275 14
	797 55	635 49	860 69	1142 74	1113 69	1013 71	514 65	226 12	838 60	722 58
	3·321	6·351	14·338	5·279	0·691	9·761	60·496	13·390	11·779	13·440
5	247 30	276 14	127 5	44 1	78 2	96 5	417 23	296 16	289 10	227 12
	191 9	307 16	195 13	67 0	63 1	138 3	281 17	420 17	123 4	272 17
	830 22	653 31	902 27	1156 60	1124 58	1031 53	559 20	233 5	851 45	753 27
	32·474	0·095	5·658	4·107	2·387	2·160	2·931	3·321	2·446	3·377
6	269 8	285 5	132 0	45 0	77 3	100 1	434 6	310 2	296 3	238 1
	188 12	318 5	202 6	65 2	63 1	137 4	293 5	416 21	126 1	283 6
	841 11	663 21	904 25	1187 29	1155 27	1058 26	559 20	232 6	872 26	756 24
	16·235	2·882	3·709	1·213	0·799	0·886	5·408	11·217	4·932	5·673
7	225 52	249 41	110 22	44 1	76 4	82 19	402 38	278 34	276 23	216 23
	186 14	296 27	185 23	65 2	62 2	123 18	283 15	413 24	120 7	264 25
	823 29	667 17	889 40	1124 92	1093 89	1026 58	537 42	225 13	833 65	733 47
	74·385	47·410	35·803	3·710	2·356	32·593	3·425	9·370	0·622	4·560
8	274 3	285 5	128 4	45 0	79 1	100 1	435 5	303 9	289 10	235 4
	198 2	318 5	205 3	65 2	63 1	136 5	289 9	428 9	126 1	279 10
	810 42	647 37	889 40	1171 45	1137 45	1043 41	547 32	223 15	863 35	747 33
	13·478	13·195	4·089	1·801	2·166	2·049	14·485	8·838	3·184	3·439
9	270 7	284 6	128 4	42 3	79 1	98 3	427 13	302 10	293 6	229 10
	195 5	318 8	203 5	66 1	63 1	136 5	285 13	424 13	118 9	283 6
	818 34	652 32	893 36	1174 42	1138 44	1046 38	559 20	224 14	867 31	750 30
	1·987	5·557	1·185	2·156	2·036	0·066	1·017	3·934	6·822	2·276
10	255 22	243 47	120 12	37 8	74 6	94 7	379 61	291 21	259 40	220 19
	186 14	285 38	191 17	66 1	54 10	132 9	265 33	391 46	116 11	265 24
	737 115	625 59	808 121	1075 141	1047 135	950 134	527 52	221 17	799 99	673 107
	10·847	12·039	4·890	8·405	2·324	6·525	6·032	4·109	2·219	9·644
11	264 13	281 9	131 1	45 0	80 0	100 1	134 6	301 11	291 8	235 4
	190 10	309 14	201 7	67 0	61 3	135 6	291 7	428 9	121 6	279 10
	833 19	665 19	895 34	1174 42	1143 39	1049 35	550 29	216 22	870 28	752 28
	6·720	1·714	3·038	3·992	3·110	2·075	3·522	20·071	1·225	2·199
12	263 14	281 9	121 11	43 2	70 10	94 7	393 47	285 27	271 28	217 22
	189 11	306 17	183 25	56 11	61 3	126 15	276 22	401 36	123 4	261 28
	782 70	616 68	882 47	1135 81	1101 81	1011 73	553 26	214 24	836 62	739 41
	4·109	16·665	14·204	9·644	4·195	2·853	14·317	0·650	5·356	8·665
13	270 7	282 8	126 6	43 2	79 1	99 2	430 10	301 11	291 8	229 10
	191 9	319 4	193 15	67 0	61 3	139 2	293 5	418 19	123 4	275 14
	824 28	651 33	909 20	1173 43	1141 41	1043 41	549 30	234 4	865 33	762 18
	1·410	8·984	14·629	2·579	1·428	2·740	9·890	3·269	0·655	5·223
14	250 27	253 37	113 19	37 8	70 10	84 17	362 78	272 40	259 40	205 34
	162 38	268 55	175 33	46 21	52 12	120 21	239 59	368 69	109 18	238 51
	716 136	581 103	791 138	1044 172	1005 177	924 160	517 62	209 29	756 142	666 114
	9·032	2·170	0·173	14·866	1·096	0·302	16·198	2·162	1·126	1·712
15	269 8	284 6	130 2	45 0	77 3	100 1	430 10	300 12	290 9	226 3
	187 13	311 12	202 6	66 1	64 0	140 1	285 13	417 20	122 5	281 8
	805 47	635 49	869 60	1149 67	1117 65	1018 66	534 45	218 20	844 54	724 56
	3·901	12·613	8·560	4·622	4·086	11·239	15·928	6·338	4·526	17·407

Values of chi² for 2df

5%	2%	1%	0·1%
5·991	7·824	9·210	13·815

College	Objective									
	41	42	43	44	45	46	47	48	49	50
1	126 16 173 12 870 129 6·208	121 25 249 28 694 95 4·434	71 18 90 16 1009 124 7·896	162 31 295 37 582 52 10·143	212 38 202 27 706 80 4·733	55 18 44 4 1070 134 12·679	194 35 251 34 724 87 3·563	74 25 82 9 1012 124 18·211	193 44 310 47 582 60 14·122	487 74 316 33 311 42 2·883
2	122 20 159 26 872 127 0·388	132 14 240 37 682 107 1·734	73 16 92 14 990 143 2·083	175 18 278 54 582 52 5·311	200 50 191 38 706 80 18·542	60 13 38 10 1054 150 4·378	200 29 245 40 707 104 0·299	75 24 70 21 1008 128 22·169	204 33 323 34 547 95 5·758	475 86 311 38 307 46 3·708
3	135 7 178 7 971 28 2·043	139 7 266 11 764 25 1·092	86 3 99 7 1100 33 4·202	187 6 323 9 618 16 0·108	239 11 216 13 775 11 15·077	71 2 41 7 1170 34 20·334	214 15 276 9 792 19 10·048	96 3 83 8 1104 32 9·547	233 4 340 17 623 19 4·582	541 20 339 10 344 9 0·792
4	138 4 176 9 937 62 2·884	143 3 272 5 723 66 20·108	89 0 104 2 1060 73 9·463	187 6 318 14 580 54 10·299	240 10 214 15 730 50 2·067	72 1 48 0 1130 74 5·911	227 2 273 12 750 61 16·192	99 0 89 2 1063 73 9·218	234 3 339 18 590 52 15·177	540 21 311 18 338 15 22·195
5	136 6 174 11 955 44 0·861	139 7 260 17 757 32 1·985	86 3 103 3 1078 55 1·186	178 15 312 20 621 13 16·299	229 21 211 18 771 15 28·357	71 2 48 0 1146 58 3·030	216 13 272 13 776 35 0·698	97 2 89 2 1079 57 3·117	223 14 342 15 617 25 1·694	528 33 330 19 345 8 6·753
6	142 0 177 8 976 23 6·536	146 0 272 5 764 25 5·774	86 3 101 5 1110 23 3·436	192 1 329 3 608 26 12·749	248 2 216 13 776 10 19·921	72 1 48 0 1174 30 1·518	227 2 279 6 788 23 3·050	99 0 88 3 1109 27 2·724	235 2 348 9 623 19 3·201	559 2 336 13 340 13 16·064
7	130 12 172 13 929 70 0·372	133 13 256 21 743 46 2·424	86 3 100 6 1047 86 2·575	172 21 310 22 590 44 3·792	227 23 214 15 731 55 1·597	68 5 47 1 1115 89 1·932	205 24 271 14 754 57 5·959	97 2 84 7 1050 86 4·236	216 21 336 21 593 49 1·966	509 52 327 22 338 15 8·707
8	137 5 182 3 960 39 2·342	142 4 269 8 755 34 1·618	85 4 102 4 1094 39 0·221	192 1 321 11 600 34 9·609	245 5 225 4 748 38 7·260	73 0 43 5 1163 41 9·519	225 4 279 6 774 37 6·307	98 1 90 1 1091 45 3·980	232 5 350 7 611 31 7·207	538 23 344 5 337 16 6·100
9	134 8 180 5 966 33 2·365	142 4 269 8 755 34 1·618	88 1 105 1 1089 44 4·026	183 10 325 7 605 29 4·336	244 6 219 10 757 29 1·404	72 1 47 1 1160 44 1·283	220 9 277 8 782 29 0·541	95 4 91 0 1095 41 1·619	231 6 351 6 610 32 8·144	542 19 343 6 332 21 9·106
10	123 19 163 22 890 109 0·814	134 12 246 31 716 73 1·231	85 4 100 6 992 141 8·886	173 20 288 44 556 78 0·941	234 16 218 11 663 123 28·831	66 7 45 3 1063 141 1·600	212 17 253 32 709 102 4·690	93 6 86 5 997 139 6·733	216 21 316 41 573 69 1·041	498 63 307 42 323 30 2·587
11	140 2 178 7 966 33 1·684	145 1 271 6 762 27 3·821	89 0 102 4 1095 38 3·123	187 6 325 7 608 26 2·664	247 3 224 5 752 34 6·870	72 1 48 0 1163 41 2·530	226 3 273 12 784 27 3·605	96 3 90 1 1098 38 1·388	230 7 345 12 624 18 0·185	545 16 337 12 341 12 0·266
12	128 14 173 12 930 69 1·755	132 14 252 25 742 47 4·470	79 10 95 11 1059 74 4·532	175 18 303 29 600 34 5·739	239 11 220 9 711 75 12·361	67 6 41 7 1123 81 4·449	204 25 264 21 763 48 6·786	89 10 78 13 1064 72 9·378	217 20 327 30 605 37 3·303	526 35 318 31 328 25 2·233
13	140 2 183 2 958 41 6·217	138 8 265 12 768 21 3·916	84 5 102 4 1097 36 1·469	188 5 326 6 600 34 8·381	242 8 217 12 779 7 17·698	71 2 47 1 1162 42 0·326	223 6 271 14 786 25 2·611	98 1 88 3 1096 40 1·788	222 15 350 7 624 18 9·436	545 16 342 7 331 22 10·584
14	122 20 150 35 855 144 2·570	118 28 228 49 677 112 3·503	72 17 86 20 972 161 2·970	160 33 283 49 537 97 0·516	216 34 201 28 651 135 4·220	59 14 40 8 1026 178· 1·117	190 39 227 58 708 103 10·426	84 15 76 15 967 169 0·156	198 39 283 74 566 76 14·285	478 83 295 54 301 52 0·088
15	135 7 172 13 951 48 1·578	140 6 263 14 744 45 0·649	87 2 103 3 1070 63 3·068	191 2 312 20 589 45 10·002	238 12 218 11 742 44 0·366	73 0 47 1 1137 67 5·302	223 6 279 6 757 54 12·474	96 3 91 0 1071 65 6·614	234 3 338 19 600 42 9·797	543 18 330 19 326 27 8·999

Values of chi² for 2df

5%	2%	1%	0·1%
5·991	7·824	9·210	13·815

X

Appendix 3

The attitude scale:
statements about educational psychology

Here are some statements about educational psychology. In the column on the right five alternative comments are represented by the following key:

a: I strongly disagree
b: I disagree
c: I am uncertain
d: I agree
e: I strongly agree

Please indicate which comment most nearly represents your personal opinion by ringing the appropriate letter. Please be sure to respond to every statement. There are no right or wrong answers.

1 The field of educational psychology is too woolly
and ill defined to be helpful to a teacher.   a   b   c   d   e

2 The study of educational psychology trains students
to consider educational problems in a logical way.   a   b   c   d   e

3 Educational psychology is the most important part
of the training of prospective teachers.   a   b   c   d   e

4 A better understanding of children is developed
through practical experience in the classroom rather
than through studying educational psychology.   a   b   c   d   e

5 Educational psychology adds nothing to the experienced teacher's skill.   a   b   c   d   e

6 Knowledge of educational psychology enhances
one's own personal development.   a   b   c   d   e

a: I strongly disagree
b: I disagree
c: I am uncertain
d: I agree
e: I strongly agree

7 There is no connection between success in a college course of educational psychology and success in practical teaching situations.　　　　　　　　a　b　c　d　e

8 The learning of rules from educational psychology is likely to produce a generation of teachers who cannot think for themselves.　　　　　　　a　b　c　d　e

9 Educational psychology is an essential study for all teachers.　　　　　　　　　　　a　b　c　d　e

10 Educational psychology enables teachers to make informed decisions about teaching.　　a　b　c　d　e

11 The rigid statements of educational psychology are a form of indoctrination.　　　　a　b　c　d　e

12 A study of educational psychology gives teachers the knowledge needed to handle difficult children.　a　b　c　d　e

13 Work in school needs to be far more formal than educational psychologists suggest.　　a　b　c　d　e

14 A study of educational psychology produces fair-minded teachers who are able to review educational controversies in a scientific way.　　a　b　c　d　e

15 The complexity and difficulty of educational psychology confuses rather than clarifies one's understanding of children.　　　　　　a　b　c　d　e

16 I find educational psychology a very interesting field of study.　　　　　　　　a　b　c　d　e

17 Educational psychology produces novelties in teaching methods which are only useful as gimmicks for those who wish to impress the theorists.　a　b　c　d　e

18 A student who fails to grasp the principles of educational psychology is unlikely to be as effective a teacher as he could be.　　　　　　a　b　c　d　e

19 Educational psychologists are too idealistic about children.   a b c d e

20 Successful teaching needs far more rigour than educational psychologists suggest.   a b c d e

21 The study of educational psychology helps teachers to develop successful teaching methods.   a b c d e

22 A study of educational psychology enables teachers to be sympathetic towards the weaknesses of children.   a b c d e

23 Educational psychology is chiefly concerned with animal learning and cannot be related to classroom situations.   a b c d e

24 The subject matter of educational psychology is so diverse that it does not present a coherent view of the whole child.   a b c d e

25 The science of educational psychology cannot be related to the art of teaching.   a b c d e

Appendix 4

Using the model to generate objectives

Here we set out the steps for developing sets of objectives according to the proposed model. The reader will probably find it helpful to refer to the set of objectives in educational psychology to exemplify the ideas set out in the various steps.

1   Determine the broad areas of the subject.
2   For each area derive the three broad types of objectives at the most general level (level 1). This step produces three fairly global objectives: one type C requiring that the student recall the general principles of the field being studied, one type B requiring that the student identify novel exemplars of the general principles in the field being studied, and one type A objective requiring that the student specify ways in which the general principles can be applied in specific novel situations. Even though these objectives are general, they should be stated in behavioural terms as should those referred to in all subsequent steps.
3   Analyse each of the three level 1 objectives to determine the constituent elements. One asks in this type of analysis: 'What does the student need to be able to do before he can achieve this objective: what are the contributory skills?' This step produces a number of second order objectives for each of the three types of first order objectives. The phraseology of the different levels of the same type of objective will tend to be similar. Thus, for example, type C objectives will tend to require the student to *recall* concepts relating to the whole field of study, the lower levels of type C objectives will tend to require the recalling of more highly specific concepts than the higher levels.
4   Analyse each of the second order objectives to determine the constituent elements using the approach suggested in step 3. This step produces a

number of third order, more specific objectives still classifiable as A, B or C types.

5 This method of analysis can proceed until the level of specificity required is reached.

6 Take each type of objective at the different levels and check that the C-type objectives contribute to the achievement of the B-type objectives at the same level and that the B-type objectives contribute to the achievement of the A-type objectives at the same level. This method of proceeding provides a check against redundancy and repetition and reveals any lacunae in the hierarchies.

7 Check the different levels and types of objectives in the different areas for overlap and congruencies which may be useful in preparing teaching sequences.

Step 7 is the link between the specifying of objectives and the preparation of teaching activities.

Name Index

Note: page numbers in bold type refer to Bibliography or Lists of References.

Name Index

Name Index

Sheffield, F. D., 260, 277
Siegel, L., 175
Simpson, E., 195
Simpson, R. S., 292
Skinner, B. F., 25, 32, 35, 175, 280, 294
Smith, B. O., 238, 241, 267, 268, 277
Snygg, D., 36, 170
Society for Curriculum Study, 216, 222, 289
Spence, K. W., 261, 277
Spens, W., 29, 175
Stake, R. E., 225, 227
Stenhouse, L., 6, 175
Stephens, J. M., 294
Stiles, L. J., 32, 175
Stolurow, L. M., 33, 175
Stones, E., 6, 12, 13, 17, 29, 43, 88, 92, 163, 175
Stow, K. R., 282, 294
Sullivan, H. J., 8, 24, 174, 175
Summerfield, A., 43, 175
Swanson, D., 10, 172, 253
Symonds, P. M., 294-5

Taylor, S. P., 281n
Thompson, G. G., 295
Thorndike, E. L., 25, 29, 176, 215, 216, 224, 227, 271
Thyne, J. M., 39, 176, 295

Tiemann, P. W., 14, 88, 173
Travers, R. M. W., 29, 45, 176, 238, 241
Trow, W. M., 34, 35, 37, 176, 244, 253, 295
Tyler, L. L., 8, 174
Tyler, R. W., 10, 11, 13, 16, 85, 87, 174, 176, 179, 207, 213, 216, 222, 224, 227

University of Hull *Library Bulletin*, 29
Unks, N. J., 176

Verduin, J. R., 176
Vernon, P. E., 176

Walbesser, H. H., 225, 228
Waples, D., 252
Watson, G., 295
Wees, W. R., 176
Wheeler, D. K., 176
Williams, D., 43, 82, 94, 164, 171
Wingo, G. M., 294
Wiseman, S., 174
Wittrock, M. C., 278n
Wolfle, D., 253
Wolters, A. W., 36, 176
Wood, R., 8, 11, 176
Woodring, P., 176

318

Subject Index

ability, different levels of, 191, 275
affective domain of educational objectives
    as component in cognitive domain, 201
    in educational psychology: in model taxonomy, 94, 104, 163; in schedule of objectives, 47–8, 72, 73, 94
    evaluation of, 201–2
    movement of curricular aims away from, 21
    taxonomy of, 18, 20, 21–2, 104, 195, 196–9, 200; instrumentation of, 211–12
affective-social factors in learning, 276
age
    of children taught, and attitudes of teachers to educational psychology, 84
    of students, and attitudes to educational psychology, 83–4
analysis of knowledge, in cognitive domain, 19, 196
animals, learning in, 70, 79, 274
application of knowledge, in cognitive domain, 19, 196
arts
    criticism of, should heighten perception, 219, 221–2
    difficulty of formulating behavioural objectives in, 6–7, 218, 226, 233
associationism, 271
associations, learning of, 25, 203, 204
attending (receiving), in affective domain, 20, 198
attitude scales, 51, 80, 93

behaviour of learners, expression of educational objectives in terms of, 10–11, 12–16, 22, 180–1, 189, 190–1
    concentrates teaching on primary responsibility of schools, 231
    difficult in some subjects, 5, 6–7, 217–18, 226, 233
    in educational psychology, 238–9; in model taxonomy, 89, 162; in schedule of objectives, 47, 67, 76
    promotes choice of important objectives, 229–30
    in taxonomies, 17, 195, 207
behavioural sciences, 227, 279, 280
behaviourist school of psychology, 72, 74, 189, 203, 271
behaviours, terminal, in programmed learning, 189–90
bias, on side of current practice, in attitude to objectives, 9–10, 46, 68

chains of responses, 25, 203–4
child-centred school of educational psychology, 31
    and aims of education, 10
    and schedule of objectives, 69, 71, 75
cognitive domain of educational objectives
    affective domain as component of, 201
    in educational psychology: future courses in, 274; in model taxonomy, 95, 104; in schedule of objectives, 47, 72
    taxonomy of, 18, 19–20, 21–2, 195–6; instrumentation of, 20–1, 208–11

319

Subject Index

cognitive factors in learning, 276

cognitive theory, 203

colleges of education

    scores on attitude scale of students from different, 81, 83, 84

    views on objectives in schedule held by students from different, 50–1, 63–4; analysis of, 74–5, 91, 307–12

    syllabuses (prospectuses) of: contents of, 31, 32–3; objectives in, 12–13, 45, 86, 90–1, 162

communication, promotion of accuracy of

    by specifying of objectives, 11

    by taxonomies of objectives, 194, 196, 200

competence, level of, written into objectives, 15

comprehension, in cognitive domain, 19, 196

concepts, learning of, 26, 203, 204

conditioned responses, 25, 51, 203

construction, in cognitive domain, 24

content in teaching

    classification of, not included in taxonomy, 18, 195

    definition of objective should include statement of, 180–1

    derived from objectives, 12, 87

    selection and organization of, facilitated by specifying of objectives, 9

criticism, of art, should heighten perception, 219, 221–2

culture, nature of, factor in selecting objectives, 182

curricula

    consensus on, more easily gained at more abstract levels, 192, 193

    projects for improvement of, 272

    research findings and, 264

    specification of objectives and development of, 5, 6, 9, 12, 189, 190, 191, 207, 214

    taxonomies as frameworks for, 194–202

    theory of, 215, 216, 217, 220–2

democracy, 38, 232–3

demonstration, in cognitive domain, 24

description

    in cognitive domain, 24

    of objectives, three levels of, 22–3

deviant children (handicapped or maladjusted), 36, 39, 47, 72, 74

discipline, problems of, 288

discovery learning, 271

dynamic system, objectives should constitute, 16

dynamics of behaviour, 244, 245

education

    an applied science, 259–61

    both art and science, 225

    definitions of, 34, 189, 238–9, 258

    philosophy of, 183–4, 282

    a psychological process, 34

    a social process, 245

educational objectives, *see* objectives, educational

educational psychology, *see* psychology, educational

emotional development of children, 47, 69, 246, 247

entry competence of learners, 12, 15–16

    factor in selecting objectives, 183–4, 191

evaluation

    in affective domain, 201–2

    of knowledge, in cognitive domain, 20, 196

    not necessarily quantitative, 7, 218–20, 226, 232

    of student learning, specifying of objectives and, 7, 9, 10, 15, 22, 89, 98–9, 225–6

    taxonomy and, 164, 166, 194, 207

examinations

    framing of questions for, 10

    syllabuses for, 12

expressive objectives, 8–9

Subject Index

objectives, educational, 1, 5
    arguments against specifying of, 5–9, 85, 214–23; probing validity of, 229–37
    characteristics of, 12–16
    definition of, 179–82; need for constant re-definition of, 187
    in educational psychology, *see under* psychology, educational
    justification for specifying of, 9–12, 85–6, 188–90, 224–7
    levels of description of, 22–3
    levels of specificity of, 13–14, 20–1, 48, 67, 181–2, 190–4
    precision in stating, 13, 14, 20–1; difficulty of, 235; reveals triviality, 230, 236
    selection of, 182–7
    systematizing of, *see* taxonomies
opportunism (serendipity) in teaching, specifying of objectives and, 6, 217, 230–1
ordering, in cognitive domain, 24

'pedagogical acumen', 71, 74
pedagogy, 2; *see* teaching
personality, 36, 37, 247, 275
    in schedule of objectives for educational psychology, 47, 67
    theory of, 90
philosophy of education, 282
    factor in selecting objectives, 183–4
philosophy of life, development of, 23, 199
physical development of children
    courses on, in teacher-training, 28–9; should be eliminated? 273
    in schedule of objectives for educational psychology, 47, 74
Piaget's developmental psychology, 33, 51, 64, 70, 72, 75
practice, in learning, 275
principles, learning of, 11, 26, 203, 204
problems, solving of, 26, 89, 191, 203, 204–5, 271

programmed learning, 5, 11, 15, 189, 190
    arguments against, 85, 232
    behavioural analysis in, 87
    in schedule of objectives in educational psychology, 73, 75, 93
Progressive Education movement, 216, 271
psychological development of children, in schedule of objectives for educational psychology, 47, 69, 74
psychology, clinical, 2, 43, 246, 271
psychology, educational, 1–2, 30
    attitudes to, 78–84, 94, 278, 303–5
    definitions of, 92; of field of, 257–77
    percentages of courses in colleges of education devoted to, 30–1
    possible methods of organizing, 290–2
    a research discipline, 248
    schedule of objectives for teaching of, 46–9, 299–302; cluster analysis of views on, 50, 54–61, 71–4, 93–4; comments on, 64–7, 75–7; correlations and divergences in views on, held by different groups, 51, 54, 70; differences between colleges in views on, 50–1, 63–4, 74–5, 91, 307–12; ranking of objectives in, 49–50, 52–4, 68–70, 306–7; specialists' views on, 49, 65–7, 76; tutors' views on, compared with their teaching practice, 50, 61–3, 70–1
    taxonomy of objectives in, 85–103, 160–6; model for, 104–60
    in teacher training: as it has been, 28–33, 243–4; evaluation of, by teachers, 281–5; justification for, 33–5; objectives of, 37–8, 244–9, 286–90; implications of objectives, 249–52; recommendations on, 35–45, 278–81; relevancy of, 238–42
    as a theory of teaching, 165
    topics for inclusion in courses on, 39, 91, 96, 254–6
psychomotor domain, in taxonomy of objectives, 18, 195

322

672